RETIREMENT
GAME-CHANGERS

Praise for *Retirement Game-Changers*

"*Retirement Game-Changers* is a terrific resource to help older workers make critical decisions to maximize the vast array of new opportunities brought about by the longevity revolution."

—**Ken Dychtwald, PhD,** author of *A New Purpose: Redefining Money, Family, Work, Retirement and Success*

"Steve Vernon knocks it out of the park with his new book, *Retirement Game-Changers*. His detailed research and positive approach make the daunting notion of navigating the challenges many boomers will tackle in the years ahead, well, manageable. He guides you through simple strategies to help you face the fear of outliving savings and worries about an uncertain economy, paying for medical bills, and finding ways to continue to work in some fashion as a pillar of a retirement plan. But this is far more than a book about your wealth. Steve also offers rich advice on ways to boost your health and well-being that will give you the confidence to navigate the next chapter of your life with a smart plan and a can-do spirit."

—**Kerry Hannon,** *New York Times* columnist and author of *Great Jobs for Everyone 50+*

"Steve Vernon is back, and he's done it again, better than ever! As always, he gets retirement planning right: putting your money in service to your life, not the other way around. I've studied Social Security for 41 years, but I learn still more in five minutes from Steve's fresh viewpoint."

—**Andy Landis,** author of *Social Security: The Inside Story*

"This comprehensive guide is packed with expert insights, real-life stories, practical tips, pitfalls to avoid, and helpful resources. *Retirement Game-Changers* is a book I will use to plan my own retirement."

—**Catherine Collinson,** CEO and President of Transamerica Institute and Transamerica Center for Retirement Studies, and Executive Director of Aegon Center for Longevity and Retirement

"Longer life expectancies are in so many ways a 'good news' story. But many retirees are reasonably concerned about outliving their money. *Retirement Game-Changers* provides concrete strategies for financial stability and sustainability in retirement. The book also weaves in valuable perspectives on other aspects of retirement wellness. It's an all-too-rare guide to living well in retirement that's truly holistic."

—**Christine Benz,** Director of Personal Finance, Morningstar, and author of *30 Minute Money Solutions*

"Steve Vernon's brilliance is apparent in his ability to take retirement subjects that are typically communicated with mind-numbing complexity and drill the critical points down to something easy to understand."

—**Allan Roth,** AARP *Money* contributor and author of *How a Second Grader Beats Wall Street*

"Steve Vernon has an uncanny ability to distill the best practices from complex research about retirement income planning into practical and usable advice for those seeking to position their assets for better retirement outcomes. His new book includes unbiased coverage of various retirement income tools, as well as further insights on the non-financial aspects of enjoying a successful and productive retirement."

—**Wade Pfau, PhD, CFA,** Professor of Retirement Income at The American College and Founder of *RetirementResearcher.com*

"In an engaging, thoughtful way, Steve Vernon offers detailed, practical advice on how to set realistic goals and achieve financial security, but he gives equal weight to your 'social portfolio' and how lifestyle decisions can shape a joyful, productive and comfortable retirement. Vernon's 'action steps' that wrap up each chapter are worth the price of admission alone—and the retirement tips from his dog are priceless."

—**Rick Smith**, former Chairman and Editor-in-Chief of *Newsweek*

"This book is a game-changer for anyone seeking advice to plan for retirement. Steve Vernon offers practical and sensible advice on everything from investing for retirement to choosing the best place to live, with plenty of helpful hints along the way."

—**Richard Eisenberg,** Managing Editor of *NextAvenue.org*

"Retirement Game-Changers is a must-read for those wanting to create a comprehensive plan for their future. It's about money and much more. This unique book helps individuals get ready to plan the rest of their lives, integrating the financial and important non-financial considerations of the retirement experience. It's a winner!"

—**Helen Dennis,** columnist, author and lecturer on aging and the new retirement, and co-author of *Project Renewment: The First Retirement Model for Career Women*

"Retirement Game-Changers provides essential information and a wealth of resources to help older workers (or their children) navigate the financial, health and social aging systems. Steve Vernon's practical guide offers a positive path to a longer life, and both women and men will benefit from his guidance."

—**M. Cindy Hounsell,** President, Women's Institute for a Secure Retirement

"Retirement Game-Changers tackles a critical planning issue facing many Americans—their rising and unknown longevity. The sections on retirement income and Social Security alone are worth the price of the book, but there's so much more. There's no one better equipped to help people navigate these challenges than Steve Vernon."

—**Mark Miller,** Reuters columnist and author of *Jolt: Stories of Trauma and Transformation*

"Retirement Game-Changers is a great book for people thinking about their own retirement and for people who are helping parents and friends. Steve Vernon is a practical, down-to-earth writer, who brings expertise from his years of consulting for employee benefit plans, retirement education and personal experience. I recommend that people start using it about 10 years before retirement age."

—**Anna M. Rappaport, FSA, MAAA,** Past-President of Society of Actuaries, internationally known retirement expert and phased retiree

"Steve Vernon's easy-to-read *Retirement Game-Changers* provides wisdom about the many ways retirees and pre-retirees can make smart choices about money, health and social engagement to build the retirement you want."

—**Kathy Kristof,** Editor of *SideHusl.com*

RETIREMENT
GAME-CHANGERS

Strategies for a Healthy,
Financially Secure,
and Fulfilling Long Life

STEVE VERNON, FSA

Rest-of-Life Communications
Oxnard, California

For more information:
Retirement Game-Changers: www.retirementgamechangers.com
Rest-of-Life Communications: www.restoflife.com

Project management: Markman Editorial Services, www.MarlaMarkman.com
Book cover and design by GKS Creative, www.gkscreative.com

Library of Congress Cataloging-in-Publication Data:

Vernon, Steven G., 1953-, author.

Retirement game-changers : strategies for a healthy , financially secure , and fulfilling long life / Steve Vernon, FSA.

Includes bibliographical references and index. | Oxnard, CA: Rest-of-Life Communications, 2018.

ISBN 978-0-9853846-4-7 | LCCN 2018935814

LCSH Retirement--United States--Planning. | Personal finance. | Retirement income. | Quality of life. | Older people--Health and hygiene. BISAC BUSINESS & ECONOMICS / Personal Finance / Retirement Planning.

LCC HQ1063.2.U6 .V47 2018 | DDC 646.7/93--dc23

ISBN: 978-0-9853846-4-7 (Print)

ISBN: 978-0-9853846-5-4 (e-Readers)

TO MELINDA

My wife and sweetie, who helped me every step of the way

ALSO BY STEVE VERNON

Money for Life: Turn Your IRA and 401(k) Into a Lifetime Retirement Paycheck

Recession-Proof Your Retirement Years:
Simple Retirement Planning Strategies That Work Through Thick or Thin

The Quest: For Long Life, Health and Prosperity (DVD/workbook set)

Live Long and Prosper!
Invest in Your Happiness, Health and Wealth for Retirement and Beyond

Don't Work Forever! Simple Steps Baby Boomers Must Take to Ever Retire

For bulk purchases of *Retirement Game-Changers, Money for Life,*
Recession-Proof Your Retirement Years, or *The Quest* DVD, please email
steve.vernon@restoflife.com.

TABLE OF CONTENTS

INTRODUCTION TO OUR
CHALLENGES AND OPPORTUNITIES

Millions of Americans will live a long time — possibly 30 years longer than our grandparents or great-grandparents. This is a game-changer for planning the last few decades of our lives, the period known as "retirement."

How do we plan for these extra decades? How do we manage our finances, health, and general well-being so that we can enjoy this gift of time and not be a burden on our families and communities? As you approach retirement age, *how* you transition from the workforce into retirement is one of the most important series of decisions you'll make. These decisions will be just as important and influential as the decisions you made as you entered adulthood, such as where you settled down, whether you married and started a family, and the career you chose.

Here are two true-life stories of folks in their retirement years that vividly illustrate the potential challenges we face and provide insightful lessons. Which of these stories would *you* like to live?

My parents' retirement

For the first 15 years of their retirement, my parents, Jim and Mary, had the stereotypical dream retirement. They retired at the same time — Jim was 65, and Mary was 61. In their 60s and 70s, they were active with their grandkids and family, traveled with close friends, volunteered for causes they believed in, and pursued hobbies and interests. At the beginning of their retirement, they were vital and healthy due to constant exercise, good nutrition, and healthy body weight. They lived the type of retirement life that you see in glossy advertisements about retirement. Perhaps this is the type of retirement you dream of.

Eventually, though, my parents aged out of their active retirement. Each developed heart conditions, and my mother suffered from breast cancer. Medical technology extended their lives by several years with bypass surgeries, modern cancer treatments, and prescription drugs. In his last few years, Jim declined physically and mentally and unfortunately needed substantial care, until he passed away at age 88.

Mary ended up living 31 years in retirement — more than one-third of her life. She survived Jim by eight years, also needing substantial care but only in her last year. When she passed away at age 92, she was amazed that she lived that long, and she was grateful for such a good life and supportive family.

My parents never worried about running out of money, due to smart choices and careful planning. They enjoyed substantial social support from nearby family and friends. They built the financial and social resources for a long retirement, and it paid off for them and all their extended family. They provided a good example for us to follow.

A different retirement

On the other hand, our neighbors Frank and Betsy had a different story. We met Frank and Betsy when he was in his early 80s and she was in her early 70s. Frank had retired, but Betsy was still working so she could pay for assisted living care for her 102-year-old mother. She also needed to work to continue saving for her own retirement. Then they learned that Betsy's 97-year-old aunt needed to move in with them because she had run out of money. The aunt lamented that she never thought she'd live that long.

Both Betsy's mother and her aunt had long retirements, but they hadn't adequately prepared because they never dreamed they would live that long. As a result, their long-life challenges substantially impacted their families. Of course, Frank and Betsy stepped up to the plate and took care of their beloved mother and aunt, but it took a toll on them. Betsy kept working until her mother passed away at age 107 — but quit soon after because she could no longer work for health reasons.

As you can see, your decisions regarding your financial security, health and well-being will significantly impact the rest of your potentially long life. It's probably sobering to realize that the decisions you make will have a ripple effect on your family and close friends.

I say this not to scare you, but to get your attention and encourage you to make the effort to design the best possible retirement for yourself. I wrote this book to help you make effective decisions that best support the life you want for *all* your retirement years. By planning ahead, I hope you'll have a positive impact on your family, friends, and community for your remaining years, and minimize any burden you might place on them.

Longevity in the 21st century

Longer lives aren't the only game-changing challenges that boomers face today. You'd have to be Rip Van Winkle to be unaware of boomers' plight as they approach their retirement years: They're facing such issues as inadequate savings, lack of pensions, poor health, an uncertain economy, and difficult job prospects. To add to the anxiety, the long-term sustainability of important programs such as Social Security and Medicare is questionable, which only increases the hurdles that boomers face as they enter their retirement years.

Let's throw him a life-saving ring!

"Help! I haven't saved enough for retirement!"

Christopher Weyant/The New Yorker Collection/The Cartoon Bank

But you may not have realized that these significant challenges exist due to one of humankind's greatest achievements. On average, Americans and citizens of other developed nations have been given a gift of 30 years or more of additional life that they can expect to enjoy compared to prior generations.

Longer lives — one of humankind's greatest achievements!

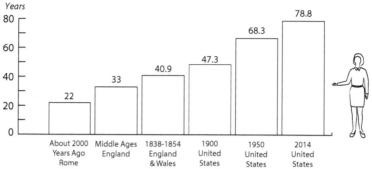

Life expectancy, from the Bronze Age to the 21st century

For example, average life expectancies at birth in the U.S. increased from 47.3 years at the beginning of the 20th century to 78.8 years by 2014 — that's more than 30 years.[1,2] Much of these gains in life expectancy came from public health advances that are widely available to most citizens — safe sanitation and efficient waste disposal, clean water, vaccinations against deadly infectious diseases, abundant supply of food, and electricity and refrigeration to keep our food fresh and safe.

Paradoxically, however, some elements of our 21st century society stack the deck against living a long, healthy and financially secure life. We're bombarded with persuasive advertisements to spend all our money, go into debt, and eat too much unhealthy processed food and beverages. We often don't get enough exercise, which has somewhat been caused by modern conveniences such as automobiles, appliances, and power tools. Many people now sit at their jobs all day long, an unexpected consequence of our "easier" lives now that research has shown that sedentary behavior is a serious health threat.

These days, society sends a powerful message that retirement is the best way to complete your life — that it's your right to retire and enjoy a work-free life — but it provides only modest support to help us achieve that goal. For example, many companies have eliminated the traditional pension and retiree medical plans that enabled the retirement of the prior generation of middle-income workers. In addition, the sustainability of important programs such as Social Security and Medicare is threatened by the inability of our political leaders to make hard but necessary decisions. And the rising cost of health care is a serious threat that we all need to address.

But that's not all we have to be concerned about. Let's look at another game-changing challenge that our gift of long life creates.

Recession-proof your retirement years

During the 20 to 30 years you'll be retired, it wouldn't be safe to assume the economy will flourish — you have to be prepared for the downturns, too. For instance, if you look at the 30-year period from 1987 to 2017, you'll see there have been four major meltdowns during this time; each one packed a potential knockout blow to retirees hoping to live on their financial resources.

It may be sobering to consider that you'll most likely experience a few more meltdowns in the economy in the next few decades. But an important part of your retirement planning should include making the right financial plans to help you survive future economic meltdowns.

Build your retirement plan to last

1987 CRASH

S & L CRISIS

TECH BUBBLE BURST

GREAT RECESSION

How many more stock market crashes in our lifetime?

1980   1990   2000   2010   2020   2030   2040

It's a good time to be aging

In spite of the serious challenges we face as retirees, I still believe it's a good time to be aging, which is why I'm enthusiastic about rolling up my sleeves and dealing with these issues. Fortunately, we won't have to do this without guidance. For instance, there's plenty of scientific and medical research that informs us how to live long, healthy lives. Social research shows what makes us happy and gives us meaning, particularly in our later years. There are many robust, efficient financial products and services, as well as nonprofit organizations like AARP, Area Agencies on Aging, and local nonprofit service groups that advocate for seniors and provide helpful resources. And these resources are at our fingertips because of the internet.

None of these resources were available to our parents' generation, so we've got a tremendous head start. We have a robust toolkit of game-changing strategies and insights we can use to address our serious challenges.

There's a big difference, however, between these recent 21st century advantages and the advances in the 20th century that contributed to the gift of 30 additional years of life. Our parents' generation automatically realized the gains in the 20th century — they didn't have to expend much effort or make decisions to take advantage of the public health advances during their lifetimes. In today's world, however, we need to make conscious choices between the elements of society that are supportive of long, healthy lives and those that work against that goal.

Because of these trends, I like to think that our gift of extra years of life came with some strings attached. That is, we'll need to spend the time and effort it will take to live well during most of these extra years, and not be a burden on society or our children. Since we're the first generation to face these challenges, we're navigating uncharted waters, and it's up to us to make the best of what we've got.

> *Nobody promised it would be easy for the millions of us living today to add 30 years to our average lifespans. Your new "retirement job" is to face up to the accompanying challenges to decide how to make the most of this gift of these extra years of life.*

Some people are enthusiastic about the possibility of living a long time. Others say they aren't, having seen their parents suffer in their later years. Regardless of your views on the topic, there's a good chance you *will* live a long time, so it only makes sense to take steps to live long and live well.

We need a plan!

You've probably heard this before: Failing to plan is planning to fail. Simply put, planning increases your chances of success. And planning for your future is a much better idea than winging it, which so many people do. According to various surveys, only half of survey respondents do any planning for their retirement years.[3,4] *This is a big mistake!*

But you'll need more than a simple retirement plan. In today's world, you'll need a detailed retirement plan that recognizes and addresses the fact that you might be living with your plan until your late 80s, 90s, or even 100s.

Money is a very important part of your retirement plan, and many retirement books focus just on your finances. *Retirement Game-Changers* covers the essential financial decisions you need to make to live a long time without going broke. However, it goes beyond finances to cover lifestyle choices and life planning that will enhance your health and well-being as well. These decisions are just as important as your financial strategies for your prosperity and longevity.

To have the most successful retirement, you'll want to make a series of essential decisions regarding your money, health, *and* well-being. All of these decisions will intertwine and reinforce each other. This multifaceted approach will be particularly important for boomers who have modest financial resources.

Planning doesn't need to be rocket science, which is why I've focused on simple strategies that most people can understand and implement on their own. To help you focus on the most important decisions you'll need to make, I've organized *Retirement Game-Changers* into four sections:

- **Prepare**, which describes the overall plan and necessary preparation
- **Secure**, which helps you build the foundation of financial security you'll need throughout your retirement
- **Engage**, which goes beyond finances with smart choices that affect the other areas of your life
- **Evaluate**, where you can track your progress with the Retirement Reality Check

Let's be clear: Planning isn't magic and it doesn't guarantee a long, healthy, financially secure life. Things can still go wrong even when you have a good plan in place. And you can't just create your plan, then file it away. Most likely, you'll need to adjust your plan to respond to events that will unfold in your life and our society over the next few decades.

You'll be in a much better position to deal with life's curveballs, however, if you have the basics covered: money in the bank, reliable and steady income, good health, the right insurance, and family and friends who can help when you need it. Planning will increase the chances that you'll achieve all these goals.

Navigating *Retirement Game-Changers*

To help you understand and remember the ideas and strategies in this book, I've created these navigational guides and icons:

- Each chapter starts with Mistakes to Avoid ⊘ and Game-Changing Strategies to try. ➡
- Each chapter ends with Action Steps ✎ and Helpful Resources. 🔧
- I've also highlighted some ideas that deserve special emphasis, along with wisdom from several experts on various topics.

- Along the way, I'll warn you about "Traps for the Unwary," which are common pitfalls that can set you back.

- To have a little fun, I'll share "Retirement Planning Tips from Your Dog."

- Finally, the book contains several checklists that can help you stay on track as you're working on your plan.

Retirement Game-Changers is packed full of insights, ideas, and strategies. It's not a book you can read and absorb in a few sittings — it will take many hours to read about the action steps and fully grasp the concepts in this book. You'll also need to spend time doing your own research about the strategies, products, and services that best meet your specific goals.

But don't let the amount of time or effort you'll need to invest dissuade you from getting started. The game-changing challenges we face and the strategies we can use deserve a certain level of detail. I encourage you to pace your reading by tackling and absorbing one chapter at a time. You're setting up your financial security and enjoyment of life for the rest of your life, and it's going to take some time and patience to do the job right.

Many readers may not choose to adopt *all* the strategies I'm suggesting in this book. The more strategies you can adopt, however, will make you better prepared to face the significant challenges in our future.

Turn our challenges into an opportunity

This book shares game-changing strategies and actions you can take to successfully address the serious challenges we face during our retirement. But there's more to a long life than just simple survival. I encourage you to view these challenges as an opportunity to make your final years really count. Use this gift of extra life to make a positive difference with your family, friends, community, and society at large.

Remember, you're planning the most important period of your life — the rest of the time you have on earth. To help, it's a good idea to include your spouse or partner in this effort, so that he or she provides input into your plans and can continue them if they should survive you. You'll also want to kick things around with your family and close friends to get their insights and gain their emotional support.

Americans will need to be resourceful and resilient to face the serious challenges that come with their gift of longevity, and to use the game-changing tools and strategies to their best advantage. Do a thorough job with your planning, and you'll have the optimism to view these challenges as an opportunity.

Boomers are up for the challenge of changing their retirement game! Over the years, they've taken pride on being informed and fully participating in their future, and not just accepting their fate. It will be no different with planning their retirement years.

About the author of *Retirement Game-Changers*

I don't sell annuities, insurance, or investments, so my recommendations aren't influenced by how I earn money; this enables me to tell it like it is. Throughout this book — and elsewhere — I'll give you an unbiased perspective on strategies you can use to help you live long and well.

I have 40-plus years of experience as an actuary, helping employers design and manage their retirement and benefit programs.* I've studied and researched retirement for my entire career, and lately I've given a lot of thought to planning for my retirement years. This book shares many of the strategies I'm applying to my own situation.

What's different about this book?

- Straightforward, workable strategies
- Holistic long-life perspective
- Research-based
- Unbiased guidance
- Insights to stay on track
- Helps you succeed

I think you're ready, so let's get started.

*Actuaries are professionals who measure the risks of important but unpredictable life events — risks such as death, serious illness, accidents, and outliving your money during retirement (living too long is considered a risk!). We design financial programs to mitigate these risks, such as life, health, and disability insurance, pension plans, and 401(k) plans. As part of our training, we study the mathematical chances of these life events happening, along with the types of investments and financial products and services that will protect individuals from the adverse consequences of these events. We've been called the "architects of financial security."

I.

PREPARE

Have you ever watched how skilled artists, carpenters, or painters start important projects? They don't just pick up their tools and start painting, sawing, or hammering. They take the time to complete the necessary planning and prep work, which are essential steps for a successful project. It's the same with your important life project — your retirement planning.

In this section, you'll start your prep work with important perspectives on retirement that have the potential to save you lots of money and increase your enjoyment of life. These perspectives will help set the stage for all the strategies that follow in *Retirement Game-Changers*.

It will take a lot of patience and persistence to carry out the steps described in this book. As a result, you'll want to pay attention to motivation and inspiration — a critical yet often overlooked aspect of retirement planning. You'll increase your chances of success if you embrace strategies to give you the strength and resilience to follow through with your planning.

One of the first necessary steps is to collect your critical documents and papers to help you implement the financial strategies in the second section of the book. You'll see a robust checklist that helps you with this task.

Have patience and proceed at your own pace. It will be a long journey, but well worth your efforts!

CHAPTER 1

PLAN FOR A LONG RETIREMENT

DON'T MAKE THESE MISTAKES:

- ⊘ Just hope that the rest of your life will turn out OK. Hope is not a strategy!

- ⊘ Plan for just the next few months or years, or just for your "go-go" years.

- ⊘ Focus exclusively on the "vacation" aspect of your retirement years.

TRY THESE GAME-CHANGING STRATEGIES:

- → Plan as if you might live to 90, 95 or even 100 – because you and/or your spouse just might live that long.

- → Develop and follow a thoughtful plan that includes strategies regarding your happiness, health, and financial security for all phases of the rest of your life.

- → Redefine your retirement to meet your unique life goals and resources.

- → Plan for a "second middle age" between your career years and full retirement.

- → Prepare for possible frail years at the end of your life.

Retirement planning sure isn't what it used to be

Until recently, the conventional definition of retirement meant "not working" for an extended period at the end of your life — an idyllic period during which you traveled, spent time with your grandkids, and pursued your hobbies and interests. Retirement was the answer for anyone who was tired of working, thought they were unable to work, or had reached the "golden" age of 65, the age many people consider to be the end of their working life.

Planning for this type of retirement was straightforward: Make sure your Social Security, pension, and savings could cover your living expenses, participate in Medicare, and possibly buy supplemental medical insurance. Then start having fun.

But the conventional definition of retirement has some problems for those of us about to enter that phase of our lives. First, people are living longer, healthier lives, which requires very high savings levels to accumulate enough money to enable us to "not work" for a very long time. To compound this problem, many older workers today don't enjoy the same economic resources or safety net that enabled the retirement of prior generations of retirees.[1]

The second problem: Evidence is accumulating that full retirement may not be the healthiest or most fulfilling way to spend your later years. Instead, research shows that people who work or volunteer in their later years are often healthier, live longer, and are less likely to develop dementia than their peers.[2,3]

Planning for the new retirement is much more involved and complex than the retirement planning that worked for our parents. This chapter gives you some broad perspectives on retirement planning to help you address the challenges mentioned above. Here we'll focus on:

- Reframing retirement planning and redefining your retirement years
- Preparing for the new arc of life in the 21st century, including the "second middle age" that many people are creating
- Planning beyond the "vacation" aspects of retirement
- Learning how long you might live, and how to plan accordingly

These perspectives will help you understand and appreciate the specific strategies described in this book.

At least he's planning! *Retirement Game-Changers* **shows you a better plan.**

"If we take a late retirement and an early death, we'll just squeak by."

Barbara Smaller/The New Yorker Collection/The Cartoon Bank

Focus on happiness, health, and fulfillment

Most people really just want to be happy, healthy, and satisfied with life, and they think that retirement will help them achieve these goals. But if full retirement isn't realistic or practical in your 50s or even your 60s, can you still achieve these goals without retiring full time? The game-changing answer is to "reframe" your retirement years — a concept advocated by design thinkers.

Since we're reframing retirement planning to figure out how to be happy, healthy, and satisfied with life rather than just how not to work, let's explore a bit about what makes people happy and fulfilled. It's a topic that's intrigued philosophers and psychologists for ages. For our purposes here, I'm proposing that you focus on two key guidelines for happiness in your retirement years.

First, start out by thinking about the ways in which you can avoid being unhappy. There are many ways you can become unhappy with your life, including with your love life, your family, your work, and so on. For the purposes of this book, we're going to focus on the ways in which not having enough money to live on in your retirement years or having poor health can affect your happiness and therefore your retirement. These are both important aspects of your life that can get disrupted when you retire from your career job. It'll be an important part of your planning to do what you can to avoid being unhappy with your finances and your health.

This brings us to the second guideline: to think about what makes you happy and satisfied with life. For most people, it's some combination of work, play, and social engagement, but finding the right combination for *you* is the key to smart planning.

Because many career workers get too much "work" and not enough "play" during their working years, playing more is an important goal for their retirement. However, there's much more to a successful retirement than just "more play." For instance, many people derive much of their social engagement and life satisfaction through work. If this is true for you, you'll need to be conscious not only about building a robust social life after your working life has ended, but also what you can do to fulfill your ambitions for life once you retire from your job.

An important retirement planning goal is to determine which of the three areas of life — work, play, and social engagement — needs improving in order to enhance your overall happiness. And remember: Only you can determine what will make you happy. So don't let anyone — family, friends, acquaintances, even so-called experts — try to tell you what you "should" do to be happy. Defining the life *you* want for your retirement years is essential to your happiness and can help you determine how much income you really need to support that life.

Define your retirement

When I tell people in their 40s, 50s, or 60s that they might need to keep working until their 70s because they won't have enough savings to retire, the most common reaction I get is, "No way! I can't see myself working that long." That's often because many older workers are unhappy with certain aspects of their work and they think that retirement will fix those problems.

Their reaction identifies a critical problem that needs to be solved as you consider when you should retire: What is it about your work that makes you think retirement is the only answer? Are you working too hard or too many hours? Are you bored with your work and ready for new things? Are you tired of the commute or the people you work with?

Then fix those problems, because full retirement in your 50s and 60s is often not the best solution. And it may not even be feasible or affordable given the meager savings many boomers have accumulated (this is another important aspect of reframing the retirement problem).

People often define retirement differently. For many people, it means transitioning from the full-time career or job they've held for many years. Beyond that, however, there are many possibilities, including these:

- The traditional retirement — "not working"
- Part-time work in your current job or career
- A new job or career, either part time or full time
- A bridge job for a few years until full-time retirement
- An encore career that may last an extended period
- Self-employment or business ownership
- A volunteer position for a cause you believe in

All these different options lead me to offer a more expansive definition of retirement for older workers to consider:

Retirement means improving your life by changing your work.

Actually, when you look at it this way, you might benefit by "retiring" at different stages throughout your life. At any age, if you really don't like the work you're doing, don't continue to live a deferred life, waiting for retirement to make your life better. Rather, look for ways to make your work support the life you want.

As you plan for your retirement, ask yourself if you'll still be happy, healthy, and fulfilled if you need to work longer than you'd planned, or if you need to spend less money compared to when you were working full time. Answering these questions can help you devise a more realistic and successful retirement plan, one that works for you.

Prepare for the 21st century arc of life

Prior generations experienced a life cycle that could be generally broken into three stages:

1. Childhood/education/early adulthood
2. Middle age/career/raising family
3. Retirement/leisure/elderhood

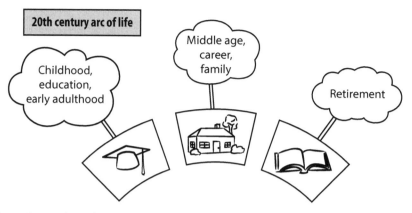

These days, it's perhaps more realistic and fulfilling to blend and/or spread out these phases. For instance, maybe you'll decide to enjoy more leisure time before a full retirement. Or maybe you'll go back to school in your 40s to learn the skills for a different career. Or you might decide that working longer is the best plan for you, although you might work differently in your later years (shorter hours, different job, or a new field of interest, for instance).

Here's another perspective on reframing the arc of life. With the extension of lifespans, we've effectively created a "second middle age" — a term popularized by a few experts.[4,5]

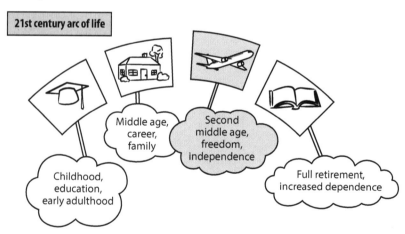

During your second middle age, you're still active, vital, and productive, but you're no longer raising a family or aggressively pursuing the career of your first middle age. As you transition out of the first middle age, it's important to distinguish whether you want to transition into full retirement or into your second middle age.

"Freedom" can be one good word to describe this second middle age. At this stage, you're free from the expectations of others. Free from preconceived notions of how you might live your life. Free from the responsibility of raising a family. Free to do what you've always wanted to do. You can break free from the advertising influences that tell you to spend your time and money in unhealthy and unfulfilling ways. You can break free from the consequences of unconscious choices you might have made earlier in your life.

Another good focus during this second middle age can be "independence." Your financial independence may come from wages, self-employment, financial resources, government benefits, efficient sharing of resources, or, more likely, a creative combination of all these solutions.

"If you asked people 'Where would you put an extra 30 years of life?' most likely they wouldn't say they'd like to make old age even longer. Fortunately, we have the opportunity to extend youth and middle age, too."

**—Laura Carstensen, PhD, Founder,
Stanford Center on Longevity**

If you're working during this second middle age, you might gain independence by redefining your career to better suit your goals and circumstances at this stage in your life. You might choose to do more work that you like and less work that you don't like. To make that happen, you'll need to keep your job skills up-to-date, which may require a recommitment to learning, obtaining new credentials, or pursuing alternative careers. You might even work fewer hours to free up time to pursue your interests.

Of course, this could also mean you'll make less money, but perhaps you'll buy less stuff because you'll be making more conscious spending choices. If so, you'd be in good company. One study from Merrill Lynch and Age Wave shows that 95% of retirees prefer enjoyable experiences rather than buying more things.[6] You'll want to think hard about this question: Are you willing to spend less money to gain your freedom in retirement? Or are you willing to work to earn more spending money? Often you can't have it both ways, so you'll need to make a choice.

The goal, not just in this second middle age but also in retirement, is to extend the life period of freedom and independence for as long as possible — to be physically fit, mentally sharp, functionally independent, and financially secure well into very old age, perhaps well into your 80s or even 90s, if possible.

Focusing just on your go-go years: A trap for the unwary

Many people focus just on the active, "vacation" phase of their retirement – travel, exercise, hobbies, possibly working part time or volunteering. Some people call these the "go-go" years, although they can also be referred to as the second middle age identified above. For many people, it's inevitable that you'll age into "slow-go" years, where you're less active and less interested in traveling or working. Eventually, you might reach the "no-go" years where you just want to stay put in your home and local community. You'll want to plan for all these different phases of your retirement.

Plan beyond your second middle age

No matter how healthy and capable you may be in your second middle age — aka the go-go years — many people may still experience a period of physical decline and illness in their late 80s or 90s. After your second middle age comes these final life stages — the slow-go and no-go years — characterized by increasing frailty and dependence. During this period, you'll most likely be unable to work for pay and will need to rely exclusively on financial resources, family, and government benefits.

You may also be relying significantly on others for care, assistance, and support with daily living. As many of us witnessed our parents' final years, we gained insight into the challenges and realities of this phase of life. This experience may have led many of you to take steps to avoid being a burden on your children or society. If you haven't already done so, it's time to start thinking seriously about what those steps will be for you.

The fact is, as you age, your needs will change. As you plan for your retirement, you'll want to plan for *all* phases of your *rest-of-life* — the go-go years, the slow-go years, and the no-go years. You'll need to make financial and life-planning decisions for all these stages, so you'll have the resources you need to support yourself no matter what stage you find yourself in.

Answer the "who-what-when-where-why" of retirement

Part of effectively planning for your retirement includes answering the following questions:

- **Who** do you want to live or spend time with?
- **What** will you do?
- **When** will you retire?
- **Where** will you live?

For each of these questions, you need to ask yourself "why" it's important to you.

There's a good chance it will take some time for you to determine the answers to these questions — that's only natural. That's why you'll want to start thinking about them well before you retire.

Your answers to the "who-what-when-where-why" of retirement will be key to helping you develop strategies that address one last question: "How" will you afford to retire? Fortunately, that's the focus of this book, and my strategies will help you discover just how to do that.

Learn how long you might live

Another key element of reframing your retirement involves thinking about how long you might live. While you may not get the exact number right, it's a critical piece of retirement planning you shouldn't ignore. By estimating the number of years you have left, you can more reasonably evaluate your finances and lifestyle.

If you're like many people, you probably suffer from two common misunderstandings about your longevity.

First misconception: You focus on average life expectancies as reported in the media. You might have heard that the average American lives until their late 70s, but that's the wrong number for aging boomers to focus on. That's the average life expectancy *at birth*, which factors in everybody who dies from childhood through mid-adulthood. But if you've lived to your 50s or 60s, you're in a more select group of people who've been healthy enough — or lucky enough — to make it that far.

Instead of relying on the average life expectancy at birth, you'll want to estimate the remaining number of years you can expect to live, given your current age. Chances are good you'll learn that you might live into your late 80s or 90s.

In addition, if you have a college degree and/or have had a steady job with good benefits throughout your working life, research shows you'll most likely live even longer than the averages that reflect the entire population.[7]

Given this information, most older workers and new retirees should be planning to live for two to three more decades. The trouble is, many people make choices that make it seem as if they're planning for short lives. In fact, research shows that most people plan ahead for just the next few months or years.[8] And while that focus might be sufficient while you're working, as you transition out of the full-time workforce, you'll want to lengthen your planning horizon to the rest of your life, which for many of you will be 20 years or more.

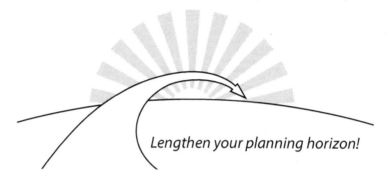

Lengthen your planning horizon!

Second misconception: You think your life expectancy is your destiny. If you use one of the available online calculators to estimate your life expectancy, keep in mind that the estimate it gives you isn't your destiny. A life expectancy is just an average period you might expect to live based on assumptions about mortality rates. Think of it more like an educated guess. It's entirely possible that you could live well beyond your calculated life expectancy — or fall well short. Using statistical terms, the standard deviation around calculated life expectancies is quite large.

To fully grasp the issues involved with life expectancy, use one of the online calculators shown in the "Helpful Resources" section at the end of this chapter to determine your own estimated life expectancy. Most likely, you'll realize that:

- You might live much longer than you think.

- Many factors will influence your longevity, including lifestyle decisions that might increase the odds that you'll live a long time.

- If you're married or in a committed relationship and you both estimate your life expectancies, you may find that one of you could outlive the other by many years. If you really care about your spouse or partner, you'll want to make sure they'll be financially secure after you're gone.

Once you have a better idea of how long you might live, it might take a lot of effort to complete the necessary planning to ensure that you have the resources you need to live that long. But that's only to be expected if you want financial security for a few more decades of your life.

Plan, plan, plan

So how do you go about starting to plan more carefully for your retirement? Financial planners often ask you to first define your living needs, so they can tell you how much money you'll need during retirement, which, in turn, tells you when you can afford to retire. The trouble with this approach is that you might end up needing a lot more money than you have now or can accumulate before a reasonable retirement age. Then you end up thinking you can't afford to retire until you're 80.

Most people, however, manage their finances the other way around: They determine how much income they have, then they manage their living expenses budget to match their income. In fact, since that's the way most people have managed their finances during their working years, it's only natural that you continue planning this way during your retirement years.

One idea might be to blend both approaches with your retirement planning. Here's how it could work: When you complete your Retirement Reality Check in Chapter 17, you might find you won't be able to afford the retirement life you'd planned for. Hopefully that will trigger some smart thinking and decisions to help you make your money last longer. The primary decision you'll need to make is to decide whether you can reduce your living expenses in retirement or whether you should work longer. But don't wait too long! I'd rather you make these decisions now, compared to winging it and then reaching your 80s and running out of money. Then you'll wish you'd planned better before you retired.

Here's a systematic process you can use to make conscious and informed decisions about your retirement[9]:

- Identify any **barriers** to retiring. Usually these are financial, such as not having enough retirement income or not having access to affordable medical insurance. These are retirement "deal-breakers," meaning that you can't retire until you figure out how to address these barriers.

- Inventory and assess your **retirement resources,** as described in Chapters 3 and 10. These are typically plans or tools that address your retirement income, such as Social Security, Medicare, retirement plans at work, IRAs, medical insurance, and so on.

- Once you develop strategies to overcome the barriers and enable your retirement, you still might not be ready to retire. So next, think about the **factors** that might influence you to **keep working**. Perhaps you enjoy your work, like your co-workers, or simply want extra spending money. Or maybe you'll feel more secure if your retirement resources grow more before you permanently leave the workforce. Write down the reasons why you might keep working. If these factors are really important, continue working if you can.

- Next, think about the **factors** that might influence you to **retire**. Do you have compelling things you want to do with your life that retirement can enable, such as traveling or pursuing your interests? On the other hand, are there negative factors about work that are compelling you to retire? Are you tired of the work you do, don't like your boss, are tired of the commute, or feel as if you're no longer appreciated? Write down both the positive aspects of retirement as well as the negative aspects of continuing to work.

- Be aware of **triggers** that can influence you to retire. This can include reaching certain milestones, such as eligibility for Social Security or Medicare, the retirement of co-workers or friends and relatives, or grandchildren being born. It can also include a frustrating experience at work – "That does it! I'm outta here!" Write down the triggers that might influence you and the strategies you'll adopt in response. But don't make a hasty decision. Instead, recognize triggers when they happen, let the immediate emotions pass, and make sure you stick to your carefully designed plans.

The people who do best in retirement have been able to "retire to" a positive vision of life they've built for their retirement years instead of "retiring from" the negative aspects of work. So think hard about what you'll enjoy by retiring rather than what you'll escape from by no longer working.

Finally, be aware of your typical decision-making style, which can influence your retirement planning. For instance, people who typically make impulsive decisions based on their feelings should consider slowing down their decision-making process and carefully considering the financial implications of working versus retiring. By contrast, people who exclusively focus on numerical calculations might benefit from reflecting on how they *feel* about work versus retirement. Or maybe they should join a discussion group and work together with the members of the group to reflect on the pros and cons of retiring versus continued work.

Are you married or in a lifelong relationship? You'll certainly want to include your spouse or partner in your planning. After all, they're sharing your life path (and most likely your finances) and may need to carry out plans you've made after you're gone. You should specifically involve them in financial decisions, especially when you're working with a financial adviser.

Not your parents' retirement plan!

The new retirement described in this chapter might not work for everybody. Many people still work in physically demanding jobs and will be unable to continue working in their later years; in that case, they'll need to transition from their first middle age directly to full retirement. Others may not have the wherewithal to make the necessary plans or changes in their lives that will help them live the retirement they want. Nevertheless, this new vision might be the most realistic for millions of workers who are approaching their retirement years.

The planning I'm suggesting here may not be easy, but it might be necessary. It might also be invigorating and exciting. After all, you're taking matters into your own hands and making plans for the rest of your life.

What's very likely is that you won't have your parents' retirement and will need to complete more planning than they did. But it will be *your* retirement, and you can make it happen with thoughtful planning.

Because we face significant retirement challenges, we'll need to sustain our motivation to remain focused on potential solutions. As a result, before we discuss the specific strategies you'll need to use to plan for your finances, health, and well-being, let's dig into the next chapter, which gives you some ideas and strategies to help motivate and inspire you for success. It's a critical part of your game-changing retirement plan.

 **ACTION STEPS:**

- Ask relatives and close friends who've retired about the steps they've taken that have worked well for them. Also ask them about any regrets they might have.

- Think about the definition of retirement that makes the most sense for you. Reflect on whether you'll want to transition directly from middle age to full retirement, or if you'll have an extended second middle age.

- Consider how important your freedom from working is compared to the need to generate income to spend during retirement.

- Answer the "who-what-when-where-why" of your retirement years. Write down your answers — they'll be key to the plans you'll be making based on this book.

- Write down the reasons why you might continue working, the reasons why you want to retire, and the triggers that might influence both of those decisions.

- Using one of the online calculators listed in this chapter's "Helpful Resources," estimate how long you might live, including the possible variance from the averages. If you're married or have a life partner, ask them to do the same so you can see how long your resources might need to last for both of you.

 HELPFUL RESOURCES:

Books

- *Aging Well: Surprising Guideposts to a Happier Life from the Landmark Harvard Study of Adult Development,* by George Vaillant. Hachette Book Group, 2002.

- *A Long Bright Future,* by Laura L. Carstensen, PhD. PublicAffairs, 2011.

- *Project Renewment: The First Retirement Model for Career Women,* by Helen Dennis and Bernice Bratter. Scribner, 2008.

- *Successful Aging,* by John W. Rowe, MD, and Robert L. Kahn, PhD. Dell Publishing, 1998.

Websites

- *Longevity Illustrator.* This website, prepared by the Society of Actuaries and the American Academy of Actuaries, provides estimates of life expectancies for both individuals and couples: www.longevityillustrator.org

- Life expectancy calculators. These websites consider your family history and lifestyle choices, and make suggestions for improving the results:

  o   www.livingto100.com

  o   www.bluezones.com

- *Managing Retirement Decisions,* maintained by the Society of Actuaries: https://www.soa.org/research-reports/2012/research-managing-retirement-decisions/

  o   "Big Question: When Should I Retire?"

  o   "When Retirement Comes Too Soon"

  o   "Women Take the Wheel: Destination Retirement"

CHAPTER 2

MOTIVATE AND INSPIRE YOURSELF

DON'T MAKE THESE MISTAKES:

⊘   Be too optimistic and just assume you'll carry through with your plans.

TRY THESE GAME-CHANGING STRATEGIES:

➜   Harness the power of your emotions to help you achieve your goals and avoid common pitfalls.

Start with motivation

How much time are you willing to spend planning for your future? It seems logical that you'd be willing to spend a lot of time, considering we're talking about the remaining 20 or 30 years of your life. But this chapter isn't going to focus on what's logical. Instead, we're discussing human nature, a factor that's often been overlooked when making important life decisions.

It will take most people many hours and days to understand the strategies I've outlined in this book, do your homework, and then implement your decisions. At first, you might start by enthusiastically devoting many hours to your planning. But then you might get frustrated or impatient and think, "I'd rather look through Facebook or watch my favorite TV show."

Indeed, studies show that most people have a limited amount of discipline and willpower to focus on any particular task.[1] And there's plenty of evidence that many people know what they need to do to improve their lives, but don't get around to taking those steps, for various reasons.[2]

So how can you stay on track to create a plan that addresses your financial security, your health, and your happiness during retirement? How can you marshal the strength to stand up to the societal influences against living a healthy, financially secure life? It might help to harness the power of emotions to make your decisions stick. For example, how often have you made New Year's resolutions to save more, eat better, or exercise more? Then, come February or March, you're back to your same old habits. If this sounds like you, read on!

It will take patience and persistence to carry out the strategies needed to live long and well. Harness the power of emotions to help you succeed.

Behavioral economics and psychological science is one of the hottest areas today in consumer finance and health promotion. For decades, traditional economists assumed that people made rational decisions, coldheartedly weighing the economic advantages and disadvantages of each option at hand. They assumed that everybody made decisions much like Mr. Spock of *Star Trek*, with logic winning out every time. Advertisers, of course, laugh at this assumption: They've been manipulating humans for decades with carefully crafted pitches to tempt you to buy the stuff they're selling. Fortunately, economists have caught on, and today, they devote a lot of attention to consumer behavior and psychology.

You can use the results of recent research in behavioral economics and psychological science to help you succeed with your retirement planning and avoid common pitfalls, including being a victim of fraud. This short chapter introduces you to a few strategies that can help motivate and inspire you to persist with your planning as you work your way through the retirement planning strategies I've outlined in this book.

Write down your hopes and dreams, your fears and concerns

Here's an easy exercise that can help guide your retirement planning: It's called the "hopes and dreams, fears and concerns" exercise and was developed by Sally Hass, who ran one of America's most comprehensive retirement readiness programs at corporate giant Weyerhaeuser for many years. Hass recommends you sit down and make a list of your hopes and dreams for your retirement life. "Think big!" she suggests. "List the things that can really get you excited about life." This list will help provide a guide to deciding how much money you need in your retirement years.

She then suggests you write down your fears and concerns about retirement and identify future events that could get in the way of realizing your hopes and dreams. Your list should identify risks that your retirement plan will later address. Running out of money and poor health are common concerns, for instance, and we'll cover both of those risks in later chapters. But you may have other concerns of your own, and you should add those to your list as well.

Once your lists are complete, Hass recommends keeping them handy so you're constantly reminded to stay on track. You should also share and discuss your lists with your spouse, partner, or close friends and relatives, who'll provide emotional support to help you carry out your plans.

Create vivid visualizations

Here's another idea to help boost your motivation: Create vivid visualizations of your future life in your retirement years. Start by thinking about past experiences that have given you joy and satisfaction, experiences you'd like to repeat in the future. For some people, this might be travel, hobbies, or working for your favorite causes. For others, it might be participating in important family events, such as attending family reunions and weddings, or being involved in grandchildren's activities.

Then, strategically place pictures of these events around your home so you see them every day to remind you of the possibilities you have for enjoying your future life. Studies show that using vivid visualizations can boost your chances of meeting the goals you set for yourself.[3]

See your future self

Psychologists contend that most people don't think much about their future selves, and as a result, they aren't motivated to take steps *now* to improve their life in the future. But studies show that people who can envision themselves in the future are more motivated to care for that future self.[4]

If you really want to ramp up your motivation to take care of your future self, it helps to see a picture of what you might look like in 10, 20, or 30 years. Using an online program, I created pictures of myself that are projected to ages 75, 85, and 95, and I keep them on my computer desktop so I see them frequently. They've helped boost my determination to take care of my future self in all aspects — money, health, and social connections.

Take care of your future self!

The "Helpful Resources" section at the end of this chapter identifies an app that will show you how you might look in a few decades. If you decide to use it, here's a hint: Start with a photo in which you're smiling. You want that future you to be happy!

Seek stories that work for you

As emotional creatures, we're generally influenced more by stories than by facts and figures.[5] Here's one real-life example: A 50-something friend of mine, Elizabeth, asked me for my thoughts on planning her retirement. She said that she most likely wouldn't live a long time, so her money wouldn't need to last very long.

I knew her history and the reason she thought she might not live long — her mother had died of cancer at age 54, so Elizabeth believed that would be her fate as well. But she had other older relatives who lived into their 80s and 90s.

Instead of just making assumptions, I suggested Elizabeth estimate her life expectancy using an online calculator that asked questions about the longevity of all close family members as well as about her lifestyle choices. It turns out she was focusing on the one big negative story in her life without considering the numerous positive stories. The calculator estimated that Elizabeth might live into her 90s, and it completely changed her perspective on her future. Now she's planning for a *long-life* retirement.

As you think about your own future, you'll want to consider both the positive and negative stories that could be influencing your thinking about how long you'll live. Do you have friends and relatives who died young? While some people die at a young age due to diseases beyond their control, others may have died due to lifestyle choices, such as smoking or obesity, that limited their lifespan. Instead of being worried about dying young, use any negative stories as motivation to avoid unhealthy behaviors. For example, you might want to think, "I don't want to end up like my poor Uncle Harry, who smoked himself to an early death from lung cancer."

Also, seek out the positive stories of older friends and relatives who are living long and well. Ask them what they did to plan for their older years. They'll probably be happy to share their experiences with you, and they'll most likely be a positive influence on you.

Help yourself to delay gratification

Standard economic theory assumes that people discount the value of future rewards, which means that the majority of people prefer to receive a good sooner rather than later. Both economists and psychologists understand that humans are hardwired to focus on providing for today — it just doesn't come naturally to think about consequences that might take years to unfold.

If you want to see a hilarious yet insightful video that illustrates this concept, find the video on YouTube titled "The Marshmallow Test." You'll see four-year-olds agonizing over whether to eat one marshmallow now or wait 15 minutes and get two marshmallows. Only about one-third of the kids ended up waiting. Most of those who waited adopted clever strategies to help them wait, usually walking around and doing something else to distract themselves — anything other than staring obsessively at the single marshmallow on the table in front of them. Subsequent studies showed that the kids who were able to wait tended to be more successful as adults than those who gave in to temptation.

I contend that a four-year-old waiting 15 minutes for a second marshmallow requires about the same willpower as a 60-something deciding whether to retire now or wait a few more years. Take a cue from the kids who waited: Keep your job, but go find something interesting to do while you're waiting to retire rather than obsessing about the joys of being retired now. (Chapter 12 offers some interesting ideas for working longer yet still improving your enjoyment of life.)

Use affirmations to help you succeed

Affirmations are statements you make about what you value that can help you cope with tricky or stressful situations. Geoff Cohen, PhD, is a professor at Stanford University who has conducted fascinating research on the power of values affirmations to achieve improvements in a few difficult situations, such as helping disadvantaged youth succeed in school, and helping women lose weight.[6]

According to Cohen, affirmations work best when they're a statement about your values. For example, you might take a moment to jot down why responsibility, family, or religion is important to you. Then take a few minutes to remember several times when these values made an impact on you. This exercise isn't about acknowledging how great you are. It's about reminding yourself what's really important to you at your core.

For instance, you can use affirmations to remind yourself that being responsible for your life and the impact on your family is a core value for you. That can help boost your motivation when you'll inevitably face some tough choices with your planning, such as retiring as soon as possible vs. deciding to work a little longer to allow your financial resources to grow. Working a little longer now might permanently increase your standard of living when you eventually retire full time.

Plan your planning

As you continue to read through this book, you might think that the decisions you need to make regarding retirement and your future are overwhelming. Fortunately, you don't need to do everything all at once. First, spend some time listing all the decisions you'll need to make and the homework you'll need to complete. Then parcel out your tasks so you don't have to decide between planning and looking at Facebook, watching your favorite TV show, or going out with friends for coffee.

Here's another idea: The average American spends three to four hours each day watching TV or perusing the internet. Think about your least favorite TV show or online activity, and then remove that from your weekly routine. Use the time you've just freed up to plan your *rest-of-life*. Do that for a few weeks, and you'll soon see just how much progress you can make.

Supercharge your planning

I've got two more ideas for you to help you succeed at planning for your retirement years.

First, reward yourself when you complete tasks or experience any small or large success. Frequent reinforcement will help you succeed! Choose small rewards that make you happy, whether that's a trip to your local Starbucks, 15 minutes of time on your favorite social media site or blog, or a walk with your favorite four-legged friend.

The second thing you could try is to do the planning together with your spouse, or with a small group of close relatives and friends. It helps to discuss the pros and cons of important decisions with people who care about you. They can offer food for thought and help you make decisions that might be more difficult for you to make on your own.

This chapter provides some basic ideas for tapping the power of emotions to help you succeed with your planning. If you're really interested in this topic, see the bonus chapter "Stay Focused" on the "Advanced Study" page of www.retirement gamechangers.com. There, you'll learn about factors that can have a significant impact on your financial decisions, such as loss aversion, framing, and confirmation bias, as well as factors that can influence your decisions regarding Social Security and deploying your savings in retirement.

Remember Popeye from our childhood, who downed spinach as a superfood to give him strength to face his challenges? Think of the tools you've read about in this chapter as the "spinach" that will give you the strength and determination to do your homework, make important decisions, and carry your plans out to completion.

Given the challenges that most of us face when planning for our retirement years, we'll need all the help we can get. We'll do best to consciously strengthen our resourcefulness and resilience. Harnessing the power of our emotions is a smart way to help ourselves do just that.

 **ACTION STEPS:**

- Make a list of your hopes and dreams for your retirement years. What will excite you about the rest of your life? Who do you want to spend time with? What do you want to be doing?

- Make another list of your fears and concerns. What might hold you back from realizing your hopes and dreams? Be sure to put in place plans to address these fears. Don't worry — this book will show you how.

- Share and discuss your lists with your spouse, partner, or close friends and relatives.

- Consider using one of the motivation strategies discussed in this chapter to help you keep your plans on track: visualizing your future, viewing a picture of your future self, or paying attention to stories that will have a positive impact on your life.

- Develop an affirmation that can give you the determination to persist and succeed.

- Form a small study group that can help you be honest with yourself, and be on the lookout for negative stories that might influence you in an unproductive way.

 **HELPFUL RESOURCES:**

Advanced Study page at www.retirementgamechangers.com

- *Stay Focused,* a bonus chapter that uses psychology to help make decisions in all aspects of your planning

App on Apple or Android smartphones

- AgingBooth can project photos of your future self.

Books

- *Decisive: How to Make Better Choices in Life and Work,* by Chip Heath and Dan Heath. Crown Business, 2013.

- *Jolt: Stories of Trauma and Transformation,* by Mark Miller. Post Hill Press, 2018.
- *Willpower: Rediscovering the Greatest Human Strength,* by Roy Baumeister and John Tierney. Penguin Books, 2011.

Website

- *The Marshmallow Test.* YouTube. https://www.youtube.com/watch?v=QX_oy9614HQ

CHAPTER 3

TAKE YOUR FINANCIAL INVENTORY

DON'T MAKE THESE MISTAKES:

- ⊘ Guess about the value of any of your assets.
- ⊘ Overlook valuable assets and resources.
- ⊘ Spend too much time on issues that won't help you very much.

TRY THESE GAME-CHANGING STRATEGIES:

- → Gather and organize your financial resources and debts, so that you have the information you need to build the foundation of your financial security.
- → Estimate your retirement income target by determining how much you'll spend on living expenses.
- → Focus on the items that will have the most positive impact on your overall financial security and well-being.

Don't guess: Know where you stand

A few years ago, I was approached at a holiday party by Elaine, a 60-something family friend. She asked me for some advice about her retirement. That often happens to me nowadays — at last, this actuary is the life of the party!

Elaine guessed that she had saved about $300,000 in various retirement accounts, although she wasn't sure about the exact amounts in each account. She assumed this money would be enough for her to retire in the next year or so, but she wanted to check with me first.

I asked her how much she would receive from Social Security. "I don't know" was her answer. Then I asked her if she'd earned any pension benefits from prior employers, and she replied, "I think so, but I don't know how much." I then asked her how much she planned to withdraw from her savings each year, and she said, "About $25,000 per year — that's what I need to cover my living expenses nowadays." After I did the math in my head, I calculated that she'd be withdrawing more than 8% of her savings each year — an amount that's far too high if she wants to make her money last for the rest of her life (a topic we'll cover in detail in Chapters 6 and 7).

I told Elaine that based on her intended withdrawals from savings, there was a very good chance she'd exhaust her savings in her 70s or 80s. And given her circumstances and health, there was also a good chance she'd live into her 90s, so she'd most likely end up old and poor — or old and broke! It wasn't the answer she wanted to hear, but to her credit, she wanted to hear more.

> *"44 percent of people who tried to figure out their financial futures ended up changing their retirement savings plans."*

> **—From *Taking the Mystery Out of Retirement Planning,*
> by the U.S. Department of Labor**

I suggested that, as a first step, she take inventory of all her financial assets and debts, her current living expenses, and how they might change when she retires. During the next few months, she did as I suggested and followed the steps described later in this book. The good news is, she now has a more realistic retirement plan. And while she's planning to continue working for a few more years, she's going to reduce her hours so she has more time to enjoy life. This compromise will make a big difference in her financial security for the rest of her life.

Just as I told Elaine, my best advice to you is, don't guess — know where you stand! Take the time *now* to realistically inventory and assess your situation. Doing so will help you make more effective decisions about the rest of your life, particularly about when you can realistically afford to retire.

The rest of this chapter describes the specific information you'll need to gather in order to implement the financial strategies described later in this book. But you don't need to stop reading while you collect this information. Instead, begin your homework as you continue to work your way through *Retirement Game-Changers* so you'll understand why it's important to track down and learn about *all* of your resources. Taking a thorough inventory can make your retirement more secure and fulfilling. And while this might take some time, please be patient and persist. Remember, you're planning your life for the next 20 to 30 years.

Ready for your first assignment? Let's proceed with an inventory of your financial assets, debts, and living expenses. To help you keep track of things more easily, you may want to use a software program to document your inventory. Popular options include Mint, Personal Capital, Quicken, planning tools at Fidelity's retirement planning website, or planning tools on NewRetirement.com. Or you can simply organize your paper files and store them where you can find them.

Inventory your financial resources

Since money — and how much of it you have — is an essential part of your retirement, your first step is to take an inventory of all your financial assets so you can realistically assess the retirement income you'll receive from Social Security, savings, and pensions. As you compile the information, be sure to include your spouse's resources if you're married, or your partner's resources if you're in a committed relationship.

> *Your financial inventory helps you implement the strategies you'll learn later, but you don't need to complete your inventory before reading the rest of* **Retirement Game-Changers**.

Here's a checklist of typical financial resources you should consider including in your inventory:

- ✓ Social Security information
  - ○ The amount of monthly income you'd receive if you started benefits at each of the following ages: your target retirement age, your full retirement age, and age 70. See Chapter 5 for details.

✓ Employer-sponsored retirement savings plans such as 401(k), 403(b), 457(b), profit-sharing, or health savings account (HSA) plans

- o Account balances
- o Descriptive material, such as summary plan descriptions
- o Online resources, including retirement planners
- o Summaries of investment funds, including expense ratios
- o Description of the payout options available to you when you retire

✓ Employer-sponsored pension plans, including cash balance plans

- o The amount of monthly retirement income you've earned at normal retirement age
- o Descriptive material, such as summary plan descriptions
- o Online resources, including a calculator that enables you to estimate your monthly retirement income at a target retirement age

✓ IRAs and investment accounts with mutual fund companies, financial institutions, or financial advisers

- o Account balances
- o Investment options, including descriptions of investment goals and specific investments
- o Disclosures on available funds, including expense ratios
- o Options for setting up retirement income. See Chapters 6 and 7 for details.
- o Online resources, including retirement planners

✓ Annuity policies

- o The amount of the cash value
- o The amount of the monthly retirement income you'll receive and the age this income starts
- o Descriptive material, including policy documents and associated expense charges

✓ Whole life insurance policies

- o The amount of the cash value
- o The amount of the death benefit

- o Any conversion options, including converting to an annuity payment
- o Descriptive material, including policy documents and associated expense charges
✓ Bank accounts
- o Account balances, including applicable fees
✓ Home equity
- o Estimated market value
✓ Any other sources of income, such as divorce settlements, including amounts and payment periods

Don't count on an inheritance

Some people think they might inherit money or assets when their parents or other relatives pass away. And for some people, that might be a reasonable assumption.

There are some problems, however, with counting on an inheritance in your retirement planning. First, your parents or relatives might be alive during your retirement years, so that could create uncomfortable thoughts if you really need that money to make ends meet. Second, these people may need to spend a lot of money on long-term care in their later years, so it's possible there might not be very much money left when they eventually pass. And finally, you'll most likely be splitting any inheritance among your siblings, and until that will is read, you won't know who gets what.

In spite of these cautions, if you think it's likely you'll receive a significant inheritance, chances are good it will be in the form of money from bank accounts or mutual funds, and stocks and bonds. You might also inherit a share of a mortgage-free home. In this case, you'll probably need to sell the house, pay all the necessary expenses, and then split the net proceeds with the other beneficiaries of the will.

Settling an estate can take many months and even years (another reason not to count on that money for immediate availability). Once the estate has been settled, you can then invest the proceeds to generate retirement income or use as a reserve for emergencies, as discussed in subsequent chapters.

Inventory your debts

Many people enter their retirement years with substantial debt obligations, which is why payments toward any debt you have need to be considered in your budget for living expenses. You'll also want to develop a plan for reducing or eliminating your debt at some point during your retirement years.

Debt repayment can profoundly influence how long you need or want to keep working. For instance, some people plan to work until they've paid off substantial amounts of their debts, so they don't have to devote retirement income toward debt repayment.

Here's the checklist for taking inventory of your debts:

- ✓ Mortgages
  - ○ Details on your mortgage, including interest rate, whether it's adjustable, and the year you're scheduled to pay it off. Be sure to include second mortgages and equity lines of credit.
- ✓ Car loans
  - ○ How much you owe, interest rate, payment term
- ✓ Student loan debt
  - ○ How much you owe, interest rate, payment term
- ✓ Credit cards and any other debt
  - ○ How much you owe, interest rate

Inventory your living expenses

In order to get an accurate picture of your living expenses in retirement, you'll want to understand what your living expenses will be for both your basic needs and your "wants," and how they might change throughout the year. For example, some expenses, such as heating and cooling bills, might be higher during certain seasons.

In addition, most likely you have both monthly expenses and other bills that are paid less frequently — such as property taxes, car and home insurance, and home repairs. In this case, you'll need to make sure you review an entire year's worth of bills in order to be sure you're including all essential expenses.

You'll also want to assess how your living expenses might change when you retire. Some expenses, such as utilities, property taxes, car and home insurance, and food might not change very much. Other expenses will most likely increase substantially, such as premiums for medical insurance, copayments, and deductibles. On the other hand, there's a good chance your income taxes will decrease substantially when you retire.

Once you estimate the amount of your retirement income, you may want to estimate the amount of federal and state income taxes you might be required to pay. To determine those amounts, you could either work with your tax accountant or use tax planning software.

When it comes to living expenses, most people spend more than three-fourths of their budget on just six categories:

- Housing
- Transportation
- Medical expenses
- Food
- Entertainment
- Taxes (federal and state income taxes, and local property taxes)

Start compiling your list of living expenses by tracking your bills for these six categories — and for other key items — as you pay them throughout the year. The software programs I mentioned previously (such as Mint, Personal Capital, and Quicken) can help make this task easier. Or you can use the basic spreadsheets identified in the "Helpful Resources" section at the end of this chapter.

You'll also want to reflect on unexpected costs you incurred in the past three to five years that might not be reflected in the budget you've prepared. Examples include home or car repairs, major appliance purchases, or financial help for adult children or dependent parents. Think how likely it is that you might incur similar unexpected expenses during your retirement years; it'll be pretty likely if you'll live for another few decades. You may want to anticipate such expenses when deciding the amount of cash you want to set aside for emergencies and unexpected costs that we'll discuss in Chapter 4.

Chapter 9 provides more ideas for inventorying and managing your living expenses.

Safely store your documents where you can find them

Once you've gone to the trouble of assembling your financial information, you'll want to safely store the documents where you can easily find them. You'll want to strike a balance between these goals:

- Can you easily access them and make changes?
- Are they safe from people who could harm you if they accessed your information?
- Are they safe from fires and other disasters?
- Will you be able to find your documents years later?

As a practical matter, you may need to compromise with some of these goals to arrive at a solution that works for you. Possibilities include:

- Paper copies in a locked file cabinet, potentially portable so you can "grab and go" if there's an emergency.
- Online storage with appropriate security protection.
- A hard drive or thumb drive with password protection, stored so you can grab and go if there's an emergency.

Careful storage will help you easily access your important documents over the years. It will also help if you need to turn over financial affairs to a trusted relative or friend in your later years, as discussed in Chapter 15.

Learn where to best focus your time and attention

Once you've completed your financial inventory, you can use it to determine where your time and focus can make the most positive difference in your retirement situation. Here are a few common scenarios that illustrate this point:

If you haven't saved very much for retirement

If you've reached your late 50s or early 60s and have less than $100,000 in retirement savings, your retirement savings won't generate much lifetime retirement income. In this situation, your three most important decisions will be when to begin collecting Social Security benefits, how long you can — and should — continue working, and how to manage your spending.

Don't let your lack of retirement funds derail your plans: In this situation, you'll still want to save as much as possible until you retire. You'll also want to learn how to deploy these savings in retirement, as discussed in Chapters 6 and 7. But you should only focus on those steps once you've spent the necessary time on the three most important decisions listed in the previous paragraph.

If you have more home equity than retirement savings

If you have substantial home equity and your other financial resources aren't enough to generate enough retirement income to meet your living expenses, you'll want to read Chapter 6 to learn some ways you can potentially use your home equity to help finance your retirement years.

If you haven't earned a substantial pension but you've accumulated substantial retirement savings

If you have more than $250,000 in retirement savings but little or no employer pension, then mission-critical tasks for you are to carefully decide when to claim Social Security benefits and how to deploy your savings to generate a retirement paycheck that lasts for the rest of your life. See Chapters 5, 6, and 7 for insights on these topics.

If you've earned a substantial pension from your employer and are offered a lump sum payment instead of a lifetime monthly income

In most situations, the lifetime monthly income will be much more valuable than the lump sum payment. If you're tempted to take the lump sum payment, proceed very cautiously. I've known some retirees who elect a lump sum, and then run out of money, either by spending the lump sum too fast or by making investing mistakes. Learn as much as possible about using retirement savings to generate a lifetime retirement paycheck first, as covered in Chapters 6 and 7.

Whew! You're done with your financial inventory — for now. You'll want to update it periodically (at least annually) as your circumstances change to reflect any fluctuations that occur during the year.

This short chapter might seem like it requires a lot of work, but it's definitely worth your time and effort to learn where you stand regarding all your financial resources. Now you're ready to start building the foundation for your financial security in retirement.

ACTION STEPS:

- Inventory your financial assets and debts.
- Inventory your current living expenses, reflecting on how they might change in retirement.
- From your inventories, identify the financial decisions that will help you the most.

 **HELPFUL RESOURCES:**

Book

- *Taking the Mystery Out of Retirement Planning,* by the U.S. Department of Labor. December 2014. Includes many helpful worksheets to track assets, debts, and living expenses, and how they might change in retirement. https://www.dol.gov/sites/default/files/ebsa/about-ebsa/our-activities/resource-center/publications/taking-the-mystery-out-of-retirement-planning.pdf

Websites

- Online programs can help you inventory your financial assets:
  - *AARP Home Budget Calculator*: https://www.aarp.org/money/budgeting-saving/home_budget_calculator.html
  - *Fidelity Income Strategy Evaluator*: https://www.fidelity.com/calculators-tools/income-strategy-evaluator
  - *Intuit Mint*: https://www.mint.com
  - *NewRetirement*: https://www.newretirement.com
  - *Personal Capital*: https://www.personalcapital.com
  - *Quicken*: https://www.quicken.com
- Simple worksheets to estimate living expenses:
  - Blackrock's retirement expense worksheet: https://www.blackrock.com/investing/literature/investor-education/retirement-expense-worksheet-va-us.pdf
  - TIAA's retirement budget worksheet: https://www.tiaa.org/public/pdf/advice-planning/tools-calculators/A125820_budgeting_worksheet.pdf

II.

SECURE

Building your financial security for a period that could last 20 to 30 years or more is a critical yet complex task, one that will take a considerable amount of time and effort to do successfully. This will be the first test of your patience and resilience, but hang in there, because it's well worth the effort. After all, you don't want to reach your 80s or 90s and find yourself broke and vulnerable to financial and medical shocks.

Many of the important financial and medical insurance decisions you'll make in your 50s and 60s are hard to change after you've made them, and some are irreversible. In most cases, you don't get a "do-over" — and poor decisions could result in "game-over."

Simply put, your "retirement job" is to make sure that you don't outlive your money or get wiped out by high bills for medical or long-term care. This job is just as important for your financial security as your career was earlier in your life, so commit to giving your new job the care that it deserves.

The series of decisions you'll need to make as you leave your career job and retire are just as important as the decisions you made at the beginning of your adult life after you graduated from high school or college. You had to make choices that affected your employment, where you would live, and who you might spend the rest of your life with. The decisions you're going to make now will be just as important because they impact your financial security, health, and enjoyment of life for the rest of your life.

In the following section, you'll learn how to build a reliable, diversified portfolio of retirement income that lasts the rest of your life, no matter how long you live and no matter what happens in the stock market. This portfolio should cover your *needs* for the rest of your life and will hopefully cover most of your *wants* as well.

You'll learn about the best time to start Social Security benefits — your most important "retirement paycheck." You'll also learn how to deploy your hard-earned retirement savings so it lasts the rest of your life. You'll see how to integrate these decisions with the groundbreaking Spend Safely in Retirement Strategy.

You'll discover tips for managing your living expenses so you can live within your means. And you'll learn some essential facts about medical insurance and Medicare so you can protect yourself from the threat of high medical bills.

After reading the chapters in this section, you might conclude that you need to work longer than you had planned. That's OK — I'd rather you come to this realization now, instead of retiring too early and then struggling financially in your 70s and 80s.

This isn't a section you want to speed through. Instead, read and absorb one chapter at a time, and reward yourself as you diligently work through the material in this section. Don't get discouraged if you don't understand a concept right away — it's only natural if you need to read the material a few times to let the ideas sink in.

Your sense of confidence in your future is well worth the time you'll devote to planning for your retirement. You'll thank yourself when you reach your 80s and 90s with enough money to enjoy your life!

CHAPTER 4

MANAGE THE MAGIC FORMULA FOR RETIREMENT INCOME SECURITY

$$I > E$$

DON'T MAKE THESE MISTAKES:

- ⊘ Wing it and use your retirement savings like a checking account.
- ⊘ Focus exclusively on your "retirement number" (the amount of money you need to save in order to retire).
- ⊘ Assume you can continue working indefinitely, earning the same pay.

TRY THESE GAME-CHANGING STRATEGIES:

- ➡ Think beyond your "retirement number" to manage the "magic formula" for retirement income security for the rest of your life: Income > Expenses, or I > E.
- ➡ Cover your basic living expenses with a series of "retirement paychecks" that are guaranteed to last the rest of your life.
- ➡ Pay for your discretionary living expenses with "retirement bonuses" that might fluctuate in value but have the potential for growth.
- ➡ Set up a cash stash for emergencies.
- ➡ Develop plans to protect yourself against common retirement risks and to withstand financial shocks.

Don't wing it

An older family relative of mine — let's call him Bill — retired in the late 1990s with a large lump sum from his employer's 401(k) plan. It was the most money Bill had ever seen in his life, and it never occurred to him that this savings might run out. During his retirement years, he just kept spending his money on all the things he'd always spent money on, without a plan to make the money last for the rest of his life. To make matters worse, Bill started his Social Security benefits at age 62, which was another mistake he made, as you'll see in Chapter 5.

Soon after Bill retired, he was hit by a devastating one-two punch. First came the 2000-2002 stock market crash that substantially reduced the value of his savings. Then the Great Recession of 2008-2009 wiped him out completely. As a result, he lost his house because he couldn't afford to make the mortgage payments. He moved to a small apartment and went back to work in his early 70s, working at night as a delivery person to make ends meet. Then he developed a serious illness that made him unable to continue working. When he passed away at age 77, his money was completely gone.

Even though Bill was a careful money manager during his working years, his "golden years" rusted out because he didn't plan to make his savings last for a long retirement. When it comes to retirement, Bill's a perfect example of what can happen when people just "wing it." By withdrawing the amounts he needed from his savings to meet his current living expenses — without putting in place a plan to make his money last for a long life — Bill ended up dying broke.

This "pay-as-you-go" retirement is a *bad way* to manage your retirement savings. The most likely result of winging it in this fashion is that retirees will experience "money death" before actually passing away.

Here's a picture worth a thousand dollars that illustrates this mistake:

Spend without planning

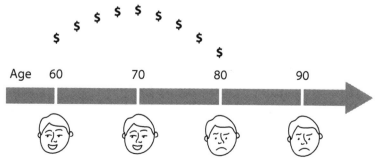

People who "plan" in this manner are *hoping* that their money will last for a lifetime without them having to do any real planning. Well, hope without planning is not a good strategy, particularly when you might live a long time.

Instead of just hoping your money will last, use this game-changing strategy: Build a portfolio of retirement "paychecks" and "bonuses" that will last the rest of your life, no matter how long you live. Then you can safely spend these paychecks and bonuses, without worrying about outliving your money or being wiped out by stock market crashes. This strategy will give you the confidence to live a long time and enjoy your life!

The goal of your retirement income portfolio should be to cover both your basic and your discretionary living expenses, in both good economic times and bad. The suggested homework in this chapter and in Chapters 5 through 8 will help you understand whether you'll need to reduce your living expenses to match your income, which many retirees may need to do.

By the way, financial security in retirement is about more than building a sufficient retirement income portfolio. You'll also want to develop strategies to protect yourself and your family from common retirement risks, such as potentially high costs for medical, dental, and long-term care expenses, as well as the death of a spouse (Chapters 10 and 15 cover these topics). You'll also want to be able to withstand predictable and unpredictable financial shocks, such as stock market crashes, home repairs, and children who need financial help.

Before talking about your retirement income portfolio, let's discuss an overall framework for managing your retirement income and living expenses.

Understand the "magic formula" for retirement income security

You might hear people talk about their "retirement number," which is the amount of money they think they need to have on hand before they can retire. But that's just too simplistic of a goal — it doesn't give you a plan to manage your income and living expenses in retirement.

Instead, you should manage the "magic formula" for retirement income security:

$$I > E$$

To translate, your **income** ("I") needs to exceed your living **expenses** ("E") for the rest of your life. As you can see, this formula really isn't magic; it's just common sense.

Retirement planners often focus on the income aspect of retirement only, wanting to talk to you solely about generating retirement income. You might hear them say, "You need a retirement income equal to 70% to 80% of your salary just before your retirement."

The problem with this rule of thumb? It ignores the element of living expenses, which can change significantly in your later years. It also assumes you want the same life in retirement that you had while you were working and that you won't change your spending habits. For many people, however, that's not the case.

Instead, you'll want to take a closer look at your expenses and determine how you might cut back. You'll also want to focus on buying just enough to meet your needs and make you happy, as discussed in Chapter 9.

Retirement planning tip from your dog

Dogs are masters at living within their means and balancing the *I* > *E* formula for retirement security. That's because dogs are content with whatever living circumstances they have, and they don't complain if they don't have as much now compared to prior years. They look for ways to be happy and satisfied.

As you read through this book, you'll find lots of ideas and strategies for managing *both* sides of the magic formula.

For now, let's get started building your retirement income portfolio.

Build the 21st century retirement income portfolio

Many retirees in the 20th century relied on the so-called "three-legged stool" of retirement, which was made up of the most common sources of retirement income: Social Security benefits, a pension from their employer, and personal savings. Unfortunately, this stool is no longer sturdy or reliable for most current older workers. Many can no longer rely on a substantial pension from their employer, and their savings might not be enough to last for a long life. In addition, this retirement stool was really designed for 20th century retirees, who didn't live as long as most current older workers and retirees will live.

Instead of a three-legged stool, we need a "21st century retirement income portfolio" that recognizes the economic realities facing many older workers today, one that will survive future stock market crashes, which are inevitable over the next few decades of our retirement years. This new plan will involve carefully deploying *all* of your financial resources.

Here's the modern retirement income portfolio that you can create using your retirement savings and other resources:

1. Set up reliable, lifetime "retirement paychecks" that you've deployed to pay yourself. These paychecks should last the rest of your life, no matter how long you live, and won't drop when the stock market crashes. Cover your basic living expenses entirely with these paychecks — or at least come close.

2. Develop "retirement bonuses" that may increase or decrease over the years, or even go away completely. Use these bonuses to pay for discretionary living expenses, such as traveling, hobbies, and spoiling your grandchildren.

3. Set up a "cash stash" to cover large, one-time expenses that would overload your retirement paychecks and bonuses. These can include predictable expenses, such as home repairs, appliances, furniture, and new cars. They can also include unforeseen emergencies, such as providing financial help to adult children and grandchildren, or large out-of-pocket medical or dental expenses. The goal is to avoid dipping into the part of your retirement savings that generates your retirement paychecks and bonuses.

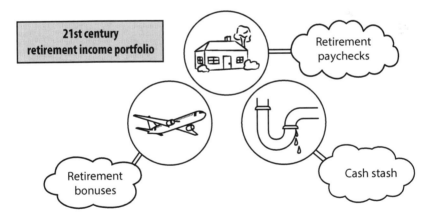

The 21st century retirement income portfolio offers a strong, three-pronged approach to managing your retirement income and living expenses. It also keeps things simple for retirees by mirroring the money management strategies you most likely used while you were working. Let me explain.

Most workers developed lifelong spending habits that were likely dependent upon a reliable paycheck. This paycheck — whether weekly, biweekly, or monthly — helped determine the amount you could spend each month on your living expenses. If you were wise, you knew you couldn't spend more than the amount of your paycheck without getting into financial trouble. Most workers counted on receiving their monthly paycheck indefinitely and planned their spending accordingly.

If you received a bonus, it most likely paid for discretionary expenses, such as vacations, home improvements, or other one-time costs, or you saved it for the future. You most likely understood the inherent nature of the bonus — it's money that isn't guaranteed year after year. It might go up in good years, it might go down in bad years, and it might even disappear altogether. As a result, most people didn't "bet the ranch" on receiving their bonus.

If you managed your money well, you most likely also had a savings account, in which you'd set aside funds for vacations, large household expenses, and any emergencies that might come up. You wouldn't use this money for everyday expenses, keeping it intact until you really needed it. As a result, you had a safety net in place should an unexpected expense arise.

Since most of you probably lived during your working years with the financial discipline of monthly paychecks, periodic bonuses, and an emergency fund, why change in retirement? You can design your retirement paychecks and bonuses to support your basic and discretionary spending for the rest of your life, no matter how long you live. And you can manage your regular living expenses so that you spend just your monthly retirement paychecks and those periodic bonuses, and keep your cash stash intact for large, one-time expenses.

Your retirement paychecks, bonuses, and cash stash are the "I" part of the magic formula for retirement security that we discussed earlier in this chapter.

Here's a graph worth a million bucks:

Plan your spending!

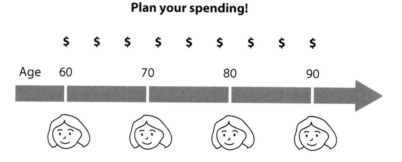

Once you estimate the amounts of the paychecks and bonuses that your retirement savings can generate, you can make important life decisions, such as when you can afford to retire, whether you need to work in retirement, and how much money you can afford to spend on both discretionary and nondiscretionary expenses. The next five chapters help you learn how to estimate these amounts.

Before we dig into the details of the modern retirement income portfolio, however, your next step should be to think about the goals you have for your retirement finances. Keep these goals in mind when you read the next five chapters about various retirement income strategies.

Determine the goals that are important to you

There are many viable retirement income generators (RIGs) you can use to deploy your hard-earned savings to generate income in retirement, whether they're for your paychecks or your bonuses. But developing an effective retirement income strategy — one that works best for you — often entails juggling goals that can conflict with each other.

Here are some common goals you may have for building your retirement income portfolio:

- Generate retirement income you can't outlive.
- Maximize the amount of retirement income expected to be paid over your lifetime.
- Provide the potential for income growth to keep up with inflation.
- Be able to handle an unexpected emergency or life event.
- Build in the flexibility to access savings so you can change course if your life circumstances change.
- Preserve the ability to apply unused funds as a legacy.
- Select solutions that are easy to use and don't need continual monitoring and adjustment.
- Protect yourself against fraud or mistakes due to cognitive decline (you'll probably appreciate this goal more when you reach your 80s and beyond — maybe even earlier).

Unfortunately, there's not one single method of developing retirement paychecks or bonuses that delivers on all these goals. As a result, you'll need to prioritize and make trade-offs between these goals in order to craft a strategy that fits your needs and circumstances. This is a valid argument for diversifying your

RIGs so your entire retirement income portfolio might address all the goals that are important to you.

Developing an effective retirement income strategy often entails juggling goals that can conflict with each other, so you'll want to make informed trade-offs.

While you're thinking about your goals, keep in mind that you might have different priorities and circumstances than your friends and family, so you'll want to consider your own specific needs, goals, and circumstances when developing your retirement income portfolio. Don't adopt a specific retirement income strategy just because your friends or relatives did! It may not work for you.

Now, let's review the basic types of retirement paychecks.

Build your portfolio of retirement paychecks to cover your basic living expenses

When it comes to their retirement years, most people aren't truly prepared to live a long time or even know how to cope with the uncertainty about the length of their lives, something the experts call "longevity risk." Yes, living too long is a financial risk, even though it might be a life goal you have. The trouble is, you just don't know whether you'll make it to age 75, 85, 95, or even 100.

That's why it's smart to set up retirement paychecks that will pay you no matter how long you live, thus protecting you against longevity risk. These paychecks won't drop if the stock market crashes and are guaranteed to last for the rest of your life, no matter how long you live (and how long your spouse or partner lives, if you're married or in a committed relationship). You'll also want a significant portion of your paychecks to increase for inflation, which is inevitable during your retirement years.

Finally, you'll want to cover most or all your basic living expenses with your retirement paychecks. This way, if you or your spouse or partner lives into your 90s or even to 100, or if the stock market crashes, you won't have to move in with your kids or friends. You'll still have a guaranteed source of income that will provide money for your basic needs.

Here are four viable sources of guaranteed retirement paychecks that help protect you against the risk of living a long time:

- **Retirement Paycheck #1:** Social Security benefits

- **Retirement Paycheck #2:** A monthly pension from a traditional pension plan or from a hybrid cash balance plan from your employer, if you participate in such a plan

- **Retirement Paycheck #3:** A low-cost payout annuity purchased from an insurance company

- **Retirement Paycheck #4:** A monthly tenure payment from a reverse mortgage on your home

This last type of retirement paycheck generator, developed by lenders to meet the needs of older Americans who have modest retirement savings but substantial home equity, has become more available in recent years. You might be able to use this option if you don't plan to move during your lifetime.

The following sequence indicates the most cost-effective sources of guaranteed income:

- Start by maxing out your Social Security benefits, usually by delaying the date you start benefits for as long as possible (but no later than age 70).

- If you participate in an employer-sponsored pension plan, elect the lifetime monthly pension.

- If you still need additional amounts of lifetime retirement paychecks, consider using a portion of your retirement savings to buy a low-cost payout annuity.

- If you need to generate even more money from your retirement paychecks, investigate whether a reverse mortgage is feasible for you.

In addition to lasting the rest of your life, another nice thing about these four retirement paycheck sources is that they're very user-friendly and worry-free. The checks for each of them come automatically in the mail or are deposited electronically. You won't need to make decisions about investing your savings or calculating withdrawal amounts. (You'll appreciate this feature more when you read about generating retirement bonuses later in this chapter.)

Retirement paychecks also protect you against financial fraud and making mistakes due to forgetfulness or cognitive decline. This is a potentially serious problem in your later years when you might not be as mentally sharp as you were in your 60s and 70s.

Chapters 5 and 6 provide many more details on these four retirement paycheck generators.

Now, let's review the basics about retirement bonuses.

Pay for discretionary living expenses with retirement bonuses

To cover your discretionary living expenses, such as travel, gifts, hobbies, and spoiling your kids and grandkids, develop one or more of the following retirement bonuses that can increase or decrease over time:

- **Retirement Bonus #1:** Invest your savings, don't touch the principal, and spend just the investment earnings, which typically consist of interest and dividends.

- **Retirement Bonus #2:** Invest your savings, and draw down the principal and investment earnings cautiously with the intent that you won't outlive your assets. Retirement experts call this method a "systematic withdrawal plan," or SWP for short. It's important to realize that with any SWP, there's no guarantee that your money will last for the rest of your life if you live a long time, or if you experience poor investment returns.

- **Retirement Bonus #3:** Generate income from working or self-employment.

- **Retirement Bonus #4:** Generate income from rental real estate or running your own business.

Each of these types of retirement bonus generators has advantages and disadvantages, and each produces a different amount of retirement income. Once again, it will be important for you to do your homework and make the best choices for you based on your needs and your circumstances. Chapter 7 covers the first two retirement bonuses in detail. Now let's briefly review a few aspects of each of these bonuses.

Depending on how you set up the first two retirement bonuses, they might look a lot like retirement paychecks. You can set them up with the goal being to have them last the rest of your life. And you can deploy investment strategies to minimize potential reductions due to stock market volatility. However, there's no guarantee that you'll achieve these goals.

If you choose to implement your retirement bonuses in this manner, you might not need to cover *all* of your basic living expenses with your retirement paychecks. Instead, you might be comfortable covering a portion of your basic living expenses with retirement bonuses.

Although it sounds like a misnomer, I classify income from working and self-employment as Retirement Bonus #3, because there's a very good chance that eventually your income from working will decrease, or go away altogether in your frail years. Some people make the mistake of assuming they can keep working indefinitely, but you can't really count on working into your 80s or 90s. Chapter 12 covers working in your retirement years in more detail.

Retirement Bonus #4 — generating income from rental real estate or running your own business — can be a good way to generate money during your retirement years, but it's not for the faint-hearted.

Rental real estate is equivalent to running a business. You'll need to spend time and effort to interview and select prospective tenants, manage relationships with your tenants, arrange for home repairs and maintenance, and make sure you have adequate insurance.

As you age into your slow-go and no-go years, you might also be less willing and able to manage your rentals or run a business. I won't cover rental real estate or businesses in this book; if these topics interest you at all, you'll want to educate yourself about the pros and cons by reading books on the subject or talking with real estate or business professionals.

Carefully set up a cash stash

In addition to setting up your retirement paychecks and bonuses, you'll need to establish a cash stash to cover large, one-time expenses that would overload your retirement paychecks and bonuses. Let's see why.

While people are working, many financial planners suggest having an emergency fund that's equal to three to six months of income. This money would help protect you if your income were to be disrupted due to unexpected job losses from layoffs or disability. Once you're retired, however, you no longer need to worry about these types of events.

But that doesn't mean you no longer need an emergency fund. Instead of setting aside the money to protect against job loss, in your retirement years you'll want to build a cash stash that can cover significant, predictable, or unforeseen expenses that can't be paid from your monthly cash flow. Examples include expensive car or home repairs or purchases, or out-of-pocket medical or dental expenses. The purpose of your cash stash is to avoid dipping into the part of your retirement savings that generates your retirement paychecks and bonuses.

The right amount for this stash is somewhat subjective, but the basic idea is to have enough ready savings on hand so that you can pay for an emergency without needing to sell any investments that are generating your retirement paychecks or bonuses. Suggestions for an adequate amount range from $10,000 to $20,000 or more, depending on your specific circumstances regarding your house, car, and medical insurance.

For instance, if you've purchased medical and dental insurance to supplement Medicare when you reach age 65, you've reduced your exposure to substantial out-of-pocket medical expenses. In this case, you might be able to finance deductibles and copayments from your monthly cash flow and not need as large of an emergency fund.

On the other hand, if you're younger than age 65, you might have chosen to participate in a high-deductible health care plan. If that's the case, you might want to have enough money on hand in your cash stash to pay the annual deductible. For more on this topic, see Chapter 10, which covers medical insurance in detail.

It's important to note that your cash stash shouldn't be used to pay for long-term care expenses. That would require an emergency fund that's simply too large for most retirees. You'll need a different strategy to address the threat of potentially ruinous long-term care expenses, and Chapter 15 covers that topic.

Depending on your circumstances, you might feel more comfortable with a reserve that's higher than the previously suggested amounts. Examples of circumstances that might dictate a larger cash stash include:

- If you anticipate moving
- If you're aware of an upcoming need for significant home repairs
- If you'll need to buy a new car at some point in the future
- If you're helping adult children and grandchildren financially

No matter your circumstances, give some careful thought to the amount of cash stash that allows you to sleep well at night.

As for where this cash stash should be maintained, you'll want to keep the money in your cash stash separate from the savings you'll use to generate retirement income. Put the money in accounts you can quickly access that aren't subject to investment fluctuations, such as savings accounts at banks or credit unions, or money market funds. You might not want to use your 401(k) or IRAs for your cash stash, since there can be delays accessing your money and because the IRS requires you to begin making withdrawals at age 70½. The exception is a Roth IRA, which might be good place for your cash stash.

If you do have to draw upon your emergency fund, you might want to consider replenishing it from future monthly retirement paychecks or bonuses, so you always have an adequate amount in it for those unexpected expenses.

One important point: Don't confuse your cash stash with the desired level of liquidity for your retirement savings. Some people think they need to be able to access *all* their retirement savings to deal with emergencies or unforeseen situations — that can be a costly mistake. The trouble is, if you access and spend more of your savings than you can afford to, it's not generating retirement income anymore. If you carefully set up your cash stash, however, you can use some RIGs for your retirement paychecks and bonuses that limit access to your savings but will generate more retirement income over your lifetime. You'll learn more about retirement paychecks and bonuses in Chapters 5, 6, and 7.

Hang in there

Building your retirement income portfolio will be one of the most complex, yet important, retirement decisions you'll make. As a result, I've devoted the most chapters to this topic. Hang in there and spend the time that's necessary to understand your options and make informed decisions. You may even need to read this chapter and Chapters 5, 6, 7, and 8 a few times to let the ideas and insights sink in.

You'll also want to coordinate your retirement income portfolio with the strategies you plan to implement to protect yourself and your family against the threat of high medical and dental expenses and long-term care. You'll want to make sure your retirement income is sufficient to pay for Medicare, medical and dental insurance premiums, and out-of-pocket expenses. You'll also want to protect against high long-term care costs that can wipe out your retirement savings. Chapters 10 and 15 discuss strategies to address these threats.

You may also find that you need professional help to carry out some of the steps in this chapter and the following chapters, but that's only natural. You'll learn how to shop for help in the "Advanced Study" bonus chapter on www.retirement gamechangers.com, identified in the "Helpful Resources" section at the end of this chapter.

So now you have a basic framework for managing your income in your retirement years. Congratulations — you're on your way to building the foundation of your financial security!

Next up: Chapters 5, 6, and 7, which discuss the details of retirement paychecks and bonuses. Then Chapter 8 puts it all together by giving you ideas to design your total retirement income portfolio.

 **ACTION STEPS:**

- Think about which retirement income portfolio goals are important to you, as discussed near the beginning of this chapter. Then prioritize these goals — this will help you make necessary trade-offs between goals that might conflict.

- Decide how much of a cash stash you might need to have on hand to feel comfortable during your retirement years.

- Read Chapters 5, 6, 7, and 8 to learn more about building a portfolio of retirement paychecks and bonuses.

 **HELPFUL RESOURCES:**

Advanced Study page at www.retirementgamechangers.com

- *Get Help*, bonus chapter which covers working with financial advisers

- *Navigating the Tax Rules*, bonus chapter that includes information on the taxation of Social Security benefits

- *Stay Focused*, bonus chapter which explains how using psychology can help you make smart financial decisions, including Social Security claiming decisions

Books

- *Money for Life: Turn Your IRA and 401(k) Into a Lifetime Retirement Paycheck,* by Steve Vernon, FSA. *Rest-of-Life* Communications, 2012.

- *Taking the Mystery Out of Retirement Planning,* by the U.S. Department of Labor. December 2014. Includes many helpful worksheets to track assets, debts, and living expenses, and how they might change when you retire. https://www.dol.gov/sites/default/files/ebsa/about-ebsa/our-activities/resource-center/publications/taking-the-mystery-out-of-retirement-planning.pdf

CHAPTER 5

OPTIMIZE YOUR BEST RETIREMENT PAYCHECK – SOCIAL SECURITY

DON'T MAKE THESE MISTAKES:

- ⊘ Ignore Social Security's significant value for financing your retirement.
- ⊘ Start Social Security benefits as early as possible, at age 62.
- ⊘ Start Social Security benefits before you've exhausted all other possibilities for generating income.
- ⊘ Allow cynicism or the belief that Social Security will go bankrupt to influence you to start benefits too early.

TRY THESE GAME-CHANGING STRATEGIES:

- → Optimize Social Security, most likely the largest portion of your total retirement income.
- → Increase your total Social Security lifetime payout by $100,000 or more with a thoughtful claiming strategy.
- → Coordinate your strategy for claiming Social Security benefits with your strategy for drawing upon your retirement savings, pensions, and other financial resources.
- → Coordinate your strategy with your spouse, if you're married.

Understand the foundation of your retirement paychecks

If you could change just one decision that would have the biggest impact on the amount of money available to you during your retirement years, what would it be? Would you choose to start saving at an earlier age? Would you max out your contributions to your employer-sponsored 401(k) plan? Would you put more money aside in an IRA? Would you live more frugally so you wouldn't worry so much about how you were going to afford to retire?

While all of those choices would be smart, the best possible decision you could make is one you may still have control over: Choose to delay your Social Security benefits for as long as possible (but no later than age 70). By doing so, you might be able to increase your lifetime payout by $100,000 or more.

I have several older friends and relatives who started Social Security income at age 62, the earliest possible age with the lowest monthly income. Now they're in their late 70s and 80s, money is tight, and they regret their decision to elect the smallest possible benefit. Much to their chagrin, they now realize that they could have put off starting their benefits by working a little longer or relying on other financial resources.

Many people just can't wait to start their Social Security income. They view it as free money that they're entitled to after paying Social Security taxes all their working lives. But starting benefits as soon as possible is a big mistake for most people, often because they don't grasp the implications of their decisions. It may also be an apt example of the inability for many people to delay gratification, as we discussed in Chapter 2.

When it comes to financing your retirement, Social Security benefits have powerful, unique features:

- They're paid for the rest of your life.
- They're increased for inflation.
- A portion of your benefits is exempt from income taxes.
- If you're married, they pay valuable survivor benefits to your spouse.
- The system is user-friendly and helps protect against fraud and mistakes.

With regard to this last point, Social Security automatically mails you the benefits check or deposits money electronically into your bank account. With Social Security, you don't need to make any decisions regarding investments or withdrawing from savings.

Simply put, Social Security is the best source for your retirement paychecks. Not a single other retirement income generator has all the desirable features listed above. For most middle-income workers, Social Security will represent anywhere from three-fourths to almost all of their total retirement income.[1] Since that's the case, it simply makes sense to optimize the value of those benefits, particularly if you're one of the millions of older workers who are approaching your retirement years with modest savings and no pension.

With so much on the line, you'll want to spend many hours learning how to get the most value out of Social Security for both yourself and your spouse, if you're married. Don't let this necessary investment of time deter you — instead, commit to devoting the time you need to maximize this valuable benefit.

Your first step? Find your estimate of your Social Security benefits. It can be a starting point for learning more about Social Security.

Find your Social Security Statement

Many of you may have received a statement in the mail from the Social Security Administration (SSA) that includes estimates of your Social Security benefits. In prior years, the SSA mailed these statements at regular intervals; lately, they're encouraging citizens to learn about their estimated Social Security benefits online. If you're like most people, you probably filed your statement away somewhere. Rummage around your house to see if you can find the latest copy of your Social Security Statement.

If you can't put your hands on your statement (or know you tossed it out), don't panic — you can view an online version of your statement by opening up a "my Social Security" account with the Social Security Administration. The "Helpful Resources" section at the end of this chapter has the link.

Your Social Security Statement will show estimates of your monthly retirement income at three possible ages: age 62, the earliest possible age you can collect retirement benefits; your "full retirement age" (more on this later); and age 70, the latest age at which to start retirement benefits. Hopefully seeing these estimates will inspire you to learn more about your options for claiming these valuable benefits so you get the most value from them.

To start your research on how you can optimize Social Security benefits, complete the checklist below (if you're married, also have your spouse complete it). Doing so will help you understand what you need to know about Social Security benefits and determine when it would be best to start your benefits.

Complete the Social Security checklist

The formulas and rules used to calculate Social Security retirement income are quite complex, so the checklist below focuses on the most important rules that will affect your benefits. Think of this checklist as your basic Social Security homework; it covers the minimum information you need to know about Social Security benefits.

Your eyes might glaze over when you work on this checklist, but hang in there! You'll discover the advantages of taking the time to understand how to get the most from your valuable Social Security benefits.

✓ Do you have at least 10 years of covered earnings?

You'll need to pay into Social Security for at least 40 calendar quarters, or 10 years, to be eligible for *any* retirement income from Social Security that's based on your earnings record.

✓ Do you have 35 years of covered earnings?

Your Social Security benefit is based on a 35-year average of your covered wages (that's wages from either an employer or self-employment income), with 10 being the minimum number of years you need to earn any retirement income. When calculating your benefit, Social Security doesn't count any wages above the Social Security Wage Base, which is adjusted each year (in 2018, it's $128,700). Each year's wages are adjusted to account for wage inflation before being used to calculate your 35-year average wage.

Social Security uses the 35 years that produced the highest average out of your entire working career; the earnings don't need to be consecutive to count. If you worked for fewer than 35 years, you'll have some zeros entered into your 35-year average, which will drag down the average earnings figure that's used to calculate your benefit.

Check to see if you have covered earnings for at least 35 years. If you don't, then you may want to continue working until you have a minimum of 35 years of earnings that can be figured into your average earnings. And if you do have enough covered earnings, you may want to continue working longer than 35 years — this can boost your Social Security income if you earn enough to drop some of your lower-earning years out of your 35-year average.

✓ What's your earnings history?

You can check your earnings history on your Social Security Statement, or online at your "my Social Security" account. Once you do that, review your numbers to make sure your earnings history is correct; it's possible that some of your earnings weren't recorded properly.

✓ What's your Full Retirement Age (FRA)?

Social Security uses a complex formula to calculate your monthly income starting at your FRA, which is also sometimes referred to as Normal Retirement Age, or NRA.

Your FRA is based on your birth year, as shown in Table 5.1 below.

Table 5.1. Social Security Full Retirement Age

If you were born in	Then your FRA is
1943-1954	66 years
1955	66 years, 2 months
1956	66 years, 4 months
1957	66 years, 6 months
1958	66 years, 8 months
1959	66 years, 10 months
1960 or later	67 years

The income that starts at your FRA is called the "Primary Insurance Amount," or PIA. You can start receiving Social Security income as early as age 62, but your benefits will be reduced using a formula that's based on the number of months that you start benefits before reaching your FRA.

You can also delay starting your Social Security benefits until after your FRA; in this case, your income will be increased using a formula that's based on the number of months you delay taking benefits beyond your FRA. However, there are no increases for delaying beyond age 70.

✓ What are the early and delayed retirement factors that apply specifically to you?

The "Helpful Resources" section at the end of this chapter contains links where you can get more detailed information about the reduction factors for starting benefits before your FRA, and the increase factors for starting your benefits after your FRA.

For example, if your FRA is age 66 and you start Social Security benefits at age 62 (48 months before your FRA), your income will be permanently reduced by 25%. If, however, your FRA is age 67, then your income at age 62 is permanently reduced by 30%, since you started your benefits 60 months before your FRA. The reduction factor is based on the number of months that your start date *precedes* your FRA; as a result, for each month that you delay starting benefits after age 62, your Social Security benefit will *increase.*

In this same example, your benefits will increase by two-thirds of 1% for each month that you delay starting Social Security benefits after your FRA. That works out to an increase of 8% for each year that you delay, up to age 70. If you're married, delaying can also improve your spouse's financial security after you're gone. The bottom line? That 8% annual increase will make a huge difference when you're in your 70s or 80s, and you can pat yourself on the back because you waited longer to collect.

It's important to note that you don't need to start your Social Security benefits when you stop working. If you have other sources of income you can rely on, it usually pays to delay starting your Social Security benefits for as long as possible, but only up to age 70. If you can't wait that long, you'll still realize significant advantages by delaying at least until your FRA.

✓ How much Social Security income will you receive?

The easiest way to estimate the amount of income you might expect from Social Security is to log into the Social Security website using the account you set up (which I mentioned previously). There you'll find an online statement showing your estimated Social Security benefits from age 62 through 70. You can also use one of the calculators available on the Social Security website:

- The **Retirement Estimator** will first estimate your Social Security income (using your actual covered earnings history) if you start benefits either at age 62, at your FRA, or at age 70. Then you can input other dates to see the impact of starting your income at different ages. The system automatically calculates your benefits using the early or delayed factors described in this chapter, if they're applicable to you. All you need to do is input your Social Security number and other requested identifying information.

- The **Quick Calculator** estimates your Social Security benefits using your date of birth and the earnings that you input. It does not access your actual earnings record. As a result, benefit estimates made by the Quick Calculator are rough at best. It will estimate your benefits at age 62, your FRA, and age 70 as well at any retirement date that you input.

- The ***Detailed Calculator*** can be downloaded to your computer. It uses information you input — your date of birth and earnings history — to calculate your benefits. It will also adjust for special situations not addressed by the previously mentioned calculators, most notably situations in which workers have a significant period of employment with state and local governments that don't participate in Social Security.

In addition to reviewing their accounts online, workers age 60 and older who haven't yet started their benefits or set up a Social Security account will have paper statements of their estimated benefits mailed to them by the Social Security Administration. You can also call the Social Security office and talk to a representative on the phone to learn how to estimate your benefits (1-800-772-1213).

If you're married, keep in mind that these calculators and statements don't link the benefits of spouses; each one of you will need to separately estimate your own benefits.

Decide when to start collecting your Social Security income

Congratulations on finishing your basic Social Security homework. Reward yourself for taking the time and effort to start your research!

Now you're ready to make a decision about when it would be best for you to begin your benefits. My yardstick for deciding when to start collecting Social Security is to estimate the total amount of income you might receive from Social Security over your lifetime. If you're married, then you and your spouse should estimate the total lifetime payout you would each be eligible to receive.

Given the complexity of Social Security benefits, the very best way to determine how to optimize your Social Security benefits is to use one of the commonly available online computer programs. Just how complex can it get? Financial Engines, a large advisory firm, estimates that married couples face more than 8,000 possible combinations of Social Security claiming strategies. Given the fact that each of us has very unique circumstances, it would be smart to let a computer work through all the possible combinations and come up with strategies that would work best for you. To help you find one that could work for you, I've listed several such programs in the "Helpful Resources" section of this chapter.

For many people, delaying benefits as long as possible will maximize their lifetime payout from Social Security. Why will most workers realize a financial advantage by delaying benefits? The reason comes from procrastination by Congress. It takes an act of Congress to change the factors that Social Security uses to adjust your benefits for an early or delayed start of your benefits. The current factors were developed many decades ago when people didn't live as long as they do today, when interest rates were much higher than they are today, and when Social Security didn't increase benefits for inflation. Because Congress hasn't updated the adjustment factors to reflect today's economic realities, you're getting a very good deal by delaying the start of your benefits.

Understand when you're money-ahead

Here's an example that illustrates the advantages with delaying your Social Security benefits. This example uses the "money-ahead" analysis, a yardstick people can use to evaluate a Social Security claiming strategy that's a favorite of Andy Landis, author of *Social Security: The Inside Story*. This analysis estimates the age at which a delay strategy pays off for a retiree.

Let's review the Social Security stories of Bob, Janice, and Mary, all born in 1960, which results in a full retirement age (FRA) of 67 for them. All three individuals currently earn about $75,000 per year, and they all earned similar amounts in prior years (adjusted for wage inflation). All three also plan to stop working at age 62.

Bob is impatient and plans to start his Social Security at age 62, the earliest possible age at which to claim benefits. He'll receive $1,400 per month in today's dollars, a result of the permanent 30% reduction in his benefits that comes from starting benefits so early. Janice, however, is very patient and plans to wait until age 70 to start her Social Security benefits. She'll receive $2,480 per month, a result of the permanent 24% increase in benefits she'll get by waiting until age 70. Mary has decided on a compromise strategy: She plans to wait until her FRA (67) to start her Social Security benefits; her initial monthly income will be $2,000.

First, let's suppose Bob, Janice, and Mary each estimate how much lifetime Social Security income they'll have received by age 75. The graph below compares the amounts and shows that so far, Bob is the winner. He's money-ahead of Mary by $26,400 and money-ahead of Janice by $69,600.

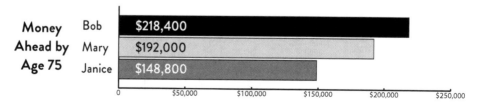

Now suppose they compare how much lifetime income they'll have received from Social Security by age 80. The graph below shows that by age 80, Mary is now in the lead — she's money-ahead of Bob by $9,600 and money-ahead of Janice by $14,400.

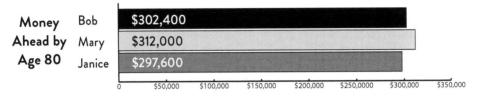

Next, suppose they compare how much lifetime retirement income they'll have received from Social Security by age 85. The graph below shows that by age 85, Janice has now pulled ahead and is money-ahead of Bob by $60,000 and money-ahead of Mary by $14,400.

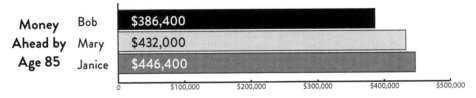

Finally, let's see what happens if they compare how much lifetime income they'll have received from Social Security by age 90. The graph below shows that by age 90, Janice is far ahead of the others. She's money-ahead of Bob by $124,800 and money-ahead of Mary by $43,200. She was smart to wait, because as people get older, there's a good chance they'll need extra money for medical and long-term care. Because she waited, Janice can draw on her Social Security to help cover her health care costs.

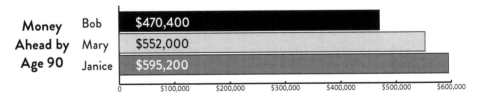

Although these examples only make comparisons at the milestone ages of 75, 80, 85, and 90, it's informative to understand the age at which one strategy pulls ahead of the other. In this example:

- Mary (who started benefits at age 67) pulls ahead of Bob (who started benefits at age 62) between ages 78 and 79.

- Janice (who started benefits at age 70) pulls ahead of Bob between ages 80 and 81 and ahead of Mary between ages 82 and 83.

You'll get similar results even if you're older than Bob, Janice, and Mary, and your FRA is still between ages 66 and 67.

Another thing that's key to remember: The money-ahead analysis shown here considers just one person's benefits. But a married couple can gain even higher amounts by carefully selecting the Social Security start date for each spouse. As you'll see later in this chapter, there's another valuable advantage to a smart delay strategy: It can help improve the financial security of your spouse if you pass away first.

And while the money-ahead analysis discussed here doesn't reflect such factors as inflation, cost-of-living increases, taxation of Social Security benefits, potential investment earnings, and wage earnings after age 62, it doesn't really matter too much. Other analyses that consider some of these factors (and significantly complicate the analysis) result in nearly the same conclusions regarding optimal Social Security claiming strategies.

Clearly, the example shows that if you're expecting (and planning) to live into your mid-80s or 90s, you'll want to delay collecting Social Security for as long as possible in order to maximize the amount of your lifetime benefits. Don't shake your head when I say you might live into your mid-80s or 90s: There's a very good chance you'll make it to these ages if you don't smoke or abuse alcohol, keep your weight at a healthy level, eat a balanced diet, have a college degree, and earned a steady income with good benefits throughout your life. All these factors improve the odds you'll live a long time. Being able to plan ahead wisely is another good reason for estimating how long you might live, as recommended in Chapter 1.

Whatever you do, don't let all the numbers intimidate you. It's well worth your time to let an online calculator do the math for you and help you make informed choices about when to start your Social Security benefits. It could put many thousands of extra dollars into your retirement pockets.

Learn about spouse's benefits

If you're married, it's critical that you and your spouse understand the Social Security rules that apply to you. Not only do these rules affect the income you'll receive while you're both alive, but they directly affect the financial security of the survivor, who is often the wife. Poverty among elderly widows is a real problem in America, so making smart decisions about your benefits now can help keep your surviving spouse out of poverty later.

FYI: Social Security now recognizes same-sex marriages. In this case, all the rules about spousal benefits described here will apply to you if you're part of a legally married same-sex couple.

The most fundamental thing you need to know is that your spouse's retirement benefit will be the *greater* of either:

- the benefit based on their own covered earnings, called the "spouse's earned benefit," or
- a benefit based on up to half of the primary worker's benefit (that's you), called the "spousal benefit."

The spousal benefit is payable even if your spouse never worked or only worked sporadically. While both of you are alive, your total Social Security benefits equal the sum of your own Social Security income plus your spouse's income. Your income will not be reduced if your spouse also receives Social Security income.

Next up: the checklist of things you need to learn, the steps you need to take, and the decisions you need to make regarding Social Security benefits for your spouse.

Complete the checklist regarding Social Security benefits for your spouse

If you're married, you'll want to keep plugging away and optimize Social Security for your spouse as well. When you reach your 70s and 80s, you and your spouse will be glad you spent the necessary time *now,* knowing that you did your best to max your Social Security benefits.

✓　Determine your spouse's expected benefit based on their earnings.

Go through the checklist described previously and check your spouse's earnings history, determine their full retirement age (FRA), and estimate the benefit your spouse will receive based on their own earnings, using the calculators on the Social Security website.

✓　Estimate the spousal benefit.

If your spouse didn't work a full career, there's a chance they could receive the spousal benefit instead of their own earned benefit, if their spousal benefit is larger.

This amount is based on the amount of your monthly benefit at the time of your FRA and the age at which your spouse starts receiving this benefit; it's not based on when you start receiving your own Social Security benefits. Note that your spouse will need to wait until they reach at least age 62 to start the spousal benefits.

Here are the steps to take to estimate your spouse's spousal benefit that's based on your earnings record:

- Estimate the monthly Social Security income you'll receive at your FRA, based on your earnings record.

- Divide that result by two. That's the amount of your spouse's spousal benefit, starting at your spouse's FRA.

- Now determine the amount your spouse will receive if they start the income before their FRA, recognizing the early retirement reductions that will apply.

The early retirement reduction is similar to the reduction that would be applied to early retirement for your own benefits, but the factors involved in determining it are slightly different. For example, if your spouse's FRA is 66, then the reduction for starting early is about 30% at age 62, 25% at age 63, 17% at age 64, and 8% at age 65. Note that there is no increase in benefits given for delaying a spouse's spousal benefit beyond their FRA. If you'd like more details on early retirement reductions, see the link in the "Helpful Resources" section for this chapter.

If the spousal benefit works out to be greater than the benefit based on your spouse's own earnings, then the spousal benefit is the income your spouse will receive while both of you are alive. (Social Security makes the determination regarding which benefit is larger; you don't need to calculate this on your own.)

✓ Determine when your spouse can start Social Security benefits.

Your spouse can start their *own* Social Security benefits based on their earnings history at any time, provided they have attained age 62. However, your spouse can only start the *spousal* benefit (based on your earning record) after you start your own benefit.

✓ Understand what happens when one of you dies.

When either you or your spouse dies, there are a number of things that will happen regarding your Social Security benefits. First, the Social Security income for the deceased person stops. Then the surviving spouse receives the *greater* of either:

1. the Social Security benefit based on their own earnings, as described previously, or
2. the full Social Security income the deceased spouse was actually receiving, based on the age the deceased spouse started Social Security benefits.

In short, the survivor gets to keep the higher of the two payments. This provides a powerful incentive for the primary wage-earner to increase the amount of benefits they get from Social Security by delaying their benefits as long as possible (but no later than age 70). If the benefit for the surviving spouse is the second item listed above, then a delay strategy provides greater financial security for the surviving spouse.

Note that after the death of a spouse, only one Social Security income is payable to the surviving spouse; they won't receive both the deceased spouse's income and their own Social Security income. Since there will be a significant reduction in household income when one spouse dies, you'll want to plan carefully for that situation.

✓ See if you'll benefit from a grandfather rule.

Here's another rule that opens the door for an interesting strategy, provided your date of birth was prior to January 2, 1954 (which means you attained age 62 by the end of 2015). Suppose your spouse starts their earned benefit. Once you've attained your FRA, you can file what is called a "restricted application" to receive the spousal benefit on your spouse's earned benefit but delay taking your own earned benefit. When you eventually file for the benefit based on your own earnings, you'll still receive the delayed retirement credit despite the fact that you've been receiving Social Security spousal benefits. That's because filing for the spousal benefit doesn't affect the amount of money you'll receive for benefits based on your own earnings.

✓ Decide when your spouse should start taking benefits.

Unlike claiming strategies for the primary wage-earning spouse, it's not always the case that delaying the secondary wage-earner's benefit as long as possible is the best strategy. There can be situations where it makes more sense to start the secondary wage-earner's Social Security benefit at their FRA, or even before. For one thing, it can help to have some money coming in while the primary wage-earner delays their own benefits. The best way to optimize the benefits for a married couple is to use one of the online calculators mentioned in the "Helpful Resources" section at the end of this chapter, or to work with an adviser who is experienced in analyzing Social Security benefits for married couples.

Learn about the earnings test

Can you have your cake and eat it, too, by working for wages and receiving your Social Security income at the same time? If so, is it a good idea? As with many financial questions, the answers to these two questions aren't black or white — the best answer to both of these questions is "It depends."

Your Social Security income might be reduced by the "earnings test" if you're receiving Social Security income before the year you attain your FRA and you're still working for pay. In this case, if your wages or self-employment income exceed a certain threshold — $17,040 per year in 2018 — then your Social Security income will be reduced by $1 for every $2 of earnings over the threshold. The spousal benefit paid to your spouse that's based on your earnings record would be reduced as well. There's no reduction if your wages or self-employment income is below this threshold.

The good news is, the earnings test only considers gross wages before withholding for taxes, and net earnings from self-employment income. It doesn't consider pension, interest, investment income, or money from inheritances, so you can receive that income without impacting your Social Security income. In addition, wages or self-employment income you earn after you reach your FRA, including during the month of your birthday, also don't count toward the earnings test. This means you can earn as much money as you want after you reach your FRA, and your Social Security income won't be reduced.

Here's one example to help make things clear. Suppose you're age 63, three years younger than your FRA of age 66, *and* you've started your Social Security income. If you earn $19,040 in wages during 2018 — $2,000 more than the threshold for that year — then your Social Security benefits will be reduced by $1,000 for the year. You'll also still pay Social Security taxes (FICA taxes) on your wages or self-employment income, regardless of whether your Social Security benefit is reduced.

It's important to understand that the amount of benefits that are reduced isn't "lost" forever. Once you reach your FRA, your monthly Social Security income will be increased permanently to make up for the months during which your benefits were stopped or reduced by the earnings test.

By the way, special rules apply for the calendar year in which you start your Social Security benefit (if it's before your FRA) and for the year you attain your FRA. The links in the "Helpful Resources" section for this chapter provide further details on this.

Another thing you'll want to understand is how the earnings test affects your spouse. First off, your spouse is subject to the same rules regarding work. So if your spouse is receiving Social Security benefits while working and hasn't yet reached their FRA, those wages earned can reduce your spouse's Social Security income, whether it's their own Social Security benefit or a spousal benefit based on your earnings record. Fortunately, if your spouse works, it won't affect any Social Security income *you* receive that's based on your own earnings record.

There's one last issue I'd like to cover in regards to your earnings record, and that's what would happen if you started to receive Social Security benefits and then decided to return to work later. In this instance, you'd be eligible for a "do-over" but only if you notified the Social Security Administration that you were working again within 12 months of starting your Social Security income. At this point, you would have to pay back all the Social Security benefits you received, and you'd be treated as if you never started your Social Security income:

- for the purpose of the earnings test, and
- for the purpose of increases in your Social Security benefit due to delaying your benefit.

If more than 12 months have passed, then you won't be eligible for the "do over" and the earnings limit will apply. But as noted previously, the amount of the benefit reduction won't be lost permanently. If you find yourself in this situation and want to take advantage of the "do-over" rule, it's a good idea to contact your Social Security Administration office and carefully follow their instructions.

The earnings test is a powerful reason for waiting at least until your FRA to begin your Social Security income. If you're working and start your Social Security benefits before your FRA, then you'll want to monitor your earnings carefully and, if possible, keep them below the threshold that applies to you.

Understand how Social Security benefits are taxed

When it comes to income taxes, part or all of your Social Security income will be excluded from your taxable income, depending on the total amount of your income in retirement from all sources. This means you'll have more money to spend after paying taxes, providing yet another reason you should try to maximize your Social Security income.

The rules on taxing Social Security benefits are quite complex, so here I'll just provide a simple overview. Most middle-income retirees will have from half to all of their Social Security income excluded from federal income taxes. The amount of your Social Security income that's subject to federal income taxes increases as your total income from all sources increases. For the very wealthiest retirees, however, at least 15% of Social Security benefits are excluded from federal income taxes.

If you want to learn more about how your Social Security benefits will be taxed, talk with your accountant, or read the bonus chapter *Navigating the Tax Rules* on the "Advanced Study" page of www.retirementgamechangers.com.

Learn about special situations

There are several special situations that can influence the amount of your Social Security benefits. While fully describing the rules that apply in these situations is beyond the scope of this book, I'll briefly describe each situation below so you can see if it applies to you. If any of them do, you'll find information in the "Helpful Resources" section that can help you learn more about each of these situations.

You have dependent children when you retire

If you have dependent children when you retire, you may receive additional income from Social Security, in addition to the benefits payable to you and your spouse.

You've been divorced

Divorced spouses who are unmarried can claim the special spousal benefit that's payable on the earnings record of an ex-spouse if they'd been married for at least 10 years. In this case, the divorced spouse would receive the greater of:

- their own earned benefit if they've worked and paid FICA taxes for a substantial period, or
- the spousal benefit based on the earnings record of their ex-spouse.

Paying benefits to an ex-spouse doesn't reduce the benefits paid to the worker, or to the worker's new spouse, if the worker remarries.

You've been collecting Social Security disability benefits

If you incur a serious disability and meet Social Security's disability requirements, you're eligible to start Social Security's disability benefits before your FRA. In this case, you can continue receiving Social Security's disability benefits until your FRA, provided you continue to meet the disability requirements. Then, when you attain your FRA, your disability benefit will convert to a retirement benefit and will be the same amount as your disability benefit.

You've had substantial employment with a state or local government that doesn't participate in Social Security

Some state and local governments and federal government organizations don't participate in Social Security. As a result, their pension plans are more generous than if their workers had participated in Social Security. Special rules apply if you have a split career, with some work at such a government employer and some work covered by Social Security. In this case, you'll want to understand how the Windfall Elimination Provision applies to you. If you're married, you'll also want to understand how the Government Pension Offset may apply to your spousal benefits.

You've worked outside the U.S.

If you spent part of your career working outside the United States, your work overseas might help you qualify for U.S. benefits if it was covered under a foreign Social Security system. The U.S. has agreements with many countries that help you avoid double taxation while working abroad and also help protect your future benefit rights.

You live abroad when you're retired

If you live somewhere other than the United States when you're retired, Social Security can send your payments abroad for most countries but not all. In this case, you'll want to understand the payment conditions for the country you're living in.

Don't worry about Social Security going bankrupt

"By the time I retire, I'll never get a cent from Social Security!" I can't tell you how many times I've heard this cynical statement.

But that thinking couldn't be more wrong. Social Security is one of the most popular government programs around, as our political leaders well understand. In other words, I expect Social Security will be around as long as we have a democracy.

The news media often don't help by running scary headlines suggesting that the Social Security Trust Fund will run out of money in the not-too-distant future — 2034 is the latest estimate from the *2017 Social Security Trustees Report*.[2] With the media crying "Wolf!" it's understandable that many people mistakenly conclude that they won't receive any benefits.

The fact is that under current law, the Social Security Trust Fund could run bone-dry and you'd still get most of your benefits. You see, the Trust Fund is only a *supplemental* source of funding for Social Security. Most of your Social Security retirement and disability benefits are actually funded from taxes collected each pay period from current workers (that's the deduction for FICA taxes on your paycheck).

The bottom line: As long as workers are paying FICA taxes, there will be money to pay for the Social Security benefits for retirees and their beneficiaries.

According to the *2017 Social Security Trustees Report*, you'd still receive about three-fourths of your benefits if the Trust Fund were completely depleted and the only source of funding was the taxes collected from current workers.[2] While this wouldn't be good news, three-fourths is certainly much bigger than zero. However, I choose to believe that our politicians will make the necessary fixes to prevent benefit reductions. Otherwise they'd be voted out of office, and they know it.

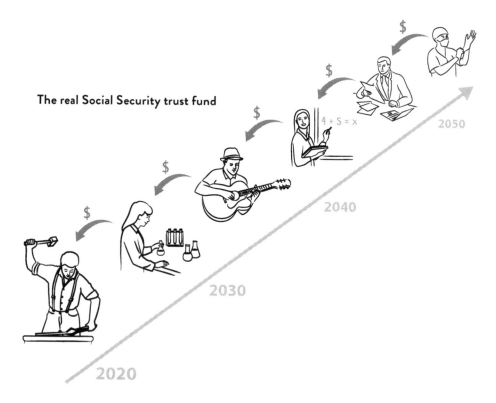

The real Social Security trust fund

It turns out that the real "trust fund" is the collective ability of current and future workers to pay their FICA taxes to support benefits for current and future retirees and beneficiaries. We all depend on the willingness of Congress to make the necessary modest benefit adjustments and tax increases to bring the program into long-term financial balance. Given the tremendous popularity of Social Security, that shouldn't be so hard.

Spend the time necessary to maximize Social Security

The most important information I hope you take away from this chapter is worth repeating: If you live a long life, you'll want to be sure to get your money's worth from Social Security!

It's well worth many hours of your time to learn as much as you can about Social Security benefits, or paying an adviser to help you understand how to get the most out of your Social Security benefits. You'll also want to coordinate your strategy for Social Security with your strategy for deploying your retirement savings, as discussed in the next three chapters.

Advisers who recommend taking Social Security early: A trap for the unwary

Some financial advisers may try to convince you to start Social Security early and invest the money you get from your benefits with them. They may "promise" they can generate higher returns. That's usually a losing strategy, given the significant financial benefits to delaying Social Security. If an adviser makes this claim, it's a warning sign to look for another adviser.

Your decisions on Social Security are particularly susceptible to the emotional issues we discussed in Chapter 2 and in the "Advanced Study" bonus chapter available on www.retirementgamechangers.com. I encourage you to read these resources to learn tips on using behavioral economics to work to your benefit, and to avoid common mistakes. And don't skip the "Helpful Resources" section: It contains a list of valuable websites and books where you can learn more, particularly about the special situations noted above.

 **ACTION STEPS:**

- Complete the checklists in this chapter for both yourself and your spouse, if you're married.

- Determine a strategy for optimizing both your benefit and your spouse's benefits, if you're married.

- Estimate the amount of annual income you might generate from your Social Security, to help make the $I > E$ formula work.

- Choose an online calculator to help you develop a strategy for claiming Social Security and estimating your income, or find an adviser who is trained on maximizing Social Security's value.

- Determine how you'll delay taking your Social Security benefits for as long as possible, either by continuing to work or by drawing on your retirement savings.

- Coordinate your strategy for starting to collect Social Security with your plans to continue working, and be sure to consider the earnings test.

- Learn how much income tax you might pay on your Social Security benefits by working with your tax adviser or tax preparation software.

 **HELPFUL RESOURCES:**

Advanced Study page at www.retirementgamechangers.com

- *Get Help*, bonus chapter which covers working with financial advisers

- *Navigating the Tax Rules*, bonus chapter that includes information on the taxation of Social Security benefits

- *Stay Focused*, bonus chapter which explains how using psychology can help you make smart financial decisions, including Social Security claiming decisions

Books

- *Get What's Yours: The Secrets to Maxing Out Your Social Security*, by Laurance J. Kotlikoff and Philip Moeller. Simon & Schuster, 2015.

- *Maximizing Your Clients' Social Security Retirement Benefits,* by Mary Beth Franklin. Investment News, 2017.
- *Social Security for Dummies, 2017 Edition,* by Jon Peterson. John Wiley & Sons, Inc., 2017.
- *Social Security: The Inside Story, 2018 Silver Edition,* by Andy Landis. Thinking Retirement, 2018.
- *When Should You Claim Social Security?,* by Wade Pfau. Retirement Researcher Media, 2017.

Social Security website: www.ssa.gov

- Benefits for dependent children: https://www.ssa.gov/pubs/EN-05-10085.pdf
- Benefits for divorced spouses: https://www.ssa.gov/planners/retire/divspouse.html
- Detailed calculator: https://www.ssa.gov/OACT/anypia/anypia.html
- Delayed retirement credits for starting benefits after your FRA: https://www.ssa.gov/planners/retire/delayret.html
- Earnings test: https://www.ssa.gov/OACT/COLA/rtea.html
- Government pension offset: https://www.ssa.gov/pubs/EN-05-10007.pdf
- Living abroad when retired: https://www.ssa.gov/pubs/EN-05-10137.pdf
- My Social Security account: https://www.ssa.gov/myaccount/
- Phone number: 1-800-772-1213
- Quick calculator: https://www.ssa.gov/OACT/quickcalc/index.html
- Reduction factors for starting benefits before FRA: https://www.ssa.gov/planners/retire/agereduction.html#chart
- Retirement estimator: https://www.ssa.gov/retire/estimator.html
- Taxation of benefits: https://www.ssa.gov/planners/taxes.html
- When disability benefits convert to retirement benefits: https://www.ssa.gov/planners/disability/dqualify.html

- Windfall elimination provision: https://www.ssa.gov/pubs/EN-05-10045.pdf
- Working outside the U.S.: https://www.ssa.gov/planners/retire/international.html

Other websites and online calculators

- AARP's Social Security calculator: http://www.aarp.org/work/social-security/social-security-benefits-calculator.html
- *Managing Retirement Decisions,* by the Society of Actuaries.
  - "Deciding When to Claim Social Security" https://www.soa.org/research-reports/2012/research-managing-retirement-decisions/
- Fidelity Investments Social Security calculator: https://www.fidelity.com/mymoneylifestyle/social-security/#/start
- Financial Engines is a large advisory firm that maintains a good Social Security planner: https://financialengines.com/education-center/social-security-planner/
- *Maximize My Social Security*: https://maximizemysocialsecurity.com
- *National Academy of Social Insurance*, a website that contains many articles and videos to learn about Social Security: https://www.nasi.org/learn/socialsecurity
- *Social Security Choices*: http://www.socialsecuritychoices.com
- *Social Security Solutions*: http://www.socialsecuritysolutions.com
- *Social Security Timing*: https://www.socialsecuritytiming.com

CHAPTER 6

COMPLETE YOUR PORTFOLIO OF RETIREMENT PAYCHECKS

DON'T MAKE THESE MISTAKES:

- ⊘ Take a lump sum from your employer pension plan (if you have one).
- ⊘ Ignore useful tools such as annuities.
- ⊘ Overlook valuable resources such as home equity.
- ⊘ Place too much importance on liquidity.

TRY THESE GAME-CHANGING STRATEGIES:

- ➜ Cover your basic living expenses with "retirement paychecks" that are guaranteed to last the rest of your life.
- ➜ Investigate viable sources of retirement paychecks to supplement your Social Security benefits.

Buy your way to happiness

While philosophers and psychologists will argue that money can't buy happiness, smart financial decisions can help increase your satisfaction with life during your retirement. Various surveys show that retirees are happier when they have sufficient sources of guaranteed lifetime retirement income.[1,2] This makes sense — with a reliable source of income, people aren't as worried about outliving their money or losing too much money when the stock market crashes. Actually, this is a good example of the "avoid being unhappy" aspect of happiness that we discussed in Chapter 1.

Before we jump into this chapter's topic — completing your portfolio of retirement paychecks — let's quickly review what we learned in Chapter 4. In that chapter, I introduced you to four retirement paychecks that are guaranteed to last the rest of your life, no matter how long you live, and won't drop if the stock market crashes:

- **Retirement Paycheck #1:** Social Security benefits

- **Retirement Paycheck #2:** A monthly pension from a traditional pension plan or from a hybrid cash balance plan from your employer, if you participate in such a plan

- **Retirement Paycheck #3:** A low-cost payout annuity purchased from an insurance company

- **Retirement Paycheck #4:** A monthly tenure payment from a reverse mortgage on your home

The previous chapter covered your most valuable retirement paycheck: Social Security. This chapter continues with the discussion of retirement paychecks by digging into the next three paychecks.

Your game-changing strategy here is to develop enough secure "retirement paychecks" so that you can survive future stock market crashes, which are inevitable during a long retirement. This will help you sleep better at night and more fully enjoy your retirement years. It also gives you the confidence to ride out stock market crashes with your invested savings; panicking and selling during a stock market crash is a common mistake to avoid.

First, let's take a look at pension benefits, a valuable benefit that some of you are lucky enough to have earned.

Make careful decisions with your pension plan

If you participate in your employer's defined-benefit pension plan or cash balance plan, then you'll want to estimate the amounts you'll receive from Retirement Paycheck #2. Most pension plans have online calculators you can use to estimate the amount of your monthly check, or you can request an estimate from your plan's administrator.

With most pension plans, while you're working, your monthly income grows as follows:

- if you earn more service at your employer
- if you get a raise that's reflected in the calculation of your benefits
- if you delay retirement until the plan's normal retirement age

Your plan's online calculator will be able to show you how much your monthly retirement paycheck might increase if you keep working, get a raise, or delay the start of your pension.

If you're married, it's usually a good idea to elect a payment option that protects your spouse by continuing part or all your retirement paycheck after you're gone; this option is called a "joint and survivor annuity." Don't fall for the strategy that some insurance agents advocate — to decline the joint and survivor annuity and instead buy a new life insurance policy with them. Although they might try to convince you it's a better deal, you must die at precisely the right time to make such a strategy work.

The only possible exception where it might make sense to decline the joint and survivor annuity is if you own existing whole life insurance policies with sufficient value to support your spouse after you pass away and you're sure you won't use this policy for another purpose, such as withdrawing the cash value at a future date. In this case, make sure your spouse is the named beneficiary of the policy.

Also, if your employer offers the choice to take your benefits in one lump sum, resist this temptation! If you've worked many years for your current employer or any other employer and have earned a substantial pension benefit, deciding between the lump sum and monthly pension will be one of the most important financial decisions you'll make for your retirement. For most people, there's a very good chance you'll receive more income over your life if you take the monthly income, compared to investing the lump sum and using a retirement income generator (RIG) to generate a retirement paycheck or retirement bonus. That's because the amount of the lump sum payment is often below the fair market value of the pension, due to the IRS regulations that dictate how plan sponsors must calculate these lump sum payments.[3]

Before deciding between a lump sum and a monthly pension paycheck, it's well worth your time to carefully consider your choices. Find out how much retirement income you can reasonably generate from the lump sum if you decide to elect the lump sum and invest it elsewhere. Compare this income to the amount of your income if you elected the monthly pension from the plan. Having a clearer idea of what you can expect to get should make your decision easier.

It's also important to note that in most cases, your election is irrevocable. So if you choose the lump sum, you permanently forfeit the right to receive a lifetime monthly check. Similarly, if you elect the monthly payment, you can't change your mind and elect a lump sum later.

The "Helpful Resources" section at the end of this chapter identifies useful sources that can help you decide what would be best for you if you're offered this choice.

 Pension lump sum cash-outs: A trap for the unwary

Many traditional pension plans and cash balance plans offer you the chance to elect a lump sum payment instead of the guaranteed lifetime monthly paycheck provided by the plan. Consider this offer very carefully! You're potentially throwing away a very valuable benefit — an income that's guaranteed for life and won't drop when the stock market crashes.

Buy a "personal pension" if you need it

If Retirement Paychecks #1 and #2 — your Social Security benefits and pension benefits — aren't enough to cover your basic living expenses and you need more money coming in via retirement paychecks, consider Retirement Paycheck #3: a monthly annuity from an insurance company. This financial asset is also known as a "single premium immediate annuity," or SPIA for short. Purchasing a monthly annuity is like buying a personal pension, and it's another way to protect against the risk of living too long.

With a SPIA, you give a portion of your retirement savings to an insurance company, and it promises to pay you a monthly retirement income for the rest of your life, no matter how long you live. You can also elect to have the income continue to your spouse or partner after you die by electing a joint and survivor annuity. The annualized amount of your paycheck usually ranges from 3.5% to 6.5% of the amount of the savings that you apply to the annuity, depending on the type of annuity you purchase, as well as your age, sex, and marital status.

You can buy an annuity in which the monthly income is fixed in dollar amount, or buy an annuity that increases the monthly payment each year at a fixed rate, such as 2%, 3%, or 4%. Such an annuity can help protect against inflation, but it costs more than a fixed annuity.

If you want to preserve flexibility with your savings during the early part of your retirement, you can postpone buying such an annuity when you first retire. You can then buy an annuity in your 70s or even later, when stability and protection against fraud may have become more important goals to you than financial flexibility.

Are you concerned that if you buy an annuity and die early in your retirement, you may not get back all the money you paid to buy the annuity? That's the wrong way to think about an annuity. Consider an annuity to be an insurance policy that covers the risk of living a long time. With any type of insurance — annuities included — if you experience an event you're insured against, you get back more in benefits than the premiums you paid. If the event doesn't occur, the reverse holds true. What's true is that an annuity will pay you more in benefits than you paid in premiums in the event you live a long time. And if you don't live a long time, you didn't need the protection and your benefits will amount to less than the premiums you paid.

Annuities sometimes get a bad rap as a result of their high transaction costs or expensive bells and whistles. But these are the expensive variety of annuity. You're better off buying simple SPIAs purchased through a competitive and transparent online bidding service, such as Income Solutions or ImmediateAnnuities.com, or through financial institutions such as Fidelity Investments, Schwab, or Vanguard. These companies don't usually charge high transaction fees, and because the annuities are simple and straightforward, you don't need to worry about paying for complicated features that you don't need. Prior to buying an annuity, you should also ask to see information on the financial stability of the insurance companies you're thinking about working with.

Annuities sometimes get a bad rap for being too expensive, but the right type of income annuity doesn't have to come with high costs or fees and can be a very useful tool for your retirement income portfolio. Educate yourself, and look beyond common misperceptions.

As with any financial product or instrument, there are always good buys and then there are lemons. Be wary of being sold an annuity from an agent who might not have your best interests at heart and instead wants to earn a high commission. Your job is to do your research and select the annuity that pays you the most retirement income, taking into consideration the strength of the insurance company. If you're working with an adviser, ask how much compensation they will receive if you buy the annuity they recommend. Make sure they find the most retirement income for you, and not the highest compensation for them. Spend as much time doing your homework as you'd spend on any important purchase, such as a car or big vacation.

Some 401(k) plans and other employer-sponsored retirement plans may offer annuities that you can buy through the plan. Often these annuities enjoy group pricing that can deliver more retirement income than buying an annuity on your own can. Investigate whether your 401(k) plan offers this feature.

Do you own a whole life insurance policy with significant cash value? This could be another possible source for buying an annuity. Often these policies let you convert the life insurance into an annuity; using this feature might make sense if your kids are grown and aren't dependent on you, or if your spouse won't be counting on receiving the life insurance proceeds.

As with all decisions you'll have to make regarding your retirement years, single premium immediate annuities come with a few downsides: They typically don't let you change your mind and withdraw your savings once you've purchased the annuity. In other words, they aren't liquid.

Also, they don't return any unused funds to your heirs after you die, unless you purchase a joint and survivor annuity, a cash refund annuity, or a period certain annuity. You'll want to investigate these features if it's important to you to pass along money to your heirs.

On the plus side, however, is the fact that these annuities will typically pay you the highest amount of income over your lifetime — a good example of trading higher income for reduced liquidity. Here's something else to consider: You might be more comfortable with the lack of liquidity if you've built a sufficient cash stash and have access to the portion of your savings that you devote to generating your retirement bonuses, as described in Chapter 7.

Finally, this lack of liquidity actually has an important advantage — you can't lose your savings due to making mistakes or being defrauded. You might appreciate this advantage when you reach your 70s and 80s, and may be less willing and able to manage your investments.

If this lack of liquidity still bothers you, however, you can buy more complex annuities that allow you to withdraw your savings at any time, yet still promise you a lifetime monthly benefit. You'll usually receive a lower monthly benefit with this type of annuity compared to a SPIA, to pay for the cost of flexibility, but you may feel more comfortable knowing you can withdraw your funds if you need them.

These more complex annuities go by the names "guaranteed lifetime withdrawal benefits" (GLWB) or "fixed index annuities" (FIA). These annuities are often sold by insurance agents with high commissions, so be very careful — shop carefully to find the lowest fees and most favorable terms. For details on these more complex annuities, see my book *Money for Life: Turn Your IRA and 401(k) Into a Lifetime Retirement Paycheck* or some of the other books and websites listed at the end of this chapter in the "Helpful Resources" section.

Pensions and annuities often get an undeserved bad rap because the monthly payout is usually fixed and doesn't increase with inflation. Studies show, however, that they often deliver the largest amount of income over your lifetime. When it comes to addressing inflation, receiving more money over your lifetime is better! If you're really worried about inflation, you can purchase annuities that increase the monthly payment each year by a specified percentage. And remember, when you consider Social Security and your retirement bonuses, a large portion of your total retirement income already has the potential to keep up with inflation.

Learn about reverse mortgages

You might have a negative impression of reverse mortgages from stories you've heard or read in the media. But recent changes in rules and regulations have addressed some of the misuses that created those negative stories, making reverse mortgages an effective tool you might be able to use strategically to improve your retirement finances. If you have substantial home equity and your financial resources aren't adequate to support your retirement, it's definitely a good use of your time to learn more about the potential uses of reverse mortgages. Let's discuss the basics.

You can tap your home equity through a federal government-insured Home Equity Conversion Mortgage that's available to homeowners age 62 and older; this type of mortgage is most commonly known as a "reverse mortgage." Reverse mortgages are loans against home equity that aren't repaid until the owner dies, moves away, or sells the home.

The loan balance accumulates with interest on the loan proceeds, and the balance is deducted from the net proceeds of the house when it's eventually sold. The loan proceeds can be paid to you in a lump sum or in periodic monthly payments, or through some combination of the two. You can also arrange for a line of credit that you can tap at a later date for emergencies, or as a purposeful strategy to make your retirement savings last longer.

There are several ways you can use reverse mortgages to help secure your retirement, according to independent retirement researcher Wade Pfau, PhD. You can:

- Generate a monthly paycheck — called a "tenure payment" — that supplements your Social Security benefits and other financial resources, similar to an annuity. This paycheck will be paid as long as you live in the house and keep up with homeowner obligations, such as property taxes and insurance.

- Generate payments for a fixed period to pay for living expenses while you're delaying Social Security, as a purposeful strategy to optimize that benefit.

- Pay off a conventional mortgage to reduce monthly housing expenses.

- Fund remodeling costs to help you age in place.

- Create a liquid asset through a reverse mortgage line of credit that can be tapped for emergencies or that grows until you need to use it late in life for medical or long-term care expenses.

- Pay for premiums for long-term care insurance premiums (see Chapter 15 for more details on the risk of needing long-term care).

- Design a strategy to reduce "sequence of returns" risk with invested assets. With this strategy, when the stock market drops, you stop withdrawing from your retirement savings. Instead, you tap the reverse mortgage line of credit for living expenses. This buys you time to allow your invested assets to recover. After the market rebounds, you can switch back to withdrawing from your invested assets.

- Pay for living expenses if your financial assets become depleted.

If you have sufficient home equity, you might be able to use more than one of these strategies. Just don't be tempted to use your reverse mortgage for extravagances! Reverse mortgages have significant upfront costs. These costs are only worth paying if you really need the money to live on and if staying in your home is very important to you.

Pfau maintains a calculator on his website that estimates how much you can borrow on your reverse mortgage, the amount of monthly tenure payment your home might generate, and your potential loan costs. For example, suppose you're age 65 and choose to amortize the upfront loan costs. Table 6.1 below shows estimates of loan amounts, monthly tenure payments, and borrowing costs from Pfau's calculator as of March 2018.

Table 6.1. Reverse mortgage illustration

Value of home	Maximum loan amount	Monthly tenure payment	Estimated upfront costs
$250,000	$107,500	$580	$7,500
$500,000	$215,000	$1,159	$12,500

There are many details on reverse mortgages that you should understand if you're considering using one to enhance your retirement. Pfau's book, *Reverse Mortgages: How to Use Reverse Mortgages to Secure Your Retirement,* does an excellent job clearing up some of the common misconceptions about reverse mortgages. Here's a quick summary of a few:

- **High costs:** Just like conventional mortgages, reverse mortgages can have substantial upfront and closing costs that can be reduced by shopping around for competitive lenders. If a reverse mortgage is the best or only way to buy your retirement freedom, it might be well worth the cost.

- **Family misunderstandings:** Given stories about angry children who thought they were inheriting a mortgage-free home, some older homeowners are reluctant to burden their children by taking out a reverse mortgage. A carefully designed strategy using a reverse mortgage, however, has the potential to increase the total legacy to adult children, or it can help prevent the unwanted legacy of a retired parent who has run out of money and needs to move in with an adult child.

- **Home title:** It's simply not true that the lender owns the title of a home with a reverse mortgage. The homeowners keep the title and aren't required to pay off the debt until they move or die. Heirs also have the right to keep the house and pay off the debt.

- **Desperate borrowers:** Some borrowers spend the proceeds of a reverse mortgage too quickly or can't keep up with required property taxes, insurance, and maintenance. To help avoid that, the U.S. Department of Housing and Urban Development now requires a counseling session for potential borrowers.

- **Non-borrowing spouses:** In the past, spouses younger than age 62 were taken off the home title to allow a reverse mortgage to proceed. Then they were surprised when the borrower died and they had to immediately repay the loan or leave the home. But in 2015, new protections were put in place for non-borrowing spouses: They can stay in the home even after the borrowing spouse has passed away, without having to immediately repay the loan.

Reverse mortgage expert Shelley Giordano's book, *What's the Deal with Reverse Mortgages?*, describes four reverse mortgage "nevers" to help alleviate common misconceptions:

- You never give up title to your home.

- You never owe more than your house is worth.

- You never need to leave your home as long as you maintain the property, the taxes on it, and the home's insurance.

- You never need to make loan repayments in advance of leaving the home, unless you choose to do so.

Of course, reverse mortgages aren't for everybody, particularly if you don't plan to stay in your home for many more years. In this case, it may not be worth incurring the upfront expenses, which can be substantial.

On the other hand, if you have considerable home equity, if your financial resources aren't sufficient to enable you to retire, and if you really want to retire, you'd be wise to explore all of your options — including a reverse mortgage — to deploy your home equity. In this case, you may need to find a professional adviser who has experience with implementing this strategy. Make sure any advisers you work with have your best interests at heart and aren't conflicted by how they're paid. In other words, hire an independent adviser who won't earn a commission on a reverse mortgage.

Congratulations on learning about your retirement paychecks! You'll enjoy your retirement more knowing that you can cover your basic living needs, no matter what happens with your life or in the economy.

Now you're ready to learn about retirement bonuses, discussed in the next chapter. Chapter 8 then gives you ideas to put it all together for your total retirement income portfolio.

 **ACTION STEPS:**

- If you participate in your employer's pension plan, estimate the amount of retirement income you might receive at various possible dates.

- If you need additional retirement paychecks, investigate annuities and monthly tenure payments from a reverse mortgage.

- Check to see if your employer's 401(k) plan offers annuities that are favorably priced.

- Estimate the amount of annual income you might generate from your retirement paychecks, to help make the $I > E$ formula work.

- Decide if you need professional help to develop your retirement income strategies. Make sure any such advisers have special training or credentials to help generate retirement income, and aren't conflicted by the manner in which they're paid.

 **HELPFUL RESOURCES:**

Advanced Study page at www.retirementgamechangers.com

- *Get Help*, bonus chapter which covers working with financial advisers

- *Navigating the Tax Rules*, bonus chapter that includes information about the taxation of Social Security benefits

- *Stay Focused*, bonus chapter which explains how using psychology can help you make smart financial decisions, including Social Security claiming decisions

Books

- *How Much Can I Spend in Retirement?*, by Wade Pfau, PhD. Retirement Researcher Media, 2017.

- *How to Make Your Money Last: The Indispensable Retirement Guide,* by Jane Bryant Quinn. Simon & Schuster, 2017.

- *Money for Life: Turn Your IRA and 401(k) Into a Lifetime Retirement Paycheck,* by Steve Vernon, FSA. *Rest-of-Life* Communications, 2012.

- *Reverse Mortgages: How to Use Reverse Mortgages to Secure Your Retirement,* by Wade Pfau, PhD. Retirement Researcher Media, 2016.

- *What's the Deal with Reverse Mortgages?,* by Shelley Giordano. People Tested Books, 2015.

Websites

- *How Much Can I Afford to Spend in Retirement?* This website is maintained by retirement researcher and actuary Ken Steiner and contains several articles on generating retirement income to meet your spending needs. It also contains a calculator to help you determine appropriate withdrawals from savings: http://howmuchcaniaffordtospendinretirement.blogspot.com

- *Immediateannuities.com.* This website enables you to buy low-cost single premium immediate annuities by competitively bidding your annuity among a number of insurance companies: https://www.immediateannuities.com

- *Income Solutions.* This is another website that enables you to buy low-cost single premium immediate annuities by competitively bidding your annuity among a number of insurance companies: https://www.incomesolutions.com

- *Managing Retirement Decisions,* maintained by the Society of Actuaries: https://www.soa.org/research-reports/2012/research-managing-retirement-decisions/
  - ○ "Designing a Monthly Paycheck for Retirement"
  - ○ "Lump Sum or Monthly Pension: Which to Take?"

- *NewRetirement.* This website contains useful tools and articles for developing a retirement income portfolio: https://www.newretirement.com

- *Retirement Researcher.* This website, maintained by Wade Pfau, PhD, contains several articles and books on retirement income planning: https://retirementresearcher.com.
His website also has a useful reverse mortgage calculator: https://retirementresearcher.com/reverse-mortgage-calculator/

- "Should You Take a Lump Sum from Your Pension Plan?" is an article by Steve Vernon on his website *Rest-of-Life Communications:* http://www.restoflife.com/PDF/TakeALumpSum.pdf

- The websites of Fidelity, Schwab, T. Rowe Price, and Vanguard all have many descriptive materials of various types of annuities and investments. They can be a good place to get started with your learning.

CHAPTER 7

DEPLOY RETIREMENT BONUSES

DON'T MAKE THESE MISTAKES:

- ⊘ Design your retirement bonuses in isolation, without considering your retirement paychecks.
- ⊘ Invest too conservatively if you've covered your basic living expenses with retirement paychecks.
- ⊘ Use high-cost mutual funds or investments.

TRY THESE GAME-CHANGING STRATEGIES:

- ➜ Pay for your discretionary living expenses with retirement bonuses that might fluctuate in value but have the potential for growth.
- ➜ Integrate your strategy for generating retirement bonuses with your retirement paycheck strategy so they work in tandem to finance your retirement.

Invest for flexibility and growth

Let's continue building your retirement income portfolio that will enable you to enjoy a long life.

Once you have your secure retirement paychecks in place, as discussed in Chapters 5 and 6, the next thing you'll want to do for your retirement security is to develop one or more "retirement bonuses." These bonuses will give you the potential for growth in your income to help protect against inflation. They also give you access to a portion of your money should you need to respond to changes in your life circumstances, or if you want to change the way you generate retirement income.

I like to refer to this part of your retirement income portfolio as "bonuses" to draw attention to the fact that this money can increase or decrease in value, much like an annual bonus you might have received from your employer. You'll use these retirement bonuses to supplement your secure retirement paychecks from Social Security, pensions, low-cost annuities, and reverse mortgages.

Let's first review the basic types of retirement bonuses. As with most of the steps in this book, it will take some time build your retirement bonuses, but it's well worth the effort.

Pay for discretionary living expenses with retirement bonuses

Here are four types of retirement bonuses that can fluctuate in value but give you the potential for growth during your retirement:

- **Retirement Bonus #1:** Invest your savings, and spend just the investment earnings. Don't touch the principal.

- **Retirement Bonus #2:** Employ a systematic withdrawal plan (SWP), where you invest your savings and draw down the principal and investment earnings cautiously with the intent that you won't outlive your assets.

- **Retirement Bonus #3:** Generate income from working or self-employment.

- **Retirement Bonus #4:** Generate income from rental real estate or from running a business, such as a franchise.

With the first two bonuses, you invest a portion of your savings and use it to generate your annual retirement bonuses. These two bonuses can fluctuate in value, depending on investment returns and how fast you draw down your savings. The third and fourth bonuses can also fluctuate in value, depending on how much you work or the profits from your business.

Each of these retirement bonuses has advantages and disadvantages, and each generates a different amount of retirement income. Once again, it will be important for you to do your homework and make the best choices for you based on your needs and your circumstances.

Retirement bonuses: A trap for the unwary

It's important to understand the dilemma posed by retirement bonuses. They have the potential to increase if the economy is strong and your investments perform well. They might produce more income over your life compared to investing in retirement paychecks. However, if the economy slows down or the stock market crashes, it's possible your retirement bonuses can drop by 50% or more. That's why you don't want to use bonuses to pay for your "must have" living expenses. It's smart to use bonuses to cover discretionary living expenses that you can afford to cut when times are tough.

A quick note: This chapter goes into detail on the first two retirement bonuses. If you want to learn more about Retirement Bonus #3: Working or Self-Employment, see Chapter 12. Discussing Retirement Bonus #4: Rental Real Estate or Running Your Own Business is beyond the scope of this book, even though it can be a viable strategy for some people. For those options, I suggest you do your own research, either online or at your local library. There are hundreds of books and easily dozens of resources that offer more information on these topics.

Now let's discuss the first two retirement bonuses in a little more detail, starting with investment earnings.

Learn more about Retirement Bonus #1: investment earnings

If you decide you'd like to invest your money and only spend your investment earnings (Retirement Bonus #1), you have many options. You can invest in a variety of mutual funds, bank accounts, individual stocks and bonds, real estate investment trusts (REITs), or limited partnerships. Some mutual funds have the stated goal to generate income from interest and dividends, and you might want to investigate those funds.

In today's environment, Retirement Bonus #1 typically pays an annual income ranging from 1% to 4% of your savings, depending on the specific investments you select and the allocation you choose between stocks, bonds, cash, and real estate investments.

Prior generations of retirees invested their money in savings accounts or CDs at banks, and they were able to live on the interest they earned. Given today's low interest rates, however, this strategy won't generate very much income. As a result, if your goal is to generate income, you'll need to consider investing in stocks, bonds, and REITs, or in mutual funds that hold these types of investments. In today's environment, the primary reason to invest in savings accounts or CDs is to temporarily park your money where it won't drop in value.

The main disadvantage of Retirement Bonus #1 is that it pays the smallest amount of current income, compared to any other retirement income generator (RIG), whether that's a retirement paycheck or a retirement bonus. But if it generates enough income for you, there are significant advantages to Retirement Bonus #1, including these:

- Your savings should last the rest of your life no matter how long you live, since you aren't withdrawing any principal.

- You maintain control over your investing choices and your ability to withdraw money from your savings.

- You have the flexibility to change to another RIG later in life, if you need more income.

- You preserve principal for a later age when you might need it to pay for health care or long-term care.

- Any unused funds at your death become a legacy to your children or charities.

You might be able to use the investment funds in your 401(k) plan or IRA for this retirement bonus. However, be aware that once you reach age 70½, the IRS required minimum distribution (RMD) rule might force you to increase your withdrawals to amounts that are higher than the investment income you earn. You're then required to include the withdrawal amounts in your taxable income, although you don't need to spend the after-tax amounts. See the "Understand the required minimum distribution (RMD) rules" section below for more details.

Learn more about Retirement Bonus #2: systematic withdrawal plans

With a systematic withdrawal plan (SWP), you invest your savings and draw down the investment earnings and principal cautiously, with the goal being not to outlive your assets.

If you decide to use an SWP, you must decide how much to withdraw and how often to withdraw it, such as monthly, quarterly, or annually, from the amount of savings you've invested for this purpose. This makes the SWP the most challenging type of RIG, because you must constantly readjust your withdrawal amounts and monitor your investment strategy.

As a result, you'll only want to implement an SWP on your own if you've educated yourself about investment strategies and effective methods for calculating your withdrawal amount. In addition, as you get older and more susceptible to making mistakes or experiencing cognitive decline, you might want to switch to a more user-friendly RIG, such as an annuity or managed payout fund.

There are several reasonable methods for calculating the monthly withdrawal, which I'll discuss in a few paragraphs below. You'll also need to decide how to invest your savings, which I discuss later in this chapter.

One user-friendly alternative to implementing an SWP is to use a managed payout fund that does the investing and withdrawing for you, such as Fidelity's Income Replacement Funds, Schwab's Managed Payout Funds, or Vanguard's Managed Payout Fund. Or you can find an advisory service that will do it for you, such as Betterment, Financial Engines, or United Income.

One important risk of an SWP that you need to be aware of is the so-called "sequence of returns" risk. This happens when you continue making significant withdrawals from your principal after the stock market drops. If you do this, you may not have enough savings remaining to fully recover when the stock market bounces back.

As a result, the best SWP strategies readjust your annual withdrawal each year to reflect investment gains or losses that have occurred. These methods apply a percentage to your remaining savings at the beginning of each year to calculate the withdrawal for the coming year. With this method, if your assets enjoy good investment returns, you can increase your withdrawals; on the other hand, you'll want to reduce your withdrawals if your assets lose money. Recent studies conducted by the Stanford Center on Longevity (SCL) and the Society of Actuaries (SOA) support these conclusions.[1,2,3]

> *The best SWP strategies readjust your annual withdrawal each year to reflect investment gains or losses that have occurred. Good returns can boost your retirement bonuses, but you'll want to cut back your bonuses when investment returns are poor.*

One such withdrawal method that's easy to use is the IRS RMD that applies to traditional IRAs and 401(k) accounts after age 70½. See the "Understand the required minimum distribution (RMD) rules" section below, which provides more details on this rule.

You can also easily implement an SWP by choosing a simple withdrawal percentage, such as 3%, 4%, or 5%. You'd then readjust your withdrawal amounts each year thereafter by multiplying your withdrawal percentage by the amount of your remaining assets each year.

Be aware that choosing the withdrawal percentage method is a "pay me now or pay me later" decision. A higher withdrawal percentage gives you more money in the early years of your retirement than a lower withdrawal percentage does, but a higher percentage also increases the risk that your withdrawals will be reduced substantially in later years. A higher withdrawal percentage also reduces any remaining assets that can be a legacy once you've passed away, if that's important to you. Just be aware, if you're using this method, that there's not a single magic number that will work for everybody, and you'll want to carefully consider the withdrawal strategy that best suits your circumstances.

Understand the required minimum distribution (RMD) rules

For most tax-advantaged retirement accounts — 401(k)s, 403(b)s, 457(b)s, and deductible IRAs — Uncle Sam wants to make sure that you eventually pay income taxes on the money you've saved in these accounts. So our good uncle applies required minimum distribution (RMD) rules that start when you turn age 70½. These rules specify the minimum amounts that you must withdraw from your retirement savings each year and include in your taxable income. Note: The RMD does not apply to Roth IRAs.

The RMD can be a straightforward method to generate retirement bonuses that last the rest of your life, as demonstrated by the SCL/SOA studies mentioned previously.[2,3] One advantage of using the RMD is that the amount of your retirement bonus will be automatically adjusted from year to year, depending on your investment returns. If you've already covered your basic living expenses with your secure retirement paychecks, any fluctuations in your bonus might not cause unacceptable reductions in your lifestyle.

There's another significant advantage to using the RMD rules to determine your retirement bonuses: Virtually any IRA or 401(k) administrator can calculate the RMD for you, and many can even pay it automatically to you in the frequency you specify (monthly, quarterly, or annually). By having your IRA or 401(k) plan administrator calculate this amount for you at the beginning of each year, you'll know the amount of your bonus for the year to come.

The RMD rules result in a withdrawal percentage that starts at 3.65% at age 70½ and increases each year thereafter (see Table 7.1 below for the exact amounts). For a given calendar year, you apply the annual withdrawal percentage to the value of your assets as of the previous December 31. As a result, you know exactly how much you're required to withdraw in the coming year. (If you're younger than age 70½ and want to use this method to generate a retirement bonus, you could use 3.5% as your annual withdrawal percentage until age 70½.)

Table 7.1. Withdrawal percentages under the IRS required minimum distribution (RMD)

Age	Payout rate
70	3.65%
71	3.77%
72	3.91%
73	4.05%
74	4.20%
75	4.37%
76	4.55%
77	4.72%
78	4.93%
79	5.13%
80	5.35%
81	5.59%
82	5.85%
83	6.13%
84	6.45%
85	6.76%
86	7.09%
87	7.46%
88	7.87%
89	8.33%
90	8.77%

Notes to the table on previous page:

- The RMD table continues beyond age 90.
- Use the account-holder's age on their birthday during the calendar year.
- If the account-holder is married and the spouse is more than 10 years younger, a different table with payout rates that are lower than the above rates applies.

While you'd have to be a tax accountant to understand all the intricacies of RMD rules, the basic concepts are fairly easy to understand if you take the time to study them. If you're interested in more details on the RMD, please see the bonus chapter titled *Navigating the Tax Rules* on the "Advanced Study" page of www.retirementgamechangers.com. Or you can investigate one of the online resources listed at the end of this chapter for more information.

The bottom line: The RMD can simplify the process for generating retirement bonuses for retirees who don't want to use more complex strategies or work with a financial adviser.

Develop an appropriate investment strategy for your retirement bonuses

When using your savings to generate a retirement bonus, you'll want to determine an investment strategy that provides a potential for growth through the stock market, yet allows you to sleep at night. The SCL/SOA studies mentioned previously support investing most or all your savings in stocks for growth potential, if you can tolerate the resulting volatility in this part of your retirement income.[2,3]

In essence, the retirement paychecks described previously become the "guaranteed" part of your retirement income portfolio, and your retirement bonuses become the part of your income portfolio that takes some risks for the potential for growth. When you consider the overall value of your retirement income portfolio, including Social Security, pensions, and annuities, you'll still receive a substantial portion — well over half in most cases — of your retirement income from guaranteed sources that won't drop if the stock market crashes.

But if you can't stomach the thought of investing most or all of your remaining assets in stocks to generate your retirement bonuses, you can always invest in target date or balanced mutual funds. These funds typically invest from one-third to two-thirds of their assets in stocks, with the remainder in conservative bond investments. Another reasonable choice is the target date fund in your 401(k) plan that's designed for retirees, provided it's a low-cost fund (see the next section for details). If you're using Retirement Bonus #1: Investment Income, you can find mutual funds that prioritize generating income from interest and dividend payments.

Consider investing your retirement bonuses in mutual funds with significant investments in stocks, or common target date or balanced funds. Although they contain some risk, these investments provide the potential for your retirement savings and bonuses to grow.

Here's one key guideline to follow: In the event of a stock market crash, don't panic and sell your stocks or mutual funds. While it can be hard for retirees to maintain this discipline since they may not be able to go back to work to make up their losses, it's not a wise move to make. By selling your stocks after a market crash, you lock in your losses and don't give your assets a chance to recover, which has happened repeatedly with prior stock market crashes.

Instead, guarantee your basic living expenses with retirement paychecks that continue no matter what happens in the stock market. This should give you the confidence to ride out the inevitable market downturns that will occur during the rest of your life. When the stock market crashes at some point in the future, this strategy might give you tremendous relief and allow you to sleep at night.

Seek low-cost investments

Do you think you need to be an investing genius or spend lots of time deciding how to invest your retirement savings? That may not be necessary. Instead, let me introduce you to a game-changing way of thinking that can simplify your retirement investments. I'll offer my own opinions — based on years of study and research — although I acknowledge that other experts may have different opinions based on their education and research.

Two well-known experts agree on the following advice: You can make your retirement investments very simple by seeking low-cost index funds at one of the large mutual fund companies or funds offered in your 401(k) plan. Many studies show there's a good chance your net return will be much greater over the long run compared to funds that are actively managed with higher investment expenses.

Both Allan Roth, a financial writer for AARP and the author of *How a Second Grader Beats Wall Street: Golden Rules Any Investor Can Learn*, and David Blanchett, director of retirement research for Morningstar Investment Management LLC, adhere to this thinking.

Reputable studies demonstrate that over the long run, you'll most likely earn a higher rate of return by investing in low-cost index mutual funds. Such funds have often outperformed mutual funds with a fund manager who actively manages the investments, or paying an adviser to select investments they think will do well.[4,5] The low-cost index mutual fund managers simply invest in all the stocks or bonds in a particular index, without trying to pick winners or sell losers. As a result, they keep their investment costs very low.

Now, it might seem counterintuitive that index funds would outperform funds where professionals actively try to buy winners and sell losers. However, studies have shown that the additional costs for paying someone to select and monitor investments usually don't result in higher returns net of expenses.[4,5]

Using low-cost index funds actually makes investing a lot simpler — you don't have to deal with complex strategies or absolutely need to work with financial advisers. You also don't need to spend a lot of time in a futile effort to find the absolute best investments. Instead, you can feel comfortable investing in the low-cost index funds that are commonly offered in many IRAs and 401(k) plans, or through a mutual fund company such as Fidelity, Schwab, or Vanguard.

For the purposes of our discussion here, I'm defining a low-cost mutual fund as having an "expense ratio" of less than 0.20% per year, although the lower it is, the better (you can find funds with expense ratios of 0.10% or lower). Many 401(k) plans and some IRA providers offer a choice of low-cost index funds. These funds may invest exclusively in stocks or offer a mix of the stocks and bonds — either balanced funds or target date funds. They might also offer index funds that invest in bonds, international stocks, or REITs.

All mutual funds, IRAs, and 401(k) plans are required to disclose the expense ratios of their funds, so if you can't easily find these disclosures in your paperwork or online, ask the provider or investment adviser for them. If they don't give them to you, that's a warning flag that you should invest elsewhere.

Any of these low-cost index mutual funds can be appropriate for Retirement Bonuses #1 and #2, and they're common at 401(k) plans of large employers (those with 1,000 or more employees). These plans typically hire experts to shop for low-cost funds that are appropriate for retirement investing. If you've worked for a large employer and your 401(k) plan has these types of funds, there's no reason you should roll your money out of your employer's 401(k) plan when you retire. In fact, your employer's 401(k) plan can also protect you against fraudsters who want to steal your retirement savings.

Reach your retirement destination faster

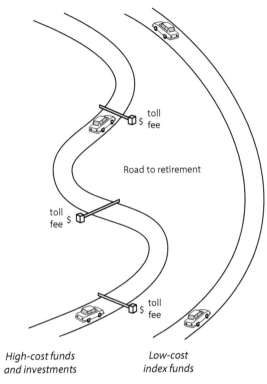

toll fee $

Road to retirement

toll fee $

toll fee $

High-cost funds
and investments

Low-cost
index funds

The 401(k) plans of small employers, typically those with less than 100 employees, may not have the resources to shop for the best funds or might offer funds with annual expenses of 1.0% or higher. In this case, when you retire, you're most likely better off rolling your savings into a low-cost IRA from such companies as Fidelity, Schwab, or Vanguard.

Before choosing to move your money, however, be sure to review the 401(k) plan disclosures to determine the expenses of the funds it offers. You may find that the funds you're invested in are reputable and have annual expenses of 0.20% or lower. If that's the case, you may not need to roll your money over to a different investment.

One caveat: The low-cost investments discussed here should work well for middle-income retirees with less than $1 million in retirement savings who have built sufficient retirement paychecks. If you have more than $1 million in savings, it could be worthwhile for you to work with an adviser who could help you determine an appropriate mix between stocks and bonds, and then help you select and monitor your retirement investments. Just make sure any adviser you work with has the training and expertise to help you generate retirement income from your savings, and isn't conflicted by how they are paid.

To learn more about other investments that are appropriate for your retirement bonuses, check out some of the books and websites listed in the "Helpful Resources" section at the end of this chapter.

Final thoughts

Here's one last point to make regarding retirement bonuses: If at any time, you no longer want to manage your investments, or if you desire more certainty in the amount of your income, you can always switch to a retirement paycheck by buying a simple, low-cost single premium immediate annuity (SPIA), as discussed in Chapter 6.

Now that you've learned more about retirement paychecks and bonuses, the next chapter wraps up our discussion of the 21st century retirement income portfolio by giving you some ideas that will help you put together your portfolio. Hang in there! Building your retirement income portfolio is one of the most complex retirement planning tasks, but you're almost finished.

 **ACTION STEPS:**

- Learn about the possible methods you can use to generate retirement bonuses, and develop strategies that will work best for you.

- Determine if your 401(k) plan or IRA provider can implement an SWP by automatically paying a specified amount or percentage of your assets, according to the frequency you select.

- Investigate if your 401(k) plan or IRA provider has low-cost index funds that you can use to implement an SWP, such as balanced funds, target date funds, or stock index funds.

- Estimate the amount of annual income you might generate from your retirement bonuses, to help make the $I > E$ formula work.

- Decide if you need professional help to develop your retirement income strategies.

 **HELPFUL RESOURCES:**

Advanced Study page at www.retirementgamechangers.com

- *Get Help*, bonus chapter which covers working with financial advisers

- *Navigating the Tax Rules*, bonus chapter that includes information about the RMD rules

- *Stay Focused*, bonus chapter which explains how using psychology can help you make smart financial decisions, including building your retirement bonuses

Books

- *How a Second Grader Beats Wall Street: Golden Rules Any Investor Can Learn,* by Allan Roth. John Wiley & Sons, Inc., 2009.

- *How Much Can I Spend in Retirement?,* by Wade Pfau, PhD. Retirement Researcher Media, 2017.

- *How to Make Your Money Last: The Indispensable Retirement Guide,* by Jane Bryant Quinn. Simon & Schuster, 2017.

- *Money for Life: Turn Your IRA and 401(k) Into a Lifetime Retirement Paycheck,* by Steve Vernon, FSA. *Rest-of-Life* Communications, 2012.

Websites

- *Diverse Risks Essay Collection,* maintained by the Society of Actuaries. The lead essay contains guidelines for determining withdrawals from savings:
  "The 'Feel Free' Retirement Spending Strategy," by Evan Inglis, FSA: https://www.soa.org/essays-monographs/2016-diverse-risk-essays/
- IRS required minimum distribution:
  - AARP: http://www.aarp.org/work/retirement-planning/required_minimuum_distribution_calculator/
  - Financial Industry Regulatory Authority (FINRA): http://apps.finra.org/Calcs/1/RMD
  - IRS website: https://www.irs.gov/retirement-plans/plan-participant-employee/retirement-topics-required-minimum-distributions-rmds
  - Many financial institutions and 401(k) administrators also have online RMD calculators and resources.
- *How Much Can I Afford to Spend in Retirement?* This website is maintained by retirement researcher and actuary Ken Steiner, FSA, and contains several articles on generating retirement income to meet your spending needs. It also contains a calculator to help you determine appropriate withdrawals from savings: http://howmuchcaniaffordtospendinretirement.blogspot.com
- *Managing Retirement Decisions,* maintained by the Society of Actuaries: https://www.soa.org/research-reports/2012/research-managing-retirement-decisions/
  - "Designing a Monthly Paycheck for Retirement"
  - "Lump Sum or Monthly Pension: Which to Take?"
- *Morningstar.* An online service that rates a variety of investments, including mutual funds, and provides a wealth of descriptive briefs and blog posts: http://www.morningstar.com

- *NewRetirement.* This website contains useful tools and articles for developing a retirement income portfolio: https://www.newretirement.com

- *Retirement Researcher.* This website, maintained by respected retirement researcher Wade Pfau, PhD, contains several articles and books on retirement income planning: https://retirementresearcher.com

- The websites of Fidelity, Schwab, T. Rowe Price, and Vanguard all have many descriptive materials regarding the various types of annuities and investments. They can be a good place to get started learning about the different types of investment options.

CHAPTER 8

BUILD YOUR RETIREMENT INCOME PORTFOLIO

DON'T MAKE THESE MISTAKES:

- ⊘ Wing it and not develop a careful strategy to deploy your hard-earned retirement savings.
- ⊘ Place too much emphasis on reducing income taxes during your retirement years.

TRY THESE GAME-CHANGING STRATEGIES:

- ➜ Build a diversified portfolio of retirement income with retirement paychecks and bonuses that work together to cover your basic and discretionary living expenses.
- ➜ Balance the goal of maximizing the amount of income you'll receive over the course of your retirement lifetime with other goals, such as desired liquidity, paying down debt, and leaving a legacy.
- ➜ Coordinate your retirement income portfolio with strategies to protect yourself against the threat of high medical bills and long-term care.

Determine if you have enough savings to retire

How will ordinary American workers retire in a world with limited or no traditional pensions, and just 401(k) plans and IRAs? How do they decide if they have enough savings to be able to afford to retire? How can they generate reliable retirement income? And how much can they afford to spend in retirement?

It's time to help you answer these crucial questions. To do that, you'll want to apply what you've learned in Chapters 4 through 7 about managing the magic formula for retirement income security ($I > E$) and building a portfolio of retirement income.

In Chapter 4, you learned that merely estimating your "retirement number" is too simplistic of a strategy for deciding when you can retire. Instead, you'll want to determine how much monthly income you'll receive from Social Security and from your self-generated retirement paychecks and bonuses. These sources of income are the "I" part of the formula for retirement income security.

To feel confident that you've done enough homework to decide if you have sufficient savings to retire, you'll want to:

- Estimate both your "I" and your "E," to make sure the formula for retirement income security will work for you, and

- Develop strategies to address the most common retirement risks regarding medical care and long-term care, as described in Chapters 10 and 15.

These steps will help you make some key life decisions, including how long you need to work, whether you should work part time for a while, and how much you can afford to spend in your retirement years (and not run out of money).

Of course, there's no guarantee that your carefully designed plans won't get disrupted by unexpected events, either in the economy or in your life. The best you can do is prepare and implement a thoughtful plan, and then be prepared to adjust your plan as your life unfolds.

Let's now look at one smart way to build your retirement income portfolio.

Consider implementing the Spend Safely in Retirement Strategy

It's only natural to be wondering how you'll put together all you've learned in the preceding chapters to build your retirement income portfolio and deploy your retirement savings. To help you with this challenge, here we'll discuss the game-changing Spend Safely in Retirement Strategy.

This straightforward strategy can be very useful for middle-income workers who have less than $1 million in retirement savings, which describes a lot of older American workers. For these people, the Spend Safely in Retirement Strategy provides many advantages:

- It helps squeeze the largest amount of income from your savings.

- It gives you some potential for growth in income to protect against inflation.

- It provides access to savings, which can provide flexibility if you should need to respond to changes in your lives.

The strategy helps address a dichotomy displayed by older workers and retirees. When it comes to spending down retirement savings, retirees tend to fall into two camps:

1. Some retirees greatly fear outliving their savings, so they conserve their savings for a rainy day, minimizing their withdrawals and treating savings as an emergency fund.

2. Other retirees "wing it" by using their savings much like a checking account to pay for their current living expenses. Often, they withdraw savings too rapidly at an unsustainable rate, running the risk of outliving their money.

Both groups of retirees can do better. The first group would be helped by a strategy that enables them to spend more in retirement and feel safe. The second group would find it useful to implement a strategy in which they spend their savings more safely, so they won't outlive their money. To give you a hand overcoming these tough challenges, I'll going to explain how you can use the Spend Safely in Retirement Strategy to develop secure retirement paychecks and flexible retirement bonuses.

The Spend Safely in Retirement Strategy enables a smooth transition into retirement and can give you flexibility if you're unsure about exactly when and how you'll retire. It also helps protect you against stock market crashes in the period leading up to your retirement. And it automates the payment of your retirement paychecks and bonuses. This can protect you from fraud and making mistakes — you'll particularly appreciate this feature when you reach your 80s and 90s and are less interested in managing your finances.

You can use virtually any IRA or 401(k) plan to implement the Spend Safely in Retirement Strategy.

The Spend Safely in Retirement Strategy is a straightforward strategy that can be used to generate retirement income from virtually any IRA or 401(k) plan. It's particularly useful for middle-income workers who have less than $1 million in retirement savings.

The Spend Safely in Retirement Strategy results from a groundbreaking research project conducted by the Stanford Center on Longevity, in collaboration with the Society of Actuaries.[1,2] This research provides a framework for assessing different retirement income generators (RIGs) and navigating the many trade-offs older workers face when making retirement income decisions. It compared 292 different retirement income strategies, including various combinations of Social Security claiming ages, systematic withdrawals from invested assets, and annuities with insurance companies. In the course of their work, the researchers prepared stochastic forecasts and efficient frontiers, analytical techniques that many large pension plans use to devise funding and investment strategies.

The Spend Safely in Retirement Strategy consists of four steps as follows:

Step 1: Delay collecting Social Security benefits.

If you're single or the primary wage-earner of a married couple, consider delaying Social Security income for as long as possible, ideally until age 70. If you're married and want to determine the optimal age to claim benefits for *both* spouses, it might make sense to use one of the popular online Social Security optimization programs, or work with a qualified financial adviser. It makes sense to take advantage of the many great features that Social Security offers, as described in Chapter 5.

For many middle-income retirees, if you delay starting your Social Security benefits at least until age 65 or 66, then a large portion of your total retirement income will be generated from Social Security — from two-thirds to more than three-fourths. If you delay starting until age 70, this proportion would most likely be three-fourths or even higher. As a result, Social Security might give you all the guaranteed lifetime retirement paychecks you need. Remember, the paycheck portion of your retirement income will help protect you against stock market crashes and living a long time. Social Security is the best way to generate such paychecks.

Step 2: Build a "retirement transition bucket."

When you're within five years of retirement, use a portion of your retirement savings to begin building a bucket within your IRA or 401(k) to smooth your transition into retirement.

This bucket provides you with several advantages:

- It enables you to delay drawing down your retirement resources, such as Social Security and your 401(k) benefits, for as long as possible, hopefully until age 70.

- It can supplement your income as you transition from working full time to working part time, and to eventual full-time retirement.

- In the period leading up to your full retirement, it provides a resource you can draw upon if you're laid off or can't find the work you need.

- It can provide a buffer against stock market crashes during this time, so you don't have to tap into long-term savings.

The "right" transition into retirement for you — whether full retirement or part-time work — will depend on your goals and circumstances. As a result, determining the amount of savings in your bucket will involve some judgement on your part. For instance:

- You might decide it should be a large enough amount to cover your estimated living expenses for a specified period, say two to five years.

- Or you might simply want enough set aside to be able to cover the amount of the Social Security benefit you plan to delay for as long as possible. As such, your strategy to optimize your Social Security can influence the amount of your retirement transition bucket.

- On the other hand, if you're absolutely sure you'll be able to continue working enough to cover your living expenses for several years until you retire full time or until age 70, then you might need a much smaller retirement transition bucket.

Your bucket can be set up as a separate account in your IRA or 401(k) plan, or you could use other investment accounts for this purpose. You could then invest this allocated money in stable, liquid investments, such as a short-term bond fund, a money market fund, or your 401(k) plan's stable value fund, if it has such a fund. You'd keep the remainder of your retirement savings invested for the long-term, often with a substantial investment in stocks.

Once you've determined how much you want in your retirement transition bucket, you can implement a schedule to make transfers to this bucket in each of the five years before your target retirement date. You could do this by *transferring* one-fifth of the target amount from your retirement savings into your retirement transition bucket. Note: There will be no tax implications if you merely transfer money from one investment fund to another within your IRA or 401(k) plan.

Step 3: Consider the rest of your savings as a long-term retirement income generator (RIG).

After you've optimized Social Security and built your retirement transition bucket, invest your remaining savings in a low-cost index fund that's significantly invested in stocks, for growth potential. Use the IRS required minimum distribution (RMD) method described in Chapter 7 to calculate your retirement bonus each year.

For this step, you could choose to invest in the target date fund at your IRA or 401(k) provider that's appropriate for your age — typically these funds invest about 50% in stocks. Remember that if you optimize Social Security as outlined in Step 1, you'll have a high portion of your retirement income portfolio provided by Social Security, money that's protected from stock market crashes. As a result, you might be able to tolerate a higher allocation to stocks for more growth potential. In that case, you could invest in a low-cost balanced index fund (typically invested about two-thirds in stocks), or even in an index fund that's invested 100% in stocks.

Your long-term RIG should give you the flexibility to access your savings at any time for any purpose, including changing the method you're using to generate your retirement bonus. For example, if you decide that you'd rather receive more secure retirement paychecks instead of flexible bonuses, or if you want to increase the amount of your income, you can buy a simple, low-cost single premium immediate annuity for that purpose, as described in Chapter 6.

Step 4: Develop a cash stash.

As you approach the age at which you'll stop working altogether, you should set aside money that you can use to cover emergencies and planned one-time expenses, as described in Chapter 4. You might want to simply adjust the emergency stash you maintained while you were working, or you could use any funds remaining in your retirement transition bucket for this purpose.

That's it! Follow these four steps and you're done. The "Helpful Resources" section identifies examples that help you understand the Spend Safely in Retirement Strategy.

If you're fortunate enough to have saved more than $1 million for retirement, the Spend Safely in Retirement Strategy can still work for you. However, you might want to consider more sophisticated methods than the RMD for generating your retirement bonuses or more elaborate investing strategies.

Let's now consider how you might refine your retirement income strategy to make it best fit your needs.

Refine your strategy

The Spend Safely in Retirement Strategy can be a good starting point for building your retirement income portfolio. You can then refine it to meet other retirement planning goals and to personalize the solution to your circumstances.

For instance, some retirees express a desire to spend more money in their early years of retirement, often for travel expenses, while they're active and healthy. If this applies to you, you could dedicate a portion of your retirement savings to a special "fun bucket" for these purposes; this bucket would not be used to generate retirement paychecks or bonuses. For example, if you plan to spend an extra $5,000 per year on travel for 10 years, you could set aside $50,000 that would not be used to generate retirement income, and then you could withdraw from this savings to pay for any travel expenses.

Here's another refinement: Some retirees may desire more guaranteed retirement paychecks than what's produced by the Spend Safely in Retirement Strategy. In this case, you could use a portion of your savings to purchase a low-cost single premium immediate annuity (SPIA). Another possibility could be to use a tenure payment reverse mortgage to generate additional monthly income, if you have significant home equity. Chapter 6 covers both these ideas.

Some retirees may want to generate retirement bonuses using a method other than the IRS required minimum distribution (RMD). In this case, you can use any of the methods described in Chapter 7, or investigate the strategies written about in some of the books listed in the "Helpful Resources" section at the end of this chapter.

If you're unable or unwilling to work longer to postpone drawing your Social Security benefits, then one possible financial strategy to address this situation would be to use a reverse mortgage line of credit as a pool of funds, which would enable you to delay your Social Security benefits, as discussed in Chapter 6.

One final note about the Spend Safely in Retirement Strategy: It works best when you delay Social Security until age 70, but delays until earlier ages, such as 67, 68, or 69, still provide significant advantages.

As you can see, there are plenty of ways to customize your retirement income portfolio to meet your unique goals and circumstances. Next up: taxes.

Don't let taxes be the tail that wags the dog

Many people obsess over reducing the income taxes they pay to federal and state governments. While that can be a desirable goal, the reality is that many retirees will fall into low-income tax brackets when they retire, and they may no longer need to spend much time investigating ways to reduce their taxes.

For example, many middle-income retirees — those with less than $1 million in retirement savings — will pay much less in income taxes when they're retired as opposed to when they were working. Most likely, they'll fall into either the 10% or 12% federal income tax bracket under the new tax law enacted near the end of 2017. Some retirees might not pay any federal income taxes at all. These individuals might pay reduced state income taxes as well. And if they're fully retired (meaning they're not even working part time), they won't be paying payroll taxes such as FICA or withholding for disability or unemployment benefits.

Most retirees will be in low-income tax brackets during
retirement, so minimizing taxes should have a lower priority
compared to maximizing your retirement paychecks and bonuses.

As a result, your most important goals as a retiree should be to build your retirement paychecks and bonuses, and select investments that support your strategies. Minimizing your taxes should take a secondary role and shouldn't get in the way of maximizing your retirement paychecks and bonuses.

Now, don't get me wrong: Even during retirement, you'll still want to learn about the tax rules that apply to you as a retiree. It's always a good idea to take reasonable steps to minimize the taxes that you pay. For more details on this topic, see the bonus chapter *Navigating the Tax Rules* on the "Advanced Study" page of www. retirementgamechangers.com. Learning more about what taxes you'll pay as a retiree — even if it's just the basics — can help you have an informed conversation with your tax accountant, or will help you develop strategies that minimize your taxes if you prepare your own taxes with tax preparation software.

Consider paying down your debt

Many older workers enter retirement with significant debt, such as mortgage debt, student debt, and credit card debt. Repayments of this type of debt represent a basic, fixed living expense. Chapter 4 recommends covering your basic living expenses with guaranteed paychecks such as Social Security and annuities. But another strategy to consider is to use retirement savings to pay off your debt, thus reducing your fixed monthly payments. This strategy makes especially good sense for credit card debt, which typically has sky-high interest rates.

Paying off mortgage and student loan debts with retirement savings might make sense if the interest rate on the loan is higher than the interest rate you might earn on your retirement savings. For instance, if you have retirement savings invested in bonds or annuities, there's a very good chance that the loan rate is higher than the rate you'd earn on your retirement savings. In this case, you might consider paying off the loans with some of your retirement savings.

Note that there are two emotional considerations to keep in mind. First, some people feel more secure having money in the bank that they can see, even if it earns a lower rate of interest than the rate on their loans. In that case, it might make sense to continue paying the monthly loan payments. On the other hand, some people feel better not owing money to anybody — this feeling would support paying off any loans you might have. So pay attention to your feelings, in addition to doing the money math.

Keep learning, and get help if necessary

Even after reading this chapter or other materials regarding retirement, many people might still want help from a professional to set up their 21st century retirement income portfolio. If this sounds like you, look for a qualified professional adviser who has your best interests at heart. For ideas and strategies that can help you shop for a skilled and unbiased adviser, see the bonus chapter *Get Help* on the "Advanced Study" page of www.retirementgamechangers.com. And if you do choose to work with an adviser, be sure to still take some time to understand the ideas in Chapters 4 through 8 so that you can have an informed conversation with your adviser.

The next chapter offers some ideas for managing the "E" part of the retirement income security formula, including estimating how your living expenses will change in retirement. This will be essential information to understand because if your estimated living expenses are more than your total estimated retirement income, you'll need to make some important decisions regarding your retirement: You'll either need to find ways to reduce your living expenses, or you'll have to find ways to increase your retirement income. To get a very good grasp on your basic financial security, I might suggest rereading all the chapters in this section of *Retirement Game-Changers*.

In addition to balancing your income and living expenses, you'll also want to take steps to protect yourself against the threat of high medical bills and long-term care. Your decisions in these areas can influence how much income you'll need, for example to pay for insurance premiums. You'll also want to coordinate how you use your assets to generate income with your strategies to protect yourself against these threats. Chapters 10 and 15 cover these topics in detail.

We're halfway through the book, and you've learned some basic, straightforward strategies you can use to deploy your hard-earned savings in retirement. If you want to learn even more about your investment choices, I devoted an entire book to this topic: *Money for Life: Turn Your IRA and 401(k) Into a Lifetime Retirement Paycheck*. It discusses the pros and cons of each type of retirement income generator (RIG) and introduces a method for selecting the RIG or RIGs that will work best for you. Although it was published in 2012, most of the ideas and tools in the book still apply today. I plan to publish a second edition in the next year or two, so keep an eye out for it.

The "Helpful Resources" section for this chapter also identifies other books and websites that I respect that can give you additional insights into generating retirement paychecks and bonuses, and establishing a cash stash.

Congratulations on reading this far and committing to developing your retirement income portfolio. By spending the time *now* to design and implement a thoughtful strategy to generate retirement paychecks and bonuses for the rest of your life, you'll thank yourself when you reach your 80s and 90s and won't have to worry about outliving your money.

 **ACTION STEPS:**

- Learn about the possible methods you can use to develop retirement paychecks and bonuses, and develop strategies that will work best for you.

- Determine if your 401(k) plan or IRA provider can pay you an automatic retirement check or bonus.

- Estimate the amounts of your retirement paychecks and bonuses, to see if they will cover your living expenses.

- Decide if you need professional help to develop your retirement income strategies.

 **HELPFUL RESOURCES:**

Advanced Study page at www.retirementgamechangers.com

- Examples of the Spend Safely in Retirement Strategy

- *Get Help*, bonus chapter which covers working with financial advisers

- *Navigating the Tax Rules*, bonus chapter that includes information about the taxation of retirement and Social Security benefits

- *Stay Focused*, bonus chapter which explains how using psychology can help you make smart financial decisions to build a retirement income portfolio, including Social Security claiming decisions

Books

- *How a Second Grader Beats Wall Street: Golden Rules Any Investor Can Learn*, by Allan Roth. John Wiley & Sons, Inc., 2009.

- *How Much Can I Spend in Retirement?*, by Wade Pfau. Retirement Researcher Media, 2017.

- *How to Make Your Money Last: The Indispensable Retirement Guide*, by Jane Bryant Quinn. Simon & Schuster, 2017.

- *Money for Life: Turn Your IRA and 401(k) Into a Lifetime Retirement Paycheck,* by Steve Vernon, FSA. *Rest-of-Life* Communications, 2012.

- *What's Your Future Worth? Using Present Value to Make Better Decisions,* by Pete Neuwirth, FSA. Berrett-Koehler Publishers, 2015.

Websites

- *How Much Can I Afford to Spend in Retirement?* This website is maintained by retirement researcher and actuary Ken Steiner, FSA. It includes several articles on generating retirement income to meet your spending needs. It also contains a calculator to help you determine appropriate withdrawals from savings: http://howmuchcaniaffordtospendinretirement.blogspot.com

- IRS required minimum distribution:

    o AARP: http://www.aarp.org/work/retirement-planning/required_minimuum_distribution_calculator/

    o Financial Industry Regulatory Authority (FINRA): http://apps.finra.org/Calcs/1/RMD

    o IRS website: https://www.irs.gov/retirement-plans/plan-participant-employee/retirement-topics-required-minimum-distributions-rmds

    o Many financial institutions and 401(k) administrators also have online RMD calculators and resources.

- *Managing Retirement Decisions,* maintained by the Society of Actuaries: https://www.soa.org/research-reports/2012/research-managing-retirement-decisions/

    o "Designing a Monthly Paycheck for Retirement"

    o "Lump Sum or Monthly Pension: Which to Take?"

- *Morningstar.* An online service that rates a variety of investments, including mutual funds, and provides a wealth of descriptive briefs and blog posts: http://www.morningstar.com

- *NewRetirement.* This website contains useful tools and articles for developing a retirement income portfolio: https://www.newretirement.com

- *Next Avenue.* The "Money & Security" page on this website contains a number of useful articles: https://www.nextavenue.org/channel/money-and-security/

- *Retirement Researcher.* This website, maintained by respected retirement researcher Wade Pfau, PhD, contains several articles and books on retirement income planning: https://retirementresearcher.com

- The websites of Fidelity, Schwab, T. Rowe Price, and Vanguard all have many descriptive materials regarding the various types of annuities and investments. They can be a good place to get started with your learning about the different types of investment options.

CHAPTER 9

BUY JUST ENOUGH

DON'T MAKE THESE MISTAKES:

- ⊘ Continue your current spending without re-examining your needs and wants in retirement.
- ⊘ Become too frugal when spending your savings.
- ⊘ Get tripped up by income taxes.

TRY THESE GAME-CHANGING STRATEGIES:

- → Manage and reduce your living expenses. It's the most common way retirees manage their finances.
- → Anticipate how your spending might change throughout the rest of your life.
- → Make conscious decisions about what is "just enough" to meet your basic living needs and make you happy.

Make every dollar count

How much money do you really need? While this question applies to almost all of us, it's an especially critical one for older Americans who might have constrained retirement resources and who'll need to make every dollar count, both before and during retirement.

One of the most common strategies that retirees use to make ends meet is to reduce the amount they spend on their living needs, according to various surveys.[1,2] So it's a good use of your time to figure out how to get the most happiness from your hard-earned retirement savings.

My parents' retirement experience provides a good example to follow. When they retired, they knew they'd be living on less income compared to when they were working and would have to cut back their spending out of necessity. To help with that, they paid off their mortgage before they retired, which significantly reduced their bills and helped them more easily make ends meet in retirement.

After my parents retired, they had much more time on their hands, which helped them shop for bargains. For example, one day my father found his favorite shoes on a deep discount sale. He did a mental calculation in his head about how long each pair of shoes would last and how long he might live. He ended up buying three more pairs of the same shoes, so that he'd have a lifetime supply of his favorite shoes at a bargain price!

They also kept up their social life but found some less expensive ways to do that. Bringing together friends and family was very important for their happiness, so they often hosted potluck family gatherings at their house that didn't cost them a lot of money. They also socialized through their hobbies and interests.

There are plenty of ways you can manage the "E" part of the magic formula for retirement income security (*I > E*), and this chapter helps you develop strategies that will help. In the process, you'll want to carefully consider your needs and wants in your retirement years and think about what is "just enough" spending to meet your needs and make you happy.

You'll also want to consider how your spending might change throughout the rest of your life. A very important task you'll want to take on is estimating your budget for living expenses throughout all your retirement years, which might lead you to consider creative alternatives for managing your spending.

Let's take a look at some of these ideas.

Carefully examine your needs and wants in your retirement years

There's a very good chance you can live on much less money compared to when you were working. While conventional wisdom from retirement planners suggests that you need a retirement income that's at least equal to 70% to 100% of your gross pay before retirement, you may not need that much. There are several good reasons why:

- You may have already paid off the mortgage to your house, or could pay off the mortgage soon into your retirement.

- You may no longer be incurring expenses for children, including college costs.

- You're no longer saving for retirement.

- You're no longer paying Social Security (FICA) taxes, which, for most people, equal 7.65% of your pay.

- Most likely you'll pay lower income taxes. Federal income taxes reduce at age 65, and part or all of your Social Security income will be exempt from income taxes. Many states reduce their income taxes for seniors as well.

- You may simply decide that you'll spend less money and can still be happy, as an acceptable price to pay for your retirement freedom.

In addition, there's evidence that many people in their 70s and 80s spend less money on clothes, household goods, travel, and hobbies.[3,4,5]

But there are also reasons why your expenses may go up at some point in your retirement. For instance, some people might need to increase their spending in their 80s and 90s on expenses for medical and long-term care. You should plan for this possibility as well.

People who have significant amounts of discretionary income while working are most likely to be able to live on reduced income when they're retired. However, the 70% to 100% guideline from retirement planners may be appropriate for you if you spend nearly all of your wage income during your career years on basic living expenses, or if you rent or won't pay off your mortgage any time soon.

Don't become too frugal

Some retirees become very concerned about outliving their money, so they make drastic reductions in their spending. They make minimal withdrawals from savings and try to preserve the principal of their savings at any cost. Then they end up dying with lots of money in the bank — money they could have enjoyed while they were alive.

While I certainly don't want to chide people for being responsible with their money, there can be a better way to manage your finances in retirement. As discussed in Chapters 4 through 8, it would be smart to set up retirement paychecks and bonuses from your savings that last the rest of your life, no matter how long you live. This strategy allows you to safely spend your paychecks and bonuses, as long as you keep your "E" less than your "I."

Common rules of thumb may not apply to you

Here's one problem with the conventional wisdom about the amount of retirement income you need. When you estimate the amount of savings you need to support your current lifestyle, as described in Chapter 8, you might find that you need a gazillion dollars to retire, and that you require a retirement savings goal that's simply unattainable. Or, you could find that you need to work into your 90s to maintain your current level of spending. Instead, it's a good idea to take a long, hard look at your living expenses and determine how much money you really need to cover basic living expenses and to afford only what truly makes you happy.

The bottom line? Do your homework to see how much income and savings you need to support the life you want. Consider your circumstances regarding your mortgage and other significant day-to-day living expenses, and take into account estimated medical expenses later in life.

Also, be prepared to make adjustments. Many people will live 20 to 30 years or more in retirement, so be ready to deal with the unexpected curveballs that life can throw your way.

Learn why spending patterns are important

As we age, some analysts predict a U-shaped pattern of expenses, as follows. They forecast that we'll spend money on travel and recreation in our 60s and early 70s, and then we'll reduce these discretionary expenses in our late 70s and early 80s. Finally, they predict that we'll spend much more money on medical and long-term care expenses in our mid-80s and beyond.

Indeed, one example — my parents — confirms this pattern. My mother and father traveled and pursued their hobbies in their 60s and 70s, then their spending tapered off in their 80s as they were less physically able to travel. Finally, they both spent a lot of money on medical bills and long-term care in their late 80s and early 90s.

Whether you expect your future retirement spending to increase, not change, or decrease over your retirement years has a dramatic impact on the amount of retirement savings you need. That's because it takes more retirement savings to generate an income that keeps up with inflation, compared to an income that's constant in dollar terms. If you require that *all* your income keeps up with inflation, then you might need more financial assets to retire. In that case, you may need to delay your retirement to accumulate the financial resources that you need.

Let me point out that in most situations, assuming you'll actually spend fewer dollars as you age is dangerous when you take inflation into account. At the very least, I'd assume level spending in dollar terms; this means you think you'll buy less stuff as you get older, but inflation will make the stuff you buy more expensive. In this case, you're assuming that your reduced spending would neutralize the impact of inflation, which allows you to rely partly on sources of income that remain constant over time, such as pensions and annuities.

Here's one possible exception where it might make sense to assume you'll actually spend fewer dollars in the future: if you'll pay off your mortgage soon into your retirement.

So what should you do about your current and future expenses when planning your retirement? When deciding how to generate retirement income from your savings, as described in Chapters 4 through 8, consider the entire picture regarding spending and income, and how you expect your spending to change during your retirement. For example, will you pay off your mortgage by the time you retire? Will you need to support dependent children or parents? Are you in good or poor health? Do you want to travel a lot, or do you have expensive hobbies? Can you use public transportation and get rid of a car? All of these factors should be taken into account when estimating your budget for living expenses in retirement.

If you expect significant increases or decreases in either your living expenses or your income in the future, you can take these changes into account when planning your retirement income generators (RIGs), as described in Chapters 6 and 7. To help you out with this refined planning, there are retirement planning software programs that allow you to build in future changes in your living expenses and income; I've listed a few systems in the "Helpful Resources" section at the end of this chapter.

Some people may feel more comfortable if they plan for most of their retirement income to increase for inflation so that they can maintain their buying power. Others may decide they don't need to plan for full inflation increases on *all* of their retirement income; after all, Social Security income is adjusted annually for cost-of-living increases, and it's an important component of most people's total retirement income. That might make them feel more comfortable about pensions or annuities, which are lifetime income sources that typically don't increase for inflation.

My conclusion on this issue: You should plan to have some increase in income in your later years to pay for increased bills for medical and long-term care expenses.

The bottom line is, you should spend the time needed to plan for sources of retirement income that meet your individual spending needs. You'll feel more confident about your retirement if you do.

Decide if you can be happy living on less income

As mentioned earlier, there's a good chance you'll live on a lower income than the one you lived on during your working years. But the key questions you need to answer are:

- How much lower? and

- Can you be satisfied with that income?

To find out, mutual fund company T. Rowe Price recently surveyed people who retired in the past five years and who had accumulated some retirement savings in either an IRA or 401(k) account.[6] These retirees were about three years into their retirement when they were surveyed, and they reported living on an income that, on average, was about two-thirds the amount of their pre-retirement income.

As the survey results show, living on less doesn't seem to necessarily reduce a retiree's quality of life:

- 57% of retirees report that they live as well or better than when they were working.

- 85% agree with the statement, "I don't need to spend as much as I did before I retired."

- 65% like spending less and see it as a newfound freedom.

- 89% are somewhat or very satisfied with their retirement so far.

These survey results provide a key insight: There's a very good chance you can live on much less money during your retirement years compared to when you were working.

Many retirees find they spend less money in
retirement, and they're still quite happy. It's an
acceptable trade-off for their retirement freedom.

Buy just enough

Economists have interesting insights into what they call "utility theory." According to this theory, if you really need something that's lacking in your life, then buying that something to meet your basic needs will most likely make you happier. For instance, if you don't own a car, then buying a basic car might truly make your life better. Once you start going beyond your basic needs, however, then going "upscale" really doesn't add much more to your happiness. So after buying a basic car that gets you where you need to go, if you trade up to a fancier car, you might not add much to your overall happiness with life.

You can see this phenomenon with the consumer ratings of cars. Inexpensive but well-made cars often have customer satisfaction ratings that are equal to — or even better than — those of much more expensive cars. But those expensive cars can cost as much as four times more than the inexpensive ones.

Understanding utility theory led me to develop a strategy you might consider using for all your purchases, whether you're purchasing large items, such as your house, cars, furniture or appliances, or you're buying smaller, everyday items, such as food and clothing. Here's my strategy:

Buy "just enough" to meet your basic needs and only what truly makes you happy.

Don't listen to the ads that tell you to buy your way to happiness. Buying your way to happiness might as well be called "futility theory"!

"Just enough" is a smart spending strategy for anyone who wants or needs to make the most of their financial resources, but especially retirees and workers approaching retirement.

Estimate your retirement budget

Prior to your retirement, you'll want to add up all your estimated retirement living expenses — your regular monthly living expenses, plus any expenses you don't pay on a monthly basis, such as insurance premiums, property taxes, and gifts. Doing so will help you understand how these will change compared to your working years.

It's also important to understand that your living expenses will inevitably change throughout your retirement. For example, at some point, you might pay off the mortgage on your house, which will significantly reduce your living expenses. On the other hand, if you received subsidized medical insurance through your employer while you were working, then your health care costs could increase significantly during retirement. And these medical expenses will be different before and after the eligibility age (65) for Medicare.

So how do you get started estimating your expenses in retirement? Some people may want to organize their living expenses using software such as Personal Capital, Mint, or Quicken; retirement planning software such as Fidelity's Retirement Income Planner; or tools on NewRetirement.com. These programs can all help you estimate how your expenses may change in retirement.

You can also use simple worksheets that help you itemize and compare your monthly living expenses before and after retirement. You should also include periodic expenses, such as property taxes, insurance premiums, and household maintenance and repairs. I've listed two helpful worksheets in the "Helpful Resources" section at the end of the chapter.

When you're estimating your anticipated retirement expenses, be sure to include the costs for basic fixed living expenses, such as housing, food, utilities, income tax withholding, and insurance, as well as for discretionary expenses, such as entertainment, hobbies, vacations, and gifts. Knowing these amounts can help you with a strategy I discussed in Chapters 5 and 6, where you generate retirement income to cover your basic living expenses with guaranteed retirement paychecks such as Social Security, pensions, and annuities. Then you'd cover discretionary expenses with your retirement bonuses, which have the potential for growth but can fluctuate in value.

Another possible budgeting refinement could be to set aside some retirement savings for a special "fun bucket" of money to pay for travel in your 60s and 70s, while you're still vital and healthy. You wouldn't use this money to generate retirement paychecks or bonuses.

Don't get tripped up by income taxes

When preparing your monthly budget for living expenses, you'll also want to include withholding amounts for your estimated income tax payments. While you were working, your employer took care of income tax withholding, but that changes when you retire. You're now responsible for withholding for income taxes if you're no longer receiving a regular paycheck as an employee.

You can't spend all the money in your IRA and 401(k) accounts: A trap for the unwary

Many people make the mistake of thinking they can spend all the money they have in their 401(k) plan and IRAs. The trouble is, if these are traditional IRAs and 401(k) accounts, they'll owe federal and possibly state income taxes on the amounts they withdraw from these accounts. (Only Roth IRAs and 401(k) accounts can be withdrawn free of income tax.) Remember: If you withdraw from your traditional IRA and 401(k) accounts throughout the year to pay for living expenses, then most likely you'll owe Uncle Sam some money when you file your income tax return.

If you usually work with a tax accountant to prepare your taxes, you'll want to review your situation with them so they can help you estimate the amount of income taxes you might pay when you're retired. Take into account how much income you'll receive from all sources, including Social Security, withdrawals from your 401(k) accounts and IRAs, and possibly employment income. Or you can use popular tax preparation software to estimate your income taxes during your retirement years. You'll also want to estimate the appropriate amount to periodically withhold for estimated taxes, so you don't face a large unexpected payment at tax time.

Make the necessary trade-offs for your retirement freedom

Estimating your fixed and discretionary expenses, and arriving at a retirement budget you believe will work for you, will help you think about the trade-offs you may need to make in order to retire when you want. It might also inspire you to see how you can reduce your retirement living expenses so you can stretch your retirement savings. Think hard about what is "just enough" to meet your needs and make you happy. For instance, would you be willing to move to a lower-cost location? Can you share housing to drastically cut your living costs?

How much is your retirement freedom really worth to you? The answer is different for everybody, but it's well worth your time to find the answer that works best for you. For many people, housing is the biggest portion of their retirement budget. As a result, carefully considering the topics in Chapter 13 can help you make decisions on the home that best meets *all* your needs in retirement. If your finances are tight, you may want to consider some creative alternatives, as discussed in the next few pages.

Living in the large home in the suburbs: A trap for the unwary

After they retire, many people stay in the same large home in the suburbs that they'd lived in for many years. They might find that they become isolated, particularly in their frail years. Isolation and loneliness are serious risks in retirement, as discussed in Chapters 14 and 15. Instead, you might want to investigate how you can downsize to a less-expensive home to maintain, one that's closer to friends, family, social activities, public transportation, shopping, and exercise opportunities. No matter what you decide, make sure your home can work for both your independent years as well as the frail periods of your retirement years.

Other people may be convinced to "retire in paradise" — either in planned retirement communities or by retiring abroad. Often the advertising for these places focuses on the "vacation" aspects of retirement. Golf and play every day! Explore exotic locales! Party in the clubhouse! These advertisements often overlook the day-to-day practicalities of living, including proximity to work or volunteer activities, medical care, and the lack of ability to mix with people of all generations.

Before deciding where you want to live, think about what will make your life happy and fulfilling. Also, focus on your daily living needs. By completing the checklists in Chapter 13, you'll create guidelines for assessing potentially enticing stories and advertisements about the best places to retire.

Consider the Golden Girls solution

Many boomers are approaching their retirement years with little or no savings, and they're wondering how they'll be able to afford to live in retirement. Many widowed and divorced women are finding themselves in this tight spot, often with modest financial resources and loneliness as a constant fear.

But four women managed to put lipstick on this challenge and came out smelling like a Rose (pun intended). The popular TV show *Golden Girls*, which ran from

1985 to 1992, offered a creative example of how to solve the "not enough money/ don't want to live alone" dilemma.

In a column for CBS *MoneyWatch*, I did the math to show that four women with just Social Security benefits and modest income from part-time work could make this type of living arrangement work.

How well did they live together? In the show, they laughed, cried, betrayed each other, lied to one another, supported each other emotionally, did things together, helped family members, shared their resources, and discussed the important issues of the day. In short, they lived their lives and lived them well.

Now let's be clear: I'm not idealizing the Golden Girls' circumstances, and of course, Hollywood glosses over real-world concerns, such as how to pool expenses. Reaching retirement age with little or no retirement savings, however, is a very unfortunate situation. While the Golden Girls solution is admittedly a radical step, it's one option to consider, should you find yourself in these circumstances.

Explore a win-win green retirement

Playing with our grandchildren awhile back, it occurred to my wife and me that there's a very good chance they'll be alive for another 90 years. As a result, they'll most likely experience the potential long-term consequences of the dire headlines we read about now, such as global warming, pollution, overcrowding, and excessive government debt. On the other hand, since we'll be dead in 30 or so years, my wife and I will most likely escape the full brunt of these trends.

This realization doesn't make us feel very good. We want to do something to leave a better world for our kids and grandkids — cleaner air and water and a sustainable environment.

What does this have to do with retirement planning? We need to make every dollar count by balancing our income and spending. But instead of viewing this as an impoverished situation, we have opportunities for enriching our retirement years while helping to improve our communities and future generations as well.

Most of us will have more time and less money in retirement compared to our working years. We can use that additional time to our advantage, along with the knowledge that many small, positive steps can lead to significant improvements over time, just as compound interest increases our savings accounts.

The win-win green retirement

With this spirit in mind, here are 10 tips for saving money during our retirement years that also will help to leave a better planet for our grandchildren:

10 tips for a green retirement

1. Downsize your house to save on maintenance and utility bills.

2. Move close to day-to-day retail and service outlets, restaurants, and social settings to reduce your energy consumption.

3. Use your car less by walking or biking. This will help reduce energy consumption and pollution. Note that you might be able to pull off a triple-header by combining tips 1, 2, and 3.

4. Take public transportation whenever possible.

5. If you need a new car, buy one that sips gas and has low emissions.

6. If you need or want to work, find work that's close to home or is accessible by public transportation.

7. Eat less meat. Factory meat production uses a lot of water and creates substantial greenhouse gases and pollution.

8. Grow your own fruits and vegetables.

9. Rip up your lawn, and replace it with landscaping that uses less water, gas (for mowing), and chemical fertilizers and pesticides.

10. Share housing to reduce your energy bills.

My wife and I have taken many of these steps, and we find it's not a sacrifice. In fact, our life has been enriched, not diminished. Making ends meet in retirement can be rewarding for your pocketbook as well as your sense of life satisfaction.

Share ideas, get help

I never cease to be amazed about American retirees' resilience and resourcefulness when it comes to managing their finances. Share your ideas and tips with your relatives, friends, and neighbors, and ask them for their favorite ways to save money on living expenses. Who knows what you'll find?

Another source of help and ideas can be financial wellness programs that have recently sprung up at many companies and financial institutions. These programs can give you ideas and tools to manage your day-to-day living expenses.

We need all the help we can get, and together we'll make it happen!

ACTION STEPS:

- Prepare a budget for your living expenses that compares before and after retirement expenses.

- Reflect on your major expenditures for housing, transportation, food, health, and entertainment. Decide what's "just enough" in each area. Are you currently spending more than "just enough"? Can you cut back in some of these areas and still be happy?

- Consider how your spending might change and evolve over *all* your retirement years for items such as travel, hobbies, medical expenses, and long-term care.

HELPFUL RESOURCES:

Books

- *Your Money or Your Life,* by Joe Dominguez and Vicki Robin. Penguin Books, revised edition 2008.

- *The Soul of Money: Transforming Your Relationship With Money and Life,* by Lynne Twist. W.W. Norton & Company, updated 2017.

Websites

- "How to Retire With No Retirement Savings: The 'Golden Girls' Solution," by Steve Vernon. CBS *MoneyWatch*, June 2011. http://www.cbsnews.com/news/how-to-retire-with-no-retirement-savings-the-golden-girls-solution/

- Online programs to help you inventory your budget for living expenses:

  ○ *AARP Home Budget Calculator*: https://www.aarp.org/money/budgeting-saving/home_budget_calculator.html

  ○ *Fidelity Income Strategy Evaluator*: https://www.fidelity.com/calculators-tools/income-strategy-evaluator

  ○ *Intuit Mint*: https://www.mint.com

- *NewRetirement*: https://www.newretirement.com
- *Personal Capital*: https://www.personalcapital.com
- *Quicken*: https://www.quicken.com

• *Mr. Money Moustache.* A great website with tips on frugal living: http://www.mrmoneymustache.com

• Worksheets to estimate living expenses:

  - Blackrock's retirement expense worksheet: https://www.blackrock.com/investing/literature/investor-education/retirement-expense-worksheet-va-us.pdf

  - TIAA's retirement budget worksheet: https://www.tiaa.org/public/pdf/advice-planning/tools-calculators/A125820_budgeting_worksheet.pdf

CHAPTER 10

MAKE SMART CHOICES FOR HEALTH INSURANCE

Ruinous medical costs

health insurance

DON'T MAKE THESE MISTAKES:

- ⊘ Allow a coverage gap with your medical insurance if you retire before Medicare eligibility at age 65.

- ⊘ Make shortsighted choices about Medicare.

- ⊘ Overlook planning for dental and vision expenses.

TRY THESE GAME-CHANGING STRATEGIES:

- → Be vigilant and persistent when exploring your options for medical insurance before age 65.

- → Make Medicare choices with the rest of your life in mind.

- → Save thousands of dollars over your lifetime by shopping smart for medical, prescription drug, and dental coverage.

- → While you're working, explore saving money in a Health Savings Account, which is a very tax-efficient way to pay for your out-of-pocket health care expenses.

Protect your well-laid plans

Remember the nursery fable about the three little pigs? The first two pigs focused too much on having fun, and built flimsy homes made of straw and sticks. They didn't plan ahead for the time when the big bad wolf would come to their door … and you know the sad result. Only the third pig thought ahead, and took the time to build a substantial brick house that protected against the big bad wolf.

It's a good lesson for planning your retirement. To fully enjoy your newfound freedom, be sure to protect yourself against the "big bad wolf of retirement" — high medical costs.

Have you ever thought, "I'm scared about large medical bills that could wipe out my savings"? If so, you're not alone — this is a common fear that I hear expressed quite often during my retirement planning workshops when we do the "hopes and dreams, fears and concerns" exercise I shared in Chapter 2.

The fact is, there's a good reason to be concerned: If you're like most people, the cost of health care is one item in your budget that will most likely increase substantially after you retire. Here's why: A recent study shows that on average, employers subsidize about 80% of the cost of medical insurance for their active employees and about two-thirds of the cost for families.[1] But for most people, these subsidies will disappear when they retire. This represents a game-changing challenge that you need to address.

By making smart choices and putting plans in place to tackle your concerns, you can help alleviate your fears and feel better about your retirement years. The first step is to make sure you've developed well-thought-out, solid strategies for your income and expenses so you can make the magic formula for retirement income security work for you.

But that's not enough: When it comes to your medical expenses, there's more planning to do. High medical expenses can blow up your well-laid plans for managing your income and expenses. As a result, you'll want to take some additional steps to protect yourself — and your spouse if you're married — against the risk of high medical expenses.

I didn't need to look very far for insightful stories about the necessity of protecting yourself against the risk of high medical expenses. I took my own advice about working and earning longer: I retired from my career job in my mid-50s to start my own business researching, writing, and teaching about retirement. I was very fortunate that my former employer offered a high-deductible medical insurance plan for eligible retirees, and I signed up. The premiums are high, but I factored them into the budget that my wife and I prepared for our living expenses.

I'm sure glad I did! My wife and I both take good care of our health, but in spite of these efforts, we each incurred rare, expensive medical conditions during the past several years. For each of us, the original bills from the hospitals exceeded $200,000. Because we're both under age 65, if we hadn't been covered by medical insurance through my former employer, we would have had to pay the full cost of these bills, which would have derailed our retirement plans. Fortunately, my former employer's medical insurance plan paid all but the deductibles and copayments, which were manageable.

Having this medical insurance was crucial to our retirement plans: It turned a potentially devastating financial event into a situation that we were able to manage by tapping our emergency savings for the deductibles and copayments.

The risk of high medical bills during retirement calls for separate strategies before and after you reach age 65, when you're eligible for universal medical coverage under Medicare. There are many crucial features regarding health insurance that have the potential to save you a lot of money — or cost a lot if you aren't paying attention. So it's smart to have the patience to persist through all the details you'll read about in this chapter.

Let's start with coverage before age 65.

Be sure you have medical and dental insurance in the years before you're eligible for Medicare

If you want to retire before age 65, which is the eligibility age for Medicare, then finding affordable medical and dental insurance must be a critical part of your retirement planning. By getting the right insurance, you help protect yourself against the threat of high, uninsured costs during the gap years between when you retire and age 65. This can be a tough challenge — you may need to be creative and persistent to obtain the medical coverage you need. However, it's a step you ignore at your own peril, as my own story illustrates.

Below are four conventional possibilities for obtaining medical, dental, and vision coverage between the time you retire and age 65. In each case, you'll want to determine the amount of your monthly premium in order to factor it into your budget for living expenses. If you have a specific health condition, you may also want to see if your preferred health care specialists are in the insurer's network.

- **Instead of retiring completely, consider semi-retirement or downshifting.** In this instance, you'll seek work from an employer that offers medical coverage for part-time employees. That may be hard to find, but some companies seek out older, experienced workers, and they offer medical insurance as part of a package to attract them.

- **Determine whether your employer or your spouse's employer offers retiree medical insurance and whether you're eligible for it.** Not many employers offer this type of insurance, but it's worth your time to find out. If your employer offers it, review the eligibility requirements to make sure you qualify and to see how much you'd pay for premiums. It's entirely possible you still won't be able to afford the monthly premiums, even considering any premium subsidies from your employer, but it doesn't hurt to check.

- **Purchase COBRA insurance coverage from your employer when you retire.** COBRA is a federal law that allows workers who are covered by their employer's medical plan to continue their medical insurance for up to 18 months after they terminate employment. The premiums are usually high, however, and the typical coverage lasts just 18 months. But COBRA coverage might enable you to close the coverage gap between age 63½ and age 65, when you'd be eligible for Medicare. One thing to keep in mind: If you're married and your spouse is covered through your medical plan at work, you'll need to wait to retire until your spouse also reaches age 63½ in order to have no gap in your spouse's coverage.

- **Purchase medical coverage on your own through exchanges under the Affordable Care Act (ACA), aka Obamacare.** You might even receive a subsidy for coverage if your income is low enough to qualify. Each state has different programs and options, so it's important that you check out the options in your state. When this book went to press, the ACA's future was in doubt for political reasons, so you'll want to follow the efforts in Congress to repeal or change the ACA. In particular, you'll want to understand whether Congress has weakened the prohibition on exclusions for pre-existing conditions.

Some people who are eligible for employer-sponsored retiree medical insurance or COBRA may be tempted to buy less-expensive coverage on their own. I prefer employer-sponsored coverage because your employer can act as an advocate on your behalf if you have disputes regarding medical claims. If you buy individual medical insurance and have a dispute, it's just you versus a big insurance company.

Don't get caught in this situation!

"Unfortunately, you have what we call 'no insurance.'"

If none of these options appeal or apply to you, I'd like to suggest three more creative possibilities. While they won't work for everybody, they might be worth investigating if you need to bridge the gap until you're eligible for Medicare.

1. Move to a state with high rankings for access to insurance, moderate insurance costs, and favorable medical outcomes. See the "Helpful Resources" section at the end of this chapter for online rankings of health care and insurance in all 50 states.

2. Move to a country with cheaper medical or insurance costs, such as Panama, Costa Rica, or Thailand.

3. Move to a country with universal health care (most European countries qualify). If you like this option, then before you cross the pond, you should determine whether you'll qualify for coverage once you're there. Note that if you stay overseas after you become eligible for Medicare, you'll need to carefully consider whether you'll enroll in Medicare at that time, as discussed next.

One last piece of advice: If you find your medical and dental insurance options are limited or too expensive, you might want to explore the downshifting strategy I discuss in Chapter 12. See if you can work part time for your current employer and still receive medical coverage. That might be a win-win alternative that provides critical medical coverage yet allows you to enjoy life more.

The bottom line: Monthly premiums for medical and dental insurance before age 65 can easily amount to several hundred dollars to more than $1,000 for yourself, and they can top $2,000 for a married couple. If you want to secure the best coverage at the most affordable prices, you'll want to explore all your options carefully. You'll also want to get a good estimate of your monthly premium costs and factor these amounts into your retirement budget. Even if you find you can't afford to retire when you'd like, you're better off finding out *before* you quit your career job. The time you spend investigating your options may just help you save a lot of money.

Understand your fundamental choice regarding Medicare

Once you're eligible for Medicare at age 65, insurance becomes more affordable and you can't be denied coverage for pre-existing conditions. Despite these benefits, managing your insurance coverage can still be complicated, and you'll need to plan carefully to make every dollar count. It will be essential for you to make some key, informed choices as you approach your 65th birthday.

First, you'll want to understand the four parts of Medicare:

- Part A covers inpatient care in hospitals, skilled nursing facility care, hospice care, and some home health care services.

- Part B covers services from doctors and other qualified health care providers, outpatient care, some home health care services, durable medical equipment, and many preventative services.

- Part C, also known as Medicare Advantage plans, is like an HMO or PPO that combines Parts A and B in one network of health care providers. Medicare Advantage plans typically also include costs for prescription drugs that are covered under Part D (described next); they might also include extra coverage for services like vision care, dental care, hearing aids, and/or wellness services.

- Part D helps pay for the cost of prescription drugs, run by Medicare-approved private insurance companies that follow rules set by Medicare. But if you enroll in a Medicare Advantage plan, you most likely won't need to buy a separate policy for Part D benefits.

Medicare doesn't cover dental or vision expenses: A trap for the unwary

Medicare doesn't cover services for dental or vision care, unless it's the result of a trauma or accident. Also, Medicare doesn't cover the cost of hearing aids. You'll want to make plans for paying for these costs out of pocket or purchasing a policy that covers these expenses.

There are many details regarding these four parts of Medicare that I just don't have the room to cover in this book. Instead, I highly recommend you visit Medicare's website, which contains some excellent descriptions of their coverage as well as some brochures. The "Helpful Resources" section at the end of this chapter contains several useful links.

In the following sections, I'll focus on the most important decisions that require your careful attention. You face a fundamental choice regarding Medicare: You can either participate in Original Medicare or elect a Medicare Advantage plan. With this fundamental choice, *you might not get a "do-over"* that would allow you to change your coverage in the future. As a result, you'll want to understand your choices as you approach eligibility for Medicare.

The main factors that will influence your choice will be costs, simplicity, and freedom to choose your health care providers. The first step is to learn more about each of these choices — the differences can be crucial!

There's a lot to learn and consider about your Medicare choices; please be patient and persist with your learning.

Learn about Original Medicare

You can elect Original Medicare, where you enroll in Medicare Parts A and B and purchase a separate prescription drug plan under Part D. Here are a few key details:

- Most retirees receive Part A without paying a monthly premium (see below for details).

- You'll need to pay a monthly premium for Part B, which is $134 per month for most new retirees in 2018. Retirees with high incomes may pay a higher premium, as discussed later in this chapter.

- Part D, which covers prescription drugs, will also require a separate premium. In 2017, the national average monthly premium for Part D coverage was $34, although actual costs vary significantly depending on the plan you choose and where you live.[2]

There are gaps in Medicare coverage due to the significant deductibles and copayments, which can amount to thousands of dollars. As a result, most people who elect Original Medicare also buy a separate Medicare Supplement Insurance plan, also known as a Medigap plan, that pays for many of the expenses not covered by Medicare. You'll pay a monthly premium for a Medigap plan, in addition to the Medicare Part B premium listed above. In 2017, costs for a separate Medigap plan ranged from $126 to $464 per month for men age 65, and from $118 to $464 for women of the same age, according to the National Medicare Supplement Price Index.[3]

One critical advantage of Original Medicare, when it's supplemented by a Medigap plan, is that you can self-refer to health care providers who accept Medicare reimbursement. This gives you some degree of freedom when choosing your providers that you may not have with a Medicare Advantage plan. This might be important if you want to have the broadest possible access to medical professionals and specialists.

Shop for a Medigap plan

Medigap plans work alongside Medicare Parts A and B, paying for much of Medicare's substantial deductibles and copayments. There are 10 standardized Medigap plans sold in most states, labeled with letters A through N. (Massachusetts, Minnesota, and Wisconsin have a different standardization model.) Plan F provides the most comprehensive coverage, and as a result, it's the most popular plan, selected by almost two-thirds of people who buy Medigap plans.[4]

When you're first eligible for Medicare Part B, you can't be excluded from buying a Medigap plan for pre-existing conditions or be charged a higher premium. As long as you continue the coverage by paying the premiums, your policy is guaranteed renewable for the rest of your life.

If you want to change plans after you're first eligible for Medicare, however, then insurance companies are allowed to apply medical underwriting. This means they can either exclude you altogether because of pre-existing conditions or charge you a higher premium if they deem you to be unhealthy. As a result, when you're first eligible for Medicare, you'll want to carefully consider the Medigap plan that will best suit your needs for the rest of your life. You may not get a "do-over" and be able to upgrade to a more generous policy in future years.

The cost of the premiums you'll pay for a Medigap plan depend on the insurance company you select, your age, gender, and where you live. According to the National Medicare Supplement Price Index, there's a very wide spread between the lowest and highest premium amounts, so it's a good use of your time to shop around for the best plan.

Remember that Medicare doesn't cover routine dental and vision care services. Medicare *might* pay for such services if you have an emergency or injury from a trauma. It also might pay for certain glaucoma screenings and cataract surgery.

Some insurance companies offer special coverage options to their Medigap plan members for routine dental and vision care, or they may offer insured members a discount program to help them save money on routine dental and vision care. You'll want to investigate whether your Medigap plan covers these items. If it doesn't, you may need to pay for these items out of pocket or look for stand-alone dental insurance or vision plans.

Medicare and Medigap plans might also cover hearing diagnostic tests if they're medically necessary, but they won't pay for the cost of hearing aids.

See the "Helpful Resources" section at the end of this chapter for links where you can learn more about Medigap plans.

Shop for a Part D Plan

Medicare Part D is a separate policy that pays for some or all of your costs for prescription drugs — these costs aren't covered by Medicare's other parts. Medicare mandates the features that must be offered in a basic Part D plan, although you can buy a policy with more generous features than the basic plan. Most, but not all, Medicare Advantage plans also cover prescription drug benefits, so if you participate in a Medicare Advantage plan, you'll want to find out if you need to purchase a separate Part D plan.

Note that you can change your Part D plan in future years without needing to satisfy medical underwriting, if you want to upgrade to a more generous plan. This is different from the rules we discussed previously that apply to Medigap plans.

There are many details about Part D plans that you can read about in the "Helpful Resources" section at the end of this chapter. But let me cover two important features here that influence the amount of benefits you'll receive and the premium costs of Part D plans:

- The Part D "donut hole"
- Drug formularies

Understand the infamous donut hole

Following are the features of a basic Part D prescription drug plan. It sounds complicated, but hang in there: It's not as bad as it looks! Note that all figures are 2018 numbers.

- Each year, you'll pay for 100% of your drug costs before you reach the prescription drug deductible, which is $405.

- After you meet the deductible ceiling, a basic Part D plan will pay for 75% of all your drug costs and you'll pay 25%, until both you and your plan have paid $3,750 for prescription drugs.

- At that point, you're then in a coverage gap, or "donut hole," and you'll pay 100% of your drug costs until you've spent $5,000 out of pocket for prescription drugs.

- After that, you're eligible for the catastrophic coverage, and you'll spend no more than 5% of the cost of drugs for the remainder of the year when you're eligible for catastrophic coverage.

If you're in the donut hole, in 2018, you can receive a 65% discount on the price of generic drugs and a 56% discount on brand-name drugs, provided you follow the procedures your plan sets. In addition, some drug plans may offer higher reimbursements if you use a network pharmacy; they may even require that you use a network pharmacy, so it's important to find out if your favorite pharmacy is a preferred provider under the plan you buy.

Note that a Part D plan can provide more generous features than the basic plan described above, but you'll spend more on monthly premiums. If you're interested in expanded coverage, you'll want to decide if the additional benefits would justify the extra premiums.

FYI the Affordable Care Act would have closed the donut hole for 2020 and thereafter, but a Congressional budget deal advanced the closing year to 2019. Instead of paying 100% of prescription drug costs that would have been in the donut hole, you'll pay 25% of these costs.

Beware of prescription drug formularies

If you're taking prescription drugs on an ongoing basis to maintain your health, you'll want to understand your plan's formulary, which you can find on your insurer's website. Prescription drug plan formularies assign drugs to a tier: the lower the tier, the higher the reimbursement (and the lower your out-of-pocket costs). Generic drugs are assigned to the lowest tiers, while more expensive, brand-name drugs are assigned to higher levels.

The lower tiers typically have fixed-dollar copayments, while the higher tiers may have "coinsurance" instead, where you pay a specified percentage of the total cost of the drug. More expensive, brand-name drugs generally have higher out-of-pocket costs, and some drug plans may not even cover certain drugs in that category.

To cut their costs, some drug plans move certain drugs from a lower tier level to a higher tier level, which reduces insurance company payments. That's one good reason you want to check the specific prescription drugs you take against your plan's formulary each year to see how much you might be paying for your medications.

If you take many expensive prescription drugs, you can save hundreds or even thousands of dollars each year by smart shopping for Part D plans during open enrollment. The good news is, you're allowed to change Part D prescription drug plans during open enrollment each year without having to satisfy medical underwriting conditions.

Medicare's plan finder can help you assess how much money you might spend on prescription drugs, considering the drugs you're taking. See the "Helpful Resources" section at the end of this chapter for the link.

Whew — it's a lot to consider! Think of the time you spend shopping for prescription drug plans as part of your "retirement job."

Now you're ready to consider Medicare Advantage plans.

Learn about Medicare Advantage plans

Medicare Part C, or Medicare Advantage, is an alternative to Original Medicare. Medicare Advantage plans are more like a Health Maintenance Organization (HMO) or Preferred Provider Organization (PPO), and they combine Parts A and B in order to provide you with integrated hospital, physician, and outpatient coverage. Medicare Advantage plans have their own deductible and coinsurance schedules, so you don't need to buy a separate Medigap policy, as you would with Original Medicare. By law, Medicare Advantage plans must provide the same services as Medicare Parts A and B, but they're in charge of how they'll deliver medical services.

Medicare Advantage plans also usually cover Part D prescription drug benefits, and they may include extra coverage for special items such as vision care, dental care, hearing aids, and/or wellness services. One goal of Medicare Advantage plans is to simplify your life by bundling health care services in a managed care environment. However, be aware that if you choose a Medicare Advantage plan, you might not be able to switch to a Medigap plan in the future, if your health or circumstances change.

In addition to your Part B premium, you'll usually pay a monthly premium for the Medicare Advantage plan. In some instances, however, there's no additional premium for so-called "zero premium plans." In this case, you only need to pay your usual Part B premium.

Shop for a Medicare Advantage plan

Medicare Advantage plans typically restrict or encourage you to use the medical providers in the plan's network. Here are the two most common types of Medicare Advantage plans:

- HMO plans usually restrict care to providers within their network. If you choose otherwise, you'll pay the full cost for providers outside the network, except possibly in the case of a medical emergency. In most cases, you'll need to select a primary care doctor, and you'll need a referral from that physician in order to see a specialist each time you need one.

- PPO plans offer the best coverage and costs for in-network services, but they also allow physician choice by covering out-of-network care. However, you'll pay higher out-of-pocket costs for out-of-network services. In most cases, you don't need to select a primary care doctor, and you don't need a referral to see a specialist.

In either case, you'll want to check whether your doctors and specialists are in the network of the Medicare Advantage plan you're considering. And you may want to consider possible future needs for specialists. You'll also want to review and understand the plan's premium amounts, deductibles, and copayments, and determine whether your Medicare Advantage plan pays for such items as dental care, vision care, hearing aids, and wellness programs.

Look beyond the premium amounts for Medicare Advantage plans: A trap for the unwary

Some people might be tempted to choose a Medicare Advantage plan that has a lower monthly premium than the combined amount of premiums for Medicare Part B, Medigap coverage, and Part D prescription drug coverage. But before you select this alternative, do your homework and think long term, because you might not be eligible for a "do-over" in the future.

First, look beyond the premium amounts and estimate your out-of-pocket expenses with either approach. It's possible that the copayments under a Medicare Advantage plan might outweigh the plan's savings on premiums. You'll also want to find out whether your current health care providers are in the network you're thinking of choosing or whether you'll be satisfied with the network's providers.

More importantly, you'll want to understand the implications of underwriting requirements that most Medigap plans apply. When you're first eligible for Medicare, Medigap plans can't exclude you for pre-existing conditions or charge higher premiums if you're not healthy. But after the initial enrollment period, if you want to switch from a Medicare Advantage plan to Original Medicare during Medicare's open enrollment period, in most cases, you won't have a guaranteed right to get a Medigap policy. *At that point, most Medigap plans are allowed to exclude you for pre-existing conditions or charge higher premiums.* This can happen if you're unhealthy according to their underwriting standards, which can be a potentially devastating disappointment.

The problems arise when people make shortsighted decisions when they're healthy at the time they're initially eligible. They might think, "I'm healthy now, and I don't see my health care providers that often, so I'll just elect the plan with the lowest monthly premium. If I develop a condition and want more freedom when choosing health care providers, I can always switch to Original Medicare and buy a Medigap plan."

But that kind of thinking could be a big mistake! If you develop a serious medical condition, you may no longer meet the underwriting requirements of Medigap plans, and then you could be denied coverage. In this case, you'll most likely be locked in to the providers in your Medicare Advantage plan's network. If you want to use a specialist who isn't in the network, you might be paying full cost for the care.

Note that in this example, you can always choose Original Medicare and self-refer to health care providers who accept Medicare. It's just likely that you won't be able to buy a Medigap policy that reimburses for Medicare's deductibles and copayments, which can add up quickly if you have a serious medical condition.

In fact, this happened to the mother of one of our close friends who developed a serious illness; she couldn't switch from a Medicare Advantage plan to a Medigap plan. As a result, she was forced to pay out-of-pocket for Medicare's deductibles and copayments for the specialists she wanted to see.

As a result of the underwriting requirements and the ability of Medigap plans to deny coverage for pre-existing conditions, many people elect to participate in Original Medicare when they're initially eligible for Medicare. They also buy separate Medigap and Part D policies in order to keep their options open in the years to come when selecting specialists and other health care providers. This may be an option you'll want to consider if you think you'll develop a serious or debilitating condition at some point in your life, and might have trouble paying for Medicare's deductibles and copayments.

The fact is, even if you're healthy now, there's a good chance you'll incur a serious medical condition at some stage in your life; at that time, you might want to have the broadest freedom to pick health care providers.

Don't get me wrong! I'm not trying to dissuade you from considering a Medicare Advantage plan. There are many such plans with robust networks of doctors, specialists, and health care practitioners, particularly in large, urban areas. A well-chosen Medicare Advantage plan has the potential to save you significant amounts of money over your lifetime, and such a plan can greatly simplify your life when selecting health care professionals. Many Medicare Advantage plans have sound prevention and wellness programs that can help keep you fit.

You might have participated in a health care plan offered by a Medicare Advantage provider while you were working, and developed trusted relationships with the health care practitioners in the network. In that case, it might make sense to continue with the Medicare Advantage plan offered by your health care provider.

I'm just advocating that you make your health insurance selections only after considering your possible needs *for the rest of your life*, and not just when you're first eligible for Medicare and are still healthy.

Check your eligibility for Medicare Part A

Whether you elect Original Medicare or a Medicare Advantage plan, you'll want to make sure either you *or* your spouse have paid FICA taxes for at least 40 calendar quarters (10 years). This qualifies both of you for free Medicare Part A coverage.

If neither of you has paid FICA taxes for 40 quarters, you can still purchase Medicare Part A, but it will be costly. The premium in 2018 is $232 per month per person if you paid FICA taxes for 30 to 39 calendar quarters, and $422 per month per person if you paid FICA taxes for fewer than 30 quarters. If you're close to these thresholds, you might consider continuing to work and paying FICA taxes until you reach these thresholds to either reduce or eliminate your Medicare Part A premiums.

Determine when you should enroll in Medicare

There are many different rules and deadlines for enrolling in the various parts of Medicare, and enrollment dates can be different for each of Medicare's four parts. For instance, if you start your Social Security income benefits before age 65, you'll be automatically enrolled in Medicare Parts A and B to be effective at age 65, and you'll receive your Medicare card three months before your 65th birthday. At that point, you'll have the option to refuse Part B, since premiums are required, but that's usually a bad idea. The only time it makes sense to delay signing up for Part B is when you're getting coverage from another source, such as a health plan offered by your employer or your spouse's employer.

If you aren't covered by a medical plan at work and if you haven't started your Social Security benefits by age 65, then it's best if you enroll in Medicare Parts A, B, and D no later than three months after your 65th birthday. *This is necessary even if you continue to delay the start of your Social Security income benefits.* If you don't sign up for coverage before this deadline, coverage can be delayed and late penalties may apply.

Warning: If you delay signing up for Medicare Part B or Part D after you're first eligible, Medicare applies a permanent penalty surcharge to your monthly premiums. The only exception is if you're eligible for a special exemption, such as coverage from the Department of Veterans Affairs.

If you decide you'd rather be covered by a Medicare Advantage plan than be covered separately by Medicare Parts A and B, you'll need to select and enroll in your Medicare Advantage plan *no later than three months after your 65th birthday,* though I always recommend doing it early so you don't forget. Once again, if you don't sign up for coverage before this deadline, coverage can be delayed and late penalties may apply. You can sign up as late as three months after your 65th birthday to avoid any penalties.

If you continue working beyond age 65 and are covered by your employer's medical plan as an active employee, make sure you understand how that plan coordinates with Medicare. The best way to do this is to consult with your HR department or benefits administrator. One key reason to look into this is that there are different rules for employers with fewer than 20 employees compared to employers with 20 or more employees. It's also important to note that many employer-sponsored plans require you to enroll in Medicare Part A but not Part B. You'll also want to determine whether your employer's plan covers prescription drugs; if so, you won't need to sign up for Medicare Part D while you're covered by your employer's plan.

If you don't enroll in Medicare Parts B and D because you're covered by your employer's plan while you're working, the late enrollment penalties mentioned here won't apply. To avoid a late penalty completely, however, you'll generally need to enroll in Medicare Part B no more than eight months after you eventually retire. You'll also need to buy a Medicare Part D plan within 63 days of your retirement date.

In most cases, you won't want to elect a Medicare Advantage plan while you're covered by your employer's medical plan as an active employee, since you'll be duplicating coverage and wasting the premiums you'd have to pay for the Medicare Advantage plan.

Whew! I know it's a lot to pay attention to, but it's well worth your time to get the coverage that's best for you.

Now let's take a look at the circumstances under which you can change your Medicare health care plan.

Learn when you can switch plans

Each year, during Medicare's open enrollment period (from October 15 to December 7), you can switch from:

- Original Medicare/Medigap to a Medicare Advantage plan
- One Medicare Advantage plan to another Medicare Advantage plan
- A Medicare Advantage plan to Original Medicare (but not necessarily to a Medigap plan; see below)

- Your Part D prescription drug plan to another Part D plan, if you're in Original Medicare

The problem arises when you want to switch from a Medicare Advantage plan to a Medigap plan that supplements traditional Medicare, or from one Medigap plan to another Medigap plan. Most states allow insurance companies to apply medical underwriting in this situation (Connecticut, Massachusetts, and New York are the exceptions). If the insurance company finds you to be in poor health, it can increase your premiums or even deny coverage outright.

In limited circumstances, you're sometimes allowed to switch out of a Medicare Advantage plan into a Medigap plan without medical underwriting. Here are a few of those particular situations:

- If your Medicare Advantage plan no longer serves your area

- If you move to an area not served by your Medicare Advantage plan

- If you enrolled in a Medicare Advantage plan for the first time and want to switch within the first 12 months

For more details regarding the various circumstances under which you can switch plans, see the links in the "Helpful Resources" section at the end of this chapter.

Determine if you'll pay a higher premium for Medicare Part B

The usual Medicare Part B premium covers about one-fourth of the costs of that coverage; the U.S. government subsidizes the rest of the cost. The government imposes higher premiums for high-income retirees, however, as one method to improve Medicare's financing.

To determine if you'll pay higher premiums for an upcoming calendar year, the Social Security Administration (SSA) looks back at your most recent available federal tax return, which is usually the tax year that's two years before the year in which you're paying Medicare premiums. The SSA uses a sliding scale to calculate the additional premiums you'll pay, based on your modified adjusted gross income (MAGI). Your MAGI is your total adjusted gross income plus tax-exempt interest income.

Here are the basic guidelines: If you file taxes as "married filing jointly" and your MAGI is greater than $170,000, you'll pay higher premiums for your Part B and Medicare prescription drug coverage. Also, if you file your taxes using the "single" or "head of household" status and your MAGI is greater than $85,000, then you'll also pay higher premiums.

Note that whether you'll pay higher premiums is determined each year based on the look-back rule described above. So it's possible that you might pay higher premiums for a specific year but subsequently drop to the regular premium levels in the future, if your MAGI drops sufficiently.

If you end up having to pay a higher premium because of your high retirement income, you'll want to factor those costs into your budget for living expenses. In limited circumstances, you can apply for a waiver of these additional costs. The most common situation that might prompt you to apply for a waiver is if your current income has dropped substantially because you retired compared to the look-back year, although there are other circumstances that apply as well.

For details on these rules, including a table that summarizes the additional premiums, see the link in the "Helpful Resources" section at the end of this chapter.

Get help

By now, it's entirely understandable if you're feeling intimidated or confused by all these details regarding medical insurance and Medicare coverage. If that's the case, you might want to find experts who can help you sort through and choose the best option.

One good source is Medicare's Star Rating System, which measures the performance of Medicare Advantage and Part D prescription drug plans. Medicare's system rates these plans in several categories, including quality of care and customer service. The ratings can be found in Medicare's online Plan Finder tool.

Another possibility is to pay an independent consultant to help you decide whether Original Medicare or a Medicare Advantage plan is right for you, and then have them help you shop for the best plan given your budget and circumstances. Such a consultant might be particularly helpful if you take a lot of prescription drugs and are shopping for a Part D plan. You'll often save much more money than the fee you pay to the consultant by choosing the right plan. One note of caution: Make sure that any consultant you hire isn't paid commissions from an insurance company or by selling your personal information!

You might also want to work with an insurance salesperson or website such as ehealthinsurance.com. They'll earn a commission on the sale of insurance to you, which means they might be restricted in the plans they offer to you, but they can help you pick the best plan for you among the plans they service.

One last suggestion: You might find help with local senior citizen centers or your local Area Agency on Aging. Be sure to determine whether they have specialized expertise with Medicare and medical insurance plans.

The "Helpful Resources" section at the end of this chapter identifies an independent consulting firm that I respect, as well as helpful resources on Medicare's website, a website that contains a directory of Medigap insurance agents, and two online health insurance agencies.

And now one last thought about preparing for medical costs during your retirement…

If you're eligible, max out your Health Savings Account (HSA)

While you're working, you might be eligible to save money in a Health Savings Account (HSA), provided that you participate in a qualified, high-deductible medical plan. If you're eligible and elect to save money this way, you make contributions to an HSA and direct the investment among funds offered by your HSA provider.

The funds in an HSA accumulate tax-free until you withdraw money from the account. If you withdraw to pay for qualified medical expenses, no income taxes are due at the time of withdrawal. In this instance, you avoid any income taxes on the amounts invested in an HSA altogether and forever. From a pure tax perspective, this beats contributions to a 401(k) plan or an IRA, because with these plans, you'll have to pay income taxes sooner (with a Roth 401(k) or Roth IRA) or later (with a deductible 401(k) or traditional IRA).

No other retirement savings vehicle offers these tax advantages. The only retirement savings opportunity that's better than an HSA would be matching contributions from your employer to your 401(k) plan.

There's even more good news: You can withdraw money from an HSA at any time to pay for qualified health care expenses, including the following:

- Medical care, dental care, prescription drug costs, and vision care expenses, including any deductibles and copayments
- Premiums paid after age 65 for Medicare or your employer's retiree medical plan (but not for Medicare supplement plans)
- COBRA premiums
- Long-term care services
- Premiums for qualified long-term care insurance

You're also allowed to withdraw money from an HSA to pay for ordinary living expenses that aren't qualified medical expenses, but you'll pay ordinary income taxes on that money. In this case, you'll also be assessed a 20% penalty if you're under age 65. After age 65, there's no penalty.

HSAs have a few significant advantages over IRAs and nonmatched 401(k) contributions:

- You can withdraw money penalty-free from an HSA to pay for qualified medical expenses at any age, whereas IRA withdrawals are typically assessed a 10% early-withdrawal penalty before age 59½.
- Once you reach age 65, you can withdraw money from an HSA penalty-free to pay for ordinary living expenses that aren't qualified medical expenses. In this case, you'll pay ordinary income taxes, which is the same outcome for any withdrawals from deductible 401(k) plans and IRAs.
- HSAs have no IRS required minimum distribution at age 70½, whereas 401(k) plans and deductible IRAs are subject to such rules.

In essence, you have maximum flexibility with an HSA. You can:

- Use it while you're working to pay for medical expenses you incur during the year or any future year.
- Let it accumulate to pay for qualified medical expenses when you retire.
- Let it accumulate until after you've attained age 65 to pay for expenses that aren't qualified medical expenses, and then pay ordinary income taxes on any withdrawals.

Your HSA withdrawal strategy will influence which of the funds offered by your HSA provider you'll invest in. If you plan to use an HSA account to pay for current medical expenses, then you'll want to avoid substantial stock market investments that can decline at any time. In this case, you'll want to look for liquid investments that conserve principal.

On the other hand, if you plan to use your HSA contributions to pay for medical expenses in retirement, you might have a long investing horizon ahead of you. Particularly, it's possible to delay withdrawing from an HSA account until your 80s, when you might have high medical or long-term care expenses. That would give you a very long investing horizon that can justify substantial stock investments.

Warning: Once you enroll in Medicare Parts A and B, you can no longer contribute to an HSA. The one exception to being able to continue to contribute to an HSA after you've reached age 65 is if you meet all of these conditions:

- You continue to work beyond age 65;

- You're covered by your employer's medical plan at work as an active employee;

- You haven't applied for Medicare Parts A or B; and

- You haven't started Social Security benefits.

The bottom line: If you're eligible, HSAs offer great tax advantages and flexibility. Many people who are eligible should consider first maxing out any matching 401(k) contributions, then max out their HSA contributions, and then finally max out their nonmatched 401(k) or IRA contributions.

You'll be glad you spent the time

Congratulations for reading this far! Like many of the other steps in this book, exploring your choices and strategies for medical insurance for your retirement years will take a lot of time and effort.

Be sure to carefully consider your own specific health care needs. Don't blindly follow the advice of a well-intentioned family member or friend — their needs might be very different from yours.

You might also need to pay to hire a qualified, objective consultant to help you shop for a plan. This can not only help you save money, but it can help you choose the best plan for you. And while it might be frustrating to spend this kind of time or money, remember: The medical procedures and drugs you'll be covered for under the right plan may be what will keep you alive and healthy!

 **ACTION STEPS:**

- If you or your spouse are retiring before age 65, investigate your options for obtaining health insurance until you're eligible for Medicare.

- Investigate your strategy for choosing Original Medicare or a Medicare Advantage plan when you reach age 65.

- If you decide to sign up for Original Medicare, shop for a Medigap plan and Part D prescription drug coverage.

- If you purchase Part D prescription drug coverage, understand how your plan's drug formulary treats your specific prescription drugs and whether your local pharmacy is a preferred pharmacy.

- Each year, determine whether to continue your Part D coverage or whether it would be advantageous for you to change your Part D plan.

- Prepare a budget of your costs for medical premiums and out-of-pocket expenses, such as deductibles, copayments, and services not covered by Medicare. Don't forget dental expenses, eyeglasses, and hearing aids.

- While you're working, investigate if you can save money in a Health Savings Account to build a fund to pay for future out-of-pocket expenses.

 **HELPFUL RESOURCES:**

Medicare's very helpful website

- Additional Part B premiums due to high income: https://www.ssa.gov/pubs/EN-05-10536.pdf

- Comparing Medigap plans: https://www.medicare.gov/supplement-other-insurance/compare-medigap/compare-medigap.html

- Finding a Medigap plan in your state: https://www.medicare.gov/find-a-plan/questions/medigap-home.aspx

- Helpful contacts to help you make decisions: https://www.medicare.gov/Contacts/

- Information regarding when an insurance company can't refuse to sell you a Medigap plan: https://www.medicare.gov/find-a-plan/staticpages/learn/rights-and-protections.aspx

- Medicare Advantage plans: https://www.medicare.gov/sign-up-change-plans/medicare-health-plans/medicare-advantage-plans/types-of-medicare-advantage-plans.html

- Medicare's costs and deductibles: https://www.medicare.gov/your-medicare-costs/costs-at-a-glance/costs-at-glance.html

- Medicare's Plan Finder: https://www.medicare.gov/find-a-plan/questions/home.aspx

- Medicare's Star Rating System: https://www.medicare.gov/find-a-plan/results/planresults/planratings/compare-plan-ratings.aspx?PlanType=MAPD

- Medigap plan overview: https://www.medicare.gov/supplement-other-insurance/medigap/whats-medigap.html

- Part D coverage for prescription drugs: https://www.medicare.gov/part-d/

- State health insurance assistance programs (SHIPs) that help you make decisions: https://www.medicare.gov/Contacts/#resources/ships

- Summary brochure: https://www.medicare.gov/medicare-and-you/medicare-and-you.html

Other websites

- The American Association for Medicare Supplement Insurance offers helpful information about Medigap plans and a directory of insurance agents: https://medicaresupp.org/medicare-supplement-insurance-costs/

- Health insurance rankings by state, including an interactive map: https://wallethub.com/edu/states-with-best-health-care/23457/#main-findings

- *Managing Retirement Decisions,* maintained by the Society of Actuaries.

    o "Securing Health Insurance for the Retirement Journey" https://www.soa.org/research-reports/2012/research-managing-retirement-decisions/

- Medicare's Star Rating System: https://www.ehealthmedicare.com/faq-what-are-medicare-plan-star-ratings/

- *My Medicare Matters*, a website maintained by the National Council on Aging, offers helpful resources.

  o Information regarding when you can switch plans: https://www.mymedicarematters.org/after-enrollment/time-to-re-evaluate/

  o Part D deductibles and copayments, and description of formularies: https://www.mymedicarematters.org/costs/part-d/

- National Association of Area Agencies on Aging often offers help navigating Medicare. This website can help you locate an agency near you: https://www.n4a.org

- Online insurance agencies that sell Medigap plans and contain useful information:

  o AARP: https://www.aarpmedicaresupplement.com/medicare-insurance/

  o ehealthinsurance.com: https://www.ehealthinsurance.com/medicare/supplement

- Sixty-Five Incorporated, a Medicare consulting firm that I respect. Its website contains a wealth of useful information: https://www.65incorporated.com

- *U.S. News and World Report* health rankings by state: https://www.usnews.com/news/best-states/rankings/health-care

III.

ENGAGE

To really thrive in your retirement years, you'll want to go beyond building your financial security as described in the previous section. The choices you make regarding working longer, your health, and your home and community all will impact your well-being, enjoyment of life, and ultimately your financial security as well.

Don't overlook the importance of the series of lifestyle decisions in this section. They're just as important as your financial security — they are game-changers. Take the time to do the job right — you won't regret it!

You'll also want to plan for your financial security and well-being in your frail and final years, to minimize your stress and the burden on your family. Think about your wishes and make them known to your loved ones. Your family will be very grateful.

Finally, if there are causes you believe in, family and friends you want to support, or values you want to pass along to your family, take the time to plan your legacy, whether it's money or your time. Now is the time to complete your life's work!

CHAPTER 11

INVEST IN YOUR HEALTH

DON'T MAKE THESE MISTAKES:

- ⊘ Give up on improving your health.
- ⊘ Think that your genes alone determine your health and longevity.
- ⊘ Fail to exercise or move enough.
- ⊘ Eat too much of the Standard American Diet (SAD).
- ⊘ Allow yourself to become obese.
- ⊘ Not get enough sleep.
- ⊘ Leave hearing loss untreated.
- ⊘ Smoke.
- ⊘ Abuse alcohol or drugs.

TRY THESE GAME-CHANGING STRATEGIES:

- ➜ Redefine what good health means to you.
- ➜ Track your progress.
- ➜ Find exercise that you enjoy.
- ➜ Seek healthy food you like to eat.
- ➜ Get enough sleep.
- ➜ Manage any health conditions that develop.
- ➜ Build your health care team.

Find your motivation to take care of your health

"I'm afraid of having poor health and not being able to enjoy my retirement years." All too often, I hear this fear expressed at my retirement planning workshops. This fear is consistent with the results of two surveys showing that the fear of poor health is one of retirees' greatest sources of stress and concern about retirement.[1,2]

So would it surprise you to learn that retirees rank health as the most important source of happiness in retirement? It's true: Two prominent surveys — different from the surveys noted above — asked retirees about the sources of their happiness in retirement, and survey respondents ranked good health ahead of financial security, enjoying typical retirement activities, and having purpose in life.[3,4]

These last survey results are good examples of the "avoid being unhappy" aspect of happiness that you read about in Chapter 1. Good health *enables* many desirable outcomes, such as enjoying friends and family, traveling, pursuing interests, volunteering, and continuing to work.

But I seriously doubt if *healthy* people wake up each morning thinking, "I sure am glad I'm healthy today!" Instead, they're most likely looking forward to the activities that make them happy. On the other hand, it's very easy to imagine *unhealthy* people waking up and having the first thing on their minds be the hope that they could feel better today.

When it comes to your health during your retirement years, you might be inspired by stories of the 96-year-old sprinter and wakeboarder, the 104-year-old marathoner, or the 97-year-old yoga instructor.[5,6,7] The encouraging examples of these active older individuals illustrate that just because you're old doesn't mean you have to be in poor health. I'm still inspired by my father, who continued pole vaulting and high jumping into his late 70s.

But if you think these examples are outliers or that these people are pursuing activities you'd never be interested in, let me tell you about some ordinary people I know who are great role models for all of us as we move into our retirement years:

- My 70-something neighbor, Paul, lost more than 100 pounds because he was scared about his poor health. His plan to lose weight wasn't hard to understand, but it took courage and determination: He started walking regularly, cut out all sugar in his diet, and restricted his meal portions.

- My 81-year-old friend, Ben, regularly attends the yoga class that I attend, primarily composed of age 50-plus regular folks. He doesn't do headstands or backbends, but neither does anybody else in the class. Ben is fit and trim, and his good health enables him to enjoy frequent travels. As he puts it, "Travel keeps me young — planning the travel taxes my brain, and I meet interesting people all over the world."

- Ben's 93-year-old sister, Audrey, attended our yoga class one day. She had never tried yoga, but she dances and practices tai chi regularly, and her good health enabled her to keep up with our yoga class just fine.

- My 78-year-old neighbor, Nomi, and her 81-year-old husband, Gerry, regularly attend their gym and take Pilates classes. Both are very active in their community and look years younger than their age. Nomi also keeps busy with a thriving portrait business.

These stories are all about regular folks who are committed to taking care of their health and whose lives are much better for their efforts. But there's another perspective that's also important to consider, as this quote illustrates:

"My friend, John, took care of his health, and he still died at an early age. You just never know!"

It's not unusual to hear stories about people who were serious about taking care of their health through good nutrition and exercise, yet still suffered from cancer or other serious medical conditions. Some pessimists cite these stories as justification for not bothering to make any effort to improve their own health. But they're missing some important points.

Taking care of your health is a game-changing challenge. You can *significantly improve the odds* that you won't incur a serious condition, but unfortunately, there's still *no guarantee* that won't happen. But if you *have* taken care of yourself and then contract a serious condition, then your overall good health can improve your odds of survival and speed your recovery.

I encourage you to reflect on your own motivations for taking care of your health. Some people act out of fear of the pain and suffering that might result from poor health or are scared of all the money they'll have to spend on medical bills. It's only natural you might feel this way, particularly if you've seen older relatives and friends suffer from serious illnesses.

On the other hand, some people choose to focus on how their good health enables all the activities that give them happiness and joy in retirement. Understanding that their good health allows them to enjoy life helps them make better choices regarding how they eat and exercise.

Both the fear of poor health and the many positive experiences that good health enables are strong motivations at any age.

Dispel common misunderstandings about your health

"None of the men in my family lived beyond age 55, so I don't need to plan for a long life."

I've heard versions of this statement more times than I can count. The fact is, many people believe their genes determine their health and longevity. But that's just not the case. Scientific evidence is accumulating that shows your lifestyle decisions have an equal or greater impact on your health and longevity. Funny enough, it's often the case that you "inherited" your family's exercise and nutrition *habits*, which as you'll see, can have a large influence on your health.

> *"For all but the most strongly determined genetic diseases, such as Huntington's disease, MacArthur Studies show that the environment and lifestyle have a powerful impact on the likelihood of actually developing the disorder. This is wonderful news for individuals with strong family histories of some cancers, heart disease, hypertension, rheumatoid arthritis, and many other conditions. We now know that diet, exercise, and even medications may delay, or completely eliminate, the emergence of the disease."*

—From *Successful Aging,* by John W. Rowe, MD and Robert L. Kahn, PhD

Are you worried that you don't have what it takes to make healthy changes in your lifestyle? While that might be a natural concern, think about prior times in your life when you made significant changes: You graduated from school, moved out of your parents' house, and got a job. Many of you got married and had children. You probably also packed up and moved a few times. All of these common life experiences required making big changes in your life.

Don't let pessimism get you down. You can do it again! Be inspired by the many stories about people from all walks of life who've made healthy life changes after putting their minds to it.

Before we move on to some specific action steps you can take to enhance your health, let's look at the financial reasons you should take care of your health.

Understand the financial consequences of poor health

Being in poor health can cost you a lot of money — an expense many people can't afford. For example, Fidelity Investment's "2014 Retiree Health Care Cost Estimate" calculated that a 65-year-old married couple in poor health would need an extra $15,200 per year just to pay for their higher medical bills, compared to a married couple the same age in good health.[8] To put this in perspective, to generate that additional $15,200 per year in income, you'd need roughly $380,000 in savings, an amount that's higher than the total retirement savings of many current older workers.

Here's another important financial consideration: Many of you might want to work into your late 60s or early 70s to help make ends meet, to allow your financial resources to grow, and/or to enjoy valuable social contacts. If this is the case for you, you'll need to be healthy to continue working that long.

Once you're motivated to take care of your health, whether for financial reasons or for enjoyment of life, you'll want to develop an overall health plan, which we'll cover in later sections of this chapter. But first, let's take a closer look at what it means to be in good health.

Redefine "good health" to mean "successful aging"

Have you ever been disturbed by the wrinkles, gray hair, and inevitable changes in your body that have occurred as you age? While it's only natural to be bothered by these obvious signs of aging, they're not what really counts. In our later years, good health should involve more than our futile attempts to fight Mother Nature. Instead, we should focus on achieving the best health that's realistic for each age that we attain.

When you were in your 30s and 40s, you probably defined "good health" as the absence of a serious disease, and you probably took for granted that you and most of your family and friends were fairly healthy. You might have seen a health care practitioner only to "fix" a specific illness or injury.

During these younger decades, you may have known a few people your age who were otherwise healthy but contracted a serious disease, such as cancer. You probably thought of them as unlucky and that the disease they contracted "just happened" to them. While it's true that some unlucky souls who are otherwise healthy will fall victim to a serious illness, it's also true that we have more influence on our health than this simplistic perspective.

"Good health is much more than the absence of disease," says John Rowe, MD, a pioneer in the healthy aging movement and co-author of the groundbreaking book *Successful Aging*, published in 1998. "As we get older, we should really think about successful aging." As a result, you'll want to move beyond seeing health care practitioners to "fix" illnesses and injuries, and also discuss your long-term health goals.

During my interview with Dr. Rowe, we both commented that his book's three-part model for successful aging has held up remarkably well over the years:

1. Avoid disease and disability.

2. Maintain high cognitive and physical function.

3. Engage with life.

In this chapter, I'll share insights and steps you can take to help you address Dr. Rowe's first two recommendations. The third recommendation, "Engage with life," can be addressed in numerous ways and will be the topic of Chapters 12 through 16.

Let's start with Dr. Rowe's first step — avoid disease and disability.

Avoid disease and disability, and track your progress

If good health is much more than the absence of a serious disease, how will you define good health so you can track the progress you make with your plan to maintain your health? Here's my suggestion: Work with your doctor or health practitioner to develop a list of some of the basic indicators of your health, along with your "numbers," so you can track how these indicators change over time.

> *"…many illnesses and disabilities, particularly the chronic diseases of old age, are preceded by signs of future problems. Among these leading warning signs are modest increases in systolic blood pressure, abdominal fat, and blood sugar, and decreases in lung, kidney, and immune function. A preventive orientation would involve periodic monitoring and action …"*

—From *Successful Aging*, by John W. Rowe, MD and Robert L. Kahn, PhD

Here's a basic list of possible health indicators to get you started:

- Do you generally feel good most days?
- Do you have the energy and well-being to carry out your normal daily tasks and enjoy life?
- Do you contract acute illnesses infrequently?
- Are you free from chronic disease?
- If you have specific health conditions that you're trying to manage, are they in check or subsiding?
- Is your digestion easy and regular?
- Is your weight (as measured by your body-mass index) at heathy levels as recommended by your doctor or health practitioner?
- Ask your doctor about healthy levels for you with regards to the following measurements:
    - Blood pressure
    - Cholesterol
    - Blood sugar
    - Any other measurement that's specific for your conditions, such as PSA, CA 125, or TSH
- Are your blood pressure and blood cholesterol at these healthy levels, without taking prescription drugs?

As a group, these health indicators can serve as an early warning system for serious diseases that might develop later in life. The fact is, no matter how diligent you are with taking steps to improve your health, as you age, you'll be increasingly vulnerable to developing one or more serious, chronic health conditions.

Ideally, you'd refine your list with your doctor or health practitioner, or through your wellness program, to include the measures that make the most sense for *your* body and *your* circumstances. This personal set of health indicators can tell you if you're on track to avoid disease and maintain optimum health, or if there are additional steps you might want to take.

The good news is, even if your numbers or indicators aren't as good as you'd hoped, many of them can be improved through healthy nutrition, exercise, and other lifestyle choices that all will impact your health. Since these choices affect both of Dr. Rowe's first two recommendations, we'll cover these steps later in this chapter.

For now, let's discuss Dr. Rowe's second step — maintaining cognitive and physical health.

Develop a game plan to maintain cognitive and physical health

"Our bodies have an amazing ability to self-heal, but our resilience decreases in our 50s and beyond, often due to the cumulative effects of unhealthy decisions we've made throughout our lives," observes Ann Marie Chiasson, MD and co-director of the Fellowship at the Arizona Center for Integrative Medicine at the University of Arizona. Her words illustrate just how complex maintaining your health gets as you reach your 50s and beyond.

Learn from research

There's overwhelming scientific evidence that taking care of your health can improve your odds of living a long, vital life. Respected doctors, scientists, and researchers have published many excellent books in recent years that reveal how we can substantially increase the odds of extending our healthy lifespans — while significantly reducing the odds of expensive conditions — through our lifestyle choices. They cite research from some of our most respected universities, including Columbia, Duke, Harvard, Stanford, and Yale.

The "Helpful Resources" section at the end of this chapter lists a dozen of these books, all by respected MDs, researchers, scientists, and journalists. These books all cite the substantial evidence that supports their conclusions, and they provide practical tips for improving your nutrition, exercise, and lifestyle habits. Many of the authors have published other excellent books as well. I encourage you to read one or more of these very engaging books as part of your long-life retirement planning; they're an example of game-changing resources that weren't available to prior generations.

In recent decades, scientists and doctors have produced substantial research on the specific steps you can take to avoid disease and disability and maintain cognitive and physical health. For instance, in 2014, the Stanford Center on Longevity (SCL) convened dozens of scientists and researchers with the intent to identify action steps that individuals could adopt to improve their health, well-being, and financial security. The result was the center's groundbreaking *Sightlines* study, published in February 2016.[9]

The scientists and researchers involved in the *Sightlines* study agreed that taking the following steps would establish a foundation for good health and vitality for most Americans:

- Exercise at least 150 minutes per week.

- Limit sedentary behavior (sitting) to less than five hours per day.

- Eat at least five servings of vegetables and fruits daily.

- Keep your body-mass index under 30.

- Get at least seven hours of sleep each night.

- Don't smoke.

- Don't binge on alcohol.

- Don't use illegal drugs.

You've probably heard many of these messages before, but they certainly bear repeating.

The *Sightlines* report also identified research citing the importance of social engagement — meaningful and supportive relationships with spouses, relatives, friends, and neighbors — for your health, providing evidence that supports Dr. Rowe's model of successful aging.

As more and more research is carried out on the topics of health and well-being, the science is becoming increasingly clear regarding the obvious mistakes people make with their health. I summarized many of these mistakes on the first page of this chapter, and I'll elaborate on them throughout this chapter. By avoiding these common mistakes, you're halfway to winning the health battle.

On the other hand, the science is less clear on the right steps each person should take in order to maintain their health. Often, what's best for you is a highly personal plan, based on your unique body and lifestyle. To help you create your own plan, I'd encourage you to go on a path of discovery to find the health habits that work best for you.

Participating in your employer's health wellness program is a
retirement planning no-brainer.

If you're still working, one easy way to start on the road to better health is to take advantage of any health wellness program that's offered by your employer or health insurance plan. These types of programs typically provide a written evaluation of your health, often called a "health risk assessment," followed by a list of action steps recommended specifically for you to help you improve your health. Participating in these programs is free, and they often pay incentives for you to participate in health-improvement activities.

If you're no longer working, many health insurance plans offer similar wellness programs, so investigate whether your plan offers a program that can help you maintain and improve your health.

For many of us, the time and stresses of our jobs may have prevented us from taking the steps needed to improve our health. Hopefully, if you're now retired or are working fewer hours, you can free up enough time to take better care of your health.

To help you do just that, let's dig into some of the details of what your overall game plan should be, starting with exercise.

Find exercise that works for you

Many people have the misconception that to be healthy, they need to run marathons or spend hours in the gym every day. Fortunately, that's not the case. The SCL *Sightlines* report identified research that supports the conclusion that moderate exercise and daily activities go a long way toward improving and maintaining your health.

Here's another misconception: Well-meaning family and friends tell you that you absolutely *must* do jazzercise/jogging/swimming/tai chi/walking/weight lifting/yoga/Zumba/you-name-it in order to be healthy. Again, that's just not the case.

Instead of doing what you think you *should* do, why not follow these two better suggestions from Anne Friedlander, PhD, a professor at Stanford University who researches physiology, exercise, fitness, and health: "First, find exercise that you like to do. And second, find ways to build more exercise into your daily routine, such as more walking, climbing stairs, and gardening."

The problem is, if you view exercise as medicine — as something mandatory that you're going to have to force yourself to do because it will improve your health — then there's a very good chance you won't continue with that activity for the long haul. What's important to remember is that just about any type of exercise and movement will provide valuable health benefits, so you should find something that's fun for you, something you really enjoy. Even better, find group activities that give you valuable social benefits as well.

"If exercise could be purchased in a pill, it would be the single most widely prescribed and beneficial medicine in the nation."

—Robert Butler, MD, world-renowned gerontologist, founder of the International Longevity Center, and founding director of the National Institute on Aging

If you're not sure where to start, consider these ideas from the National Institute on Aging. With input from research studies and experts, the institute developed its Go4Life program, which recommends four types of exercise to help mitigate the impacts of aging:

- Endurance or aerobic exercises that increase your heart rate. Examples include brisk walking, jogging, yard work, or dancing.

- Strength exercises to make your muscles stronger, which can help you live independently for longer. Examples include lifting weights, using a resistance band, or doing exercises that use your own body weight, such as push-ups, pull-ups, yoga, or Pilates.

- Balance exercises to help prevent falls. Examples include standing on one leg, heel-toe walking, tai chi, dancing, and yoga.

- Flexibility exercises to help your body stay limber and give you more freedom of movement. Examples include stretching, yoga, and tai chi.

See the "Helpful Resources" section at the end of this chapter for Go4Life's website to find out more about this valuable program.

If you're concerned about finding the time to do all four types of exercise, I have good news for you: Many forms of exercise combine two or more of the above types of exercise. For example, yoga or Pilates typically address at least three types: strength, balance, and flexibility. Dancing also combines three: endurance, strength, and balance. Cross-fit and some gym programs might address all four. Simple brisk walking combines two: endurance and balance. Add some stretches before your walk, and now you have three types of exercise. See? It won't be as hard as you think to get the different types of exercise that can help keep you healthy.

Retirement planning tip from your dog

"Still, a brisk walk can be just as effective."
Danny Shanahan/The New Yorker Collection/The Cartoon Bank

Before we move on to nutrition, there's one more thing you should know about movement and exercise.

Avoid sedentary behavior

There's a growing body of evidence showing that sitting for long periods of time just isn't good for you, even if you exercise regularly.[9] As a result, you'll want to find ways to break up any long periods of sitting. If you're at home watching TV, scrolling through Facebook or Instagram, or working on sedentary hobbies like knitting or quilting, make it a habit to stand up and walk around during commercials or at least once an hour.

If you work in an office, for instance, set an alarm to remind you to stand or walk around for a few minutes every hour. Also, stand up for phone calls. And stand behind your chair during staff meetings — you can tell your colleagues you've heard it's good for your health. Some people might even join you.

Now let's take a look at some steps you can take to improve your nutrition.

Become food literate

"Most deaths in the United States are preventable, and they are related to what we eat. Our diet is the number-one cause of premature death and the number-one cause of disability."

These powerful words are from a fascinating book, *How Not to Die: Discover the Food Scientifically Proven to Prevent and Reverse Disease*, by Michael Greger, MD.

Dr. Greger is not alone in his beliefs. Numerous health researchers have linked the Standard American Diet (SAD) to many chronic, debilitating, expensive conditions, including heart disease, cancer, strokes, inflammation, obesity, and digestive disorders.[10,11,12] The fact is, the SAD is high in meat, dairy, fat, sugar, corn syrup, and sodium, as well as in refined, processed, and junk foods, all washed down with sodas and other sugary beverages. Consumed frequently, it's a recipe for disaster!

What's the alternative? Science is showing that switching to a diet that emphasizes plants can help prevent and even reverse some of the most debilitating, chronic diseases. It may even be more effective than medication and surgery at improving your health. And it's never too late to begin making changes to improve your health: Even after years of eating the SAD, it's possible to reduce chronic disease risk by eating healthier, as you'll discover by reading any of the books on the topic by the widely respected Dean Ornish, MD.[13]

When it comes to nutrition, the science is pretty clear about the mistakes you can make: eating the SAD frequently — or simply eating too much food, too much sugar, and too much sodium — and becoming overweight and diabetic. Another conclusion is clear: Most Americans need to eat more fresh vegetables and fruits, which provide essential fiber, vitamins, and nutrients. The previously mentioned *Sightlines* project found that only about one in four Americans eats the recommended five daily servings of vegetables and fruits, so there's plenty of room for improvement.

Christopher Gardner, PhD, a nutrition researcher at the Stanford University Medical School, contends that many Americans have become food illiterate. "They don't know what goes into the food that they're putting in their mouths, nor are they aware of the health consequences of the food they eat," Gardner says. "As a result, many people are eating food-like substances, not real food, and it's making them sick."

There's another benefit to healthy eating: It's more sustainable and healthy for our environment than the SAD is. Hopefully this amps up your motivation for enhancing your health through better nutrition.

Instead of remaining food illiterate, commit to going on an adventure of discovery to become food literate and, in the process, improve your health, look better, increase your energy, and reduce the time you spend in doctor's offices, as well as the money you spend on medical bills. And don't just go it alone: You're more likely to succeed if you band together with other like-minded individuals. So enlist your spouse, partner, or close friends and relatives to join you and learn to eat healthier.

Seek healthy food you like to eat

A good place to start with improving your nutrition is to significantly reduce the SAD elements and add the recommended servings of vegetables and fruits to your daily meals. Take these steps, and you'll be well on your way to better health.

Beyond that, however, there's less consensus on which healthy foods will work for you. Should you eat eggs or not? Eliminate red meat but eat chicken and fish? Should you eat a vegetarian or vegan diet? Should you drink red wine, eat kale, or enjoy chocolate? Is coffee good or bad for you? Should you eat organically grown or conventionally grown food? Should you try the Atkins/low-carb/low-fat/Mediterranean/Ornish/Paleo/raw diets? It seems like every day, you read articles that offer conflicting opinions on all these questions and more.

Don't lose faith if new research seems to contradict prior findings and conclusions. Nutrition science is a relatively recent research area, so it only makes sense that it's constantly evolving as scientists complete new research. To help navigate our nutrition decisions, my wife and I base our eating habits on the latest research and constantly keep an eye out for new findings as they emerge.

For example, you might see research that shows there's not much difference in the nutritional value of organically vs. conventionally grown foods. What these studies often don't measure, however, is the long-term effects of ingesting the potentially unhealthy pesticide and fertilizer residues that may be on or in conventionally grown food. To help you make decisions on this issue, Dr. Chiasson recommends that you follow the shopping guidelines on the website www.ewg.org, paying particular attention to the "dirty dozen" and "clean fifteen" lists for fruits and vegetables.

But there's much more to staying on top of the latest findings regarding healthy eating than deciding whether to eat organically grown food. To provide more insights on the topic of healthy nutrition, Gardner recently conducted a fascinating 12-month study that provides key insights into the "best diet" question by comparing the results of two different diets among the volunteer subjects. Some subjects consumed a healthy low-fat diet, while others consumed a healthy low-carb diet. Which diet "won" the weight loss test?

The results showed that some subjects lost weight with the low-fat diet, and some lost weight with the low-carb diet, but others didn't lose weight with either diet — or even gained weight! The conclusion? The right food for you is specific to your body type, metabolism, and constitution.

Also, consider that most diets have at least two important components: identifying foods you should avoid and recommending foods you should eat. So, it may be the case that many of the benefits of a specific diet come from avoiding unhealthy foods rather than eating specific foods. For example, several popular diets recommend avoiding many elements of the SAD. For those diets, the foods you avoid may have more of an effect than the ones you're asked to consume.

To help you cut through the confusion about the right nutrition for you, Gardner recommends that you experiment with different foods to see what works best for you. Keep in mind there are three key behavioral elements that his research suggests strongly influence people's eating habits: taste, convenience, and cost. In other words, if the food you eat tastes bland or awful, or if it takes hours to prepare, or if it's a stretch for your budget, there's a good chance you won't stick with a new eating program.

As with exercise, if you view healthy eating as a form of medicine you need to take to improve your health, there's a good chance you might not stick to a healthier diet. Gardner's suggestions about figuring out which foods work best for you can be particularly helpful for people who enthusiastically dive into a new diet but lose their commitment just a few weeks later.

Let's see what other steps Gardner suggests you take to improve your nutrition.

Try a gradual approach to better nutrition

While you can try to strictly adhere to a new eating regimen, Gardner suggests you're more likely to succeed if you gradually introduce the following principles and steps into your daily diet:

- Buy fresh, local, seasonal produce.
- Focus on minimally processed foods.
- Eat foods made with whole grains instead of white flour.
- Limit white potatoes and white rice.
- Choose healthier oils, such as extra virgin olive oil, canola oil, flaxseed oil, or avocado oil.
- Eat more seafood.
- Consume dairy, poultry, and eggs in moderation.
- Serve red meat less often.
- Reduce your intake of added sugar and salt.
- Introduce flavorful and healthy spices.
- Substantially reduce your consumption of sugary beverages.
- Drink healthy by consuming water, coffee, and tea.
- Consume alcohol in moderation.

In addition, you should reduce the number of meals you eat in your car or while on the go, or meals you eat from a package. Instead, carve out some time to prepare and leisurely enjoy your own meals. This could be a good use of the extra time you might have when you retire.

My wife and I have been experimenting with improving our eating habits for 10 years now, and we've tried most of the steps discussed here. It's been a fun, common interest that we share, and we feel much healthier than before we started our journey on improving our nutrition.

Don't accept obesity or diabetes

There's a lot of research that links obesity to expensive, chronic diseases, such as heart disease, cancer, strokes, diabetes, and Alzheimer's.[14] You can determine if you're obese — and therefore at risk — by calculating your body-mass index (BMI), a simple measure of the appropriate weight for your height. A BMI of 30 or higher is considered obese, subjecting you to increased risk for disease. The higher your BMI, the higher your risk.

If you discover that your BMI is 30 or higher, begin taking the necessary steps to reduce your weight. Since obesity is often caused by a combination of poor eating habits and lack of exercise, improving your diet and increasing your activity levels can go a long way toward making a difference.

There are several reliable BMI calculators on the internet; I've listed one website maintained by the National Institutes of Health in the "Helpful Resources" section at the end of this chapter.

One more thing: Many people think they'll use prescription drugs to manage the resulting conditions of their obesity, including high blood pressure, high cholesterol, and diabetes. If this describes you, I suggest you reconsider your position, as you'll see next.

Be cautious with prescription drugs

"Pills are not the answer for conditions that are related to lifestyle problems," says Dr. Chiasson. "In many situations, prescription drugs won't protect large numbers of patients from serious diseases. And thousands of people die each year from drug interactions. For many people, it's safer to try lifestyle remedies for the conditions that prescription drugs typically treat."

If you're taking lifetime prescription drugs for one or more of the common conditions of old age, such as the ones I just mentioned, you'll want to learn as much as possible about the potential risks and benefits. A good place to start is the excellent book *Mind Over Meds: Know When Drugs Are Necessary, When Alternatives Are Better — and When to Let Your Body Heal on Its Own,* by Andrew Weil, MD.

This book goes into detail about the risks and benefits of various prescription drugs for the conditions mentioned above. For example, heart disease remains the most prevalent and expensive disease among people of retirement age, and it's been associated with high cholesterol levels. As a result, more than one-fourth of Americans take a statin to help reduce their cholesterol levels, according to Dr. Weil.

Yet he provides this caution in his book: "Medication alone affords only limited protection against heart disease. Statins are very effective at reducing LDL cholesterol, but that is only one of many risk factors. Furthermore, half of those who have a first heart attack have *normal* blood cholesterol levels. Stress, anger, a sedentary lifestyle, and a diet that favors inflammation also predispose to blockages of coronary arteries." Dr. Weil's book details the many side effects that can result from taking statins regularly, including muscle aches and pains, cognitive impairment, diabetes, and liver dysfunction.

But there's even more to be concerned about: In addition to the recognized side effects, medical science doesn't yet know the consequences of taking many of these drugs for 20 years or more, or about the potential drug interactions from taking multiple prescriptions. By using these drugs, you may be unwittingly participating in a vast experiment to determine the long-term health consequences, including possible drug interactions, of taking multiple lifetime maintenance drugs.

So if drugs aren't always the answer, what is? The good news is, most of the common conditions of old age have possible lifestyle remedies that might help prevent or mitigate these conditions. These include improving your nutrition, increasing the amount of exercise you do, stopping smoking, reducing stress, and being sure to get enough sleep.

If you're debating whether to begin or continue taking a lifetime prescription drug or whether to adopt possible lifestyle remedies, ask your doctor about an important statistic called the "number needed to treat," commonly abbreviated as NNT. The NNT is the average number of patients who need to be treated to prevent one additional bad outcome. Dr. Weil's book provides an example of the significance of this number with respect to preventing hip fractures, a common, devastating event among the elderly.

"When comparing strategies for fracture prevention, the number of osteoporotic patients needed to receive treatment to prevent *one hip fracture* [added emphasis is mine] is forty-five for vitamin D, forty-eight for strontium ranelate, and ninety-one for bisphosphonates," Dr. Weil notes. "A lower score means a more effective treatment."

The result is that the vast majority of people who are ingesting drugs for lifetime maintenance of common old age conditions won't benefit from the treatment, yet they're incurring a lifetime of costs and increasing their vulnerability to side effects and possible drug interactions. The fact is, the NNT is high for many prescription drugs. Ask your doctor or look for research on the internet to learn more about NNT for specific drugs you might be considering.

There's also an important financial reason to be careful with the prescription drugs you might need to take for the rest of your life. The copayments for these drugs are often $5, $10, or $20 per month. While each copay may seem like a small amount, the cost of several drugs taken over your lifetime will add up to thousands of dollars — money you could have spent on things that give you more enjoyment, like a trip to Hawaii or a family cruise. Continuing your reliance on prescription drugs also leaves you vulnerable to future predatory price increases by the pharmaceutical industry.

Now don't get me wrong: Many of the lifetime prescription drugs people take are keeping them alive. Don't ever go off your prescription drug regimen cold-turkey! Instead, Dr. Chiasson recommends, "Ask your doctor or health care practitioner about a supervised lifestyle program to safely wean you off many of your lifetime prescription drugs."

If you're taking multiple prescriptions, Dr. Chiasson also recommends consulting with your pharmacist about possible drug interactions — it's formally called a medication therapy management (MTM) review. A trained pharmacist can review all the drugs you take, then inform you of possible drug interactions, side effects, and alternative treatments. Even if you continue your current drug regimen, you might learn about less-expensive generic alternatives. If you participate in a Medicare Part D drug plan as described in Chapter 10, you may be eligible for an MTM review.

If you're successful with lifestyle remedies to reduce your reliance on prescription drugs, you'll feel better, save money, and will no longer be participating unwittingly in the vast experiment to see what happens when people take lifetime maintenance drugs for many years.

Now let's move on to a few more wise moves you could make to help improve your health.

Get enough sleep

There's a lot of research that links insufficient sleep to many chronic conditions and diseases.[9,15] To sum it up, doctors recommend that you regularly get at least seven hours of sleep each night. Of course, each person might require different amounts of sleep, but the science is showing that regularly skimping on sleep is a long-term health risk.

One goal for your retirement years might be to look for ways to free up your schedule so you actually carve out enough time to get sufficient sleep every night. Or look for ways to get a *better* night's sleep. For instance, if stress is disrupting your sleep, find ways to eliminate or reduce the stress in your life.

Don't smoke or abuse alcohol or drugs

Most people already understand the dangers of smoking and substance abuse — there's really not much new to say on this topic. If you're doing either of these things, most health care programs or employer-sponsored employee assistance programs offer free programs to help you stop smoking or address the continued abuse of drugs or alcohol. If this is a problem for you, please find the motivation to seek help. Your spouse or partner, friends, and family will be glad you did.

Don't leave hearing loss untreated

Do you find yourself needing to crank up the volume on your TV, computer, or music system? Do you often ask people to repeat themselves and they end up talking loudly and slowly to you? These could all be warning signals of the need to pay attention to an important problem.

More than half of all people age 75 or older have some form of hearing loss, according to Amy Yotopoulous, the director of the Mind Division at the Stanford Center on Longevity. Yet most of these people don't use hearing aids. Hearing loss can lead to social isolation and less brain stimulation, which in turn can be a contributing factor to dementia.

Medicare and most health insurance plans might pay for hearing diagnostic tests but not the hearing devices themselves. These devices usually require a prescription and can be expensive. According to Yotopoulous, we may see many creative over-the-counter products in the next few years that might address hearing loss problems through the use of smartphones, earbuds, and other smart options. Hopefully these varieties of devices will drive down the cost of existing and future solutions, and improve their convenience. Stay tuned!

Now let's talk about how to pull together a team of people who can help monitor you and encourage better health.

Build your health care team

Our current health care system is primarily a "disease management system," good at diagnosing illnesses, treating the acute illnesses of childhood and adolescence, and repairing your body if you're injured. But our disease management system isn't yet very effective at enhancing health and longevity, or preventing chronic diseases that impact your later years.

Fortunately, there's an emerging view in medical science that calls for more holistic remedies to treat the expensive, chronic conditions of our later years. This holistic approach is more complex than simply treating the acute diseases that are common in childhood, adolescence, and early adulthood, which often respond well to vaccinations, prescription drugs, or even surgery.

Research has found that chronic conditions might be better treated by complementing traditional drugs and surgery with the lifestyle interventions discussed in this chapter. In fact, one survey found that half of all baby boomers use complementary medicine, such as acupuncture, chiropractic medicine, or herbal supplements, to treat a variety of conditions.[3]

In recent years, two medical specialties have emerged that you might want to investigate to help you avoid disease and maintain your health:

- Geriatric medicine is a specialty that focuses on the health care of elderly people. It aims to promote health by preventing and treating diseases and disabilities in older adults.

- Integrative medicine calls for treating the entire person — often with different modalities — to complement the drugs and surgery that might focus just on a specific health condition. In addition, improving your emotional well-being can positively influence the healing process if you incur a specific condition.

If you experience one of the common chronic conditions that affect those of us in our later years, you might consider complementing the help you get from traditionally trained doctors and nurses with care from other health practitioners, such as chiropractic, geriatric, integrative, or naturopathic specialists, nurse practitioners, nutritionists, physical therapists, exercise trainers, herbalists, health coaches and counselors, and acupuncturists.

Once again, don't get me wrong: If I was in a car accident, I'd want a good surgeon who could put me back together. But it's important to understand *all* the traditional and complementary treatments that are available to you to treat your conditions. One of the wisest moves you can make is to become an informed medical consumer!

A quick note: Many health plans recognize the value of integrative, geriatric, and complementary medicine, and they might pay for the specialists discussed here. Be sure to look into it if the need arises — the resources you need may be at your fingertips.

Put the fear of scary diseases to good use

Many people become fearful about aging when they see older relatives and friends contract serious, debilitating diseases such as heart disease, cancer, or Alzheimer's. I've experienced this fear myself after watching my father suffer from dementia in his mid-80s in spite of his accomplishments as a senior athlete. It was a difficult time for him, my mother, and our entire family. My grandfather also suffered the same fate. But rather than be paralyzed by the fear of contracting Alzheimer's and dementia, I've harnessed it to help motivate me to do whatever I can to take care of myself.

Alzheimer's is the disease most feared by people of all ages, according to a recent report from Merrill Lynch and Age Wave. It's more feared than heart disease, cancer, strokes, diabetes, and arthritis combined.[3] And while Alzheimer's has no cure, we're learning that many of the steps discussed in this book that can improve your health can also reduce the odds of contracting Alzheimer's as well as other debilitating diseases. It seems that what's good for your body — exercise, eating plenty of fruits and vegetables, getting sufficient sleep, reducing inflammation, not smoking or abusing alcohol, and enjoying a rich social life — is also good for your brain.[16]

It's only natural to feel afraid of growing older because you've seen your relatives and friends suffer from serious and painful conditions. Go ahead and feel the fear that comes with expensive, debilitating chronic diseases. But don't just be afraid — *do something about it!*

Respect what you're up against

If it seems overwhelming to address all the steps you learned here about improving your health, consider this wise advice from Dr. Chiasson: "Choose one thing to change every three months. You don't need to do everything at once." Since it will take a concerted effort to change your eating, exercise, and sleep habits to make necessary improvements in your life, taking it one step at a time seems like a manageable task.

Certain aspects of our current culture work against our health and longevity. We're constantly bombarded with persuasive advertising to eat unhealthy, processed food and drink sugary beverages. Or we might eat what's prominently displayed in grocery stores or what's common to the region we live in. Modern life also provides amazing conveniences that mean we don't have to exercise very much, yet this same modern life can add a lot of unhealthy stress to our lives.

For my later years, I've adopted a healthy view of the aging process that motivates me to keep focused on my health. I think of myself much like a classic car: I have a timeless look, and I still get where I want to go. But I also need to diligently adhere to a frequent maintenance schedule, I may need new parts now and then, and I'm not as fast as the new models. If I don't take care of myself, I'll end up in the junkyard!

As you approach your older years, the best advice I can offer is to do whatever it takes to find the motivation to take care of your health. You deserve to be happy in your retirement years and live the life you want to live. Being healthy will help you do both.

By the way, Dr. Rowe, the co-author of *Successful Aging,* takes his own advice and is still fit and vital in his mid-70s. I asked him how his views have evolved in the 20 years since he wrote the book, and his answer is insightful. He's now adding an emphasis on community, noting that "most likely you will age better in a lively town or city with supportive services, compared to being isolated in the suburbs or rural areas." And he's still working on projects that interest him; he shared that he might have been fully retired by now if he hadn't learned about the importance of remaining engaged with life.

That's a great preview of the next two chapters on working longer and choosing the best place for you to live.

 **ACTION STEPS:**

- Consider your motivation for improving your health. Share the reasons you want to be healthy with your spouse, family, and close friends.

- Get a health risk assessment from either your wellness plan at work, your health insurance plan, or your doctor.

- With help from your doctor or health care provider, develop your list of health indicators to track your progress. Store these indicators in a handy place so you have a history of your results.

- Develop an action plan that includes steps for improving your nutrition, exercise, stress levels, sleep, and other lifestyle choices.

- Assess whether you need to expand your health care team.

 HELPFUL RESOURCES:

Books
- *Aging Well: Surprising Guideposts to a Happier Life from the Landmark Harvard Study of Adult Development,* by George Vaillant. Hachette Book Group, 2002.

- *The Blue Zones: 9 Lessons for Living Longer from People Who've Lived the Longest,* by Dan Buettner. Penguin Random House, 2012.

- *The China Study: Revised and Expanded Edition: The Most Comprehensive Study of Nutrition Ever Conducted and the Startling Implications for Diet, Weight Loss, and Long-Term Health,* by T. Colin Campbell, PhD, and Thomas M. Campbell II, MD. BenBella Books, 2016.

- *Dr. Dean Ornish's Program for Reversing Heart Disease: The Only System Scientifically Proven to Reverse Heart Disease Without Drugs or Surgery,* by Dean Ornish, MD. Ivy Books, 2010.

- *The First 20 Minutes: Surprising Science Reveals How We Can Exercise Better, Train Smarter, Live Longer,* by Gretchen Reynolds. Penguin Group, 2012.

- *Healthy Aging: A Lifelong Guide to Your Well-Being,* by Andrew Weil, MD. Random House, 2008.

- *Healthy at 100: The Scientifically Proven Secrets of the World's Healthiest and Longest-Lived Peoples,* by John Robbins. Ballantine Books, 2008.

- *How Not to Die: Discover the Food Scientifically Proven to Prevent and Reverse Disease*, by Michael Greger, MD. Flatiron Books, 2015.

- *Mind Over Meds: Know When Drugs Are Necessary, When Alternatives Are Better – and When to Let Your Body Heal on Its Own*, by Andrew Weil, MD. Little, Brown and Company, 2017.

- *The Okinawa Program: How the World's Longest-Lived People Achieve Everlasting Health — And How You Can Too,* by Bradley J. Willcox, MD, Craig Willcox, PhD, and Makoto Suzuki, MD. Three Rivers Press, 2002.

- *Prevent and Reverse Heart Disease: The Revolutionary, Scientifically Proven, Nutrition-Based Cure,* by Caldwell B. Esselstyn, MD. Avery Publishing, 2007.

- *Successful Aging,* by John W. Rowe, MD and Robert L. Kahn, PhD. Dell Publishing, 1998.

Websites

- *Aim for a Healthy Weight.* This body-mass index calculator is maintained by the National Institutes of Health: https://www.nhlbi.nih.gov/health/educational/lose_wt/BMI/bmicalc.htm

- *Environmental Working Group.* This website contains research and shopping guidelines for deciding which fruits and vegetables should be consumed that are organically grown: https://www.ewg.org

- *Go4Life.* This website, maintained by the National Institute on Aging, contains lists, stories, and helpful videos: https://www.nia.nih.gov/health/exercise-physical-activity

- *National Center for Complementary and Integrative Health.* This website is a good resource to learn about your health treatment options: https://nccih.nih.gov

- *National Institutes of Health's Office of Dietary Supplements.* This website is a good resource to learn about dietary supplements: https://ods.od.nih.gov

- *NutritionFacts.* This website is maintained by Dr. Michael Greger and contains a wealth of articles and short video clips that share the research on healthy nutrition: https://nutritionfacts.org

- *Standard American Diet.* This website details the research on the risks of the SAD, and is maintained by Nutritionfacts.org: https://nutritionfacts.org/topics/standard-american-diet/

CHAPTER 12

FIND WORK THAT'S RIGHT FOR YOU

DON'T MAKE THESE MISTAKES:

- ⊘ Retire too soon.
- ⊘ Assume that retirement can be an endless vacation.
- ⊘ Assume you'll keep working in the same career or in the same way you've been working for many years.
- ⊘ Assume there's no work available for you because you're old.
- ⊘ Give up looking for work.

TRY THESE GAME-CHANGING STRATEGIES:

- ➜ Work longer to substantially improve your financial security, health, and well-being.
- ➜ Consider downshifting instead of full retirement. Find a way to earn just enough money to cover your living expenses and allow your other financial resources to grow until you fully retire.
- ➜ Invest the time to find work that best fits your life. There are many creative ways you can continue working.
- ➜ Explore volunteering as a way to remain engaged and productive.

Make work part of your retirement plan

If you live into your 90s, it doesn't make financial sense to fully retire in your 60s — unless you've saved a gazillion dollars. The fact is, it simply takes too much money to be retired for 20 years or more, and most people haven't saved enough to make that feasible.

But that's not the only reason to consider working longer: It may not be good for your health and well-being to go on vacation for 30 years, as you'll see later in this chapter.

While working during your retirement might sound like an oxymoron, it really depends on how you define "retirement." It's indeed an oxymoron if you adhere to the traditional definition of retirement as "not working," but it may not be so far-fetched if you define retirement as "being happy, fulfilled, and financially secure." And if you believe retirement to be "doing more of what you want to do and less of what you don't want to do," then working longer to earn longer doesn't need to be inconsistent with retirement.

> *"Working longer and fully retiring at a later age is a common-sense solution for mitigating retirement saving shortfalls."*

> **—Catherine Collinson, president of the Transamerica Center for Retirement Studies (TCRS)**

Planning to extend your earning years by finding work that's right for you should be a critical part of your retirement plan. This is a serious game-changing challenge, yet also an important game-changing opportunity. For many people, continuing to work has the potential to significantly improve your financial security, enhance your health, and provide valuable social benefits.

Be inspired by insightful stories

"I enjoy visiting my customers, and my work gets me out of the house, which my wife appreciates." Allan is one of many older friends of mine who've creatively extended their earning lives. For several decades, he owned a successful pet store. Then he sold the store when he was in his early 60s and took a job at a pet supply store as a customer representative. With this new job, he's still in the pet business that he loves, using his prior experience and contacts to successfully transition to and maintain this new job. He's now in his early 70s and works about 20 hours per week. His earnings at this new job allowed him to delay taking Social Security until age 70 and also allowed his savings to grow.

In addition to the financial aspects of his job, Allan has also benefited from the social aspects that come with being employed.

Retirement planning tip from your dog

Dogs have important responsibilities, like guarding the house and nurturing the emotional well-being of the family. But they don't work hard right up to an artificial milestone, then pack it in and retire to the doghouse, lying around all day long and wasting their later years. Instead, they continue to be as active as their aging bodies allow. They gradually decrease their activities and dog duties in their later years. Likewise, humans should consider downshifting or a phased retirement as a more natural life transition than fully retiring from their jobs and spending their later years completely unemployed.

"I love working with the kids. I can work as little or as much as I want, and the income gives me money to spend on vacations." My neighbor, Don, provides another creative example of working longer. He worked a full career for the federal government, retiring in his late 50s. Then he made a 180-degree turn and has been working as a substitute teacher at the local public schools for the past 10 years.

"Special projects keep me engaged, and I have money to spend on my grand-kids." Another friend, Debra, worked as an editor until her early 70s. While she might have been able to make ends meet if she'd retired in her 60s, she enjoyed her work, the social contacts, and the extra income. As a result, she decided to keep working. Her employer was glad to continue her employment for several years beyond age 65, their normal retirement age, because Debra was reliable and well-liked. Now, at age 76, she works as an independent contractor and takes on consulting assignments.

Be open to the new career trajectory

Retirement planning can quickly morph into career planning and life planning, a topic we often discuss during my retirement planning workshops. The reasons? When most people realistically assess their financial resources, as discussed in

Chapters 3 through 10, they realize they won't be able to generate a lifetime retirement income that covers all the living expenses they had during their working years. And while they realize they might need to continue working longer than they'd expected, they also begin to understand that they might not need to continue working the same number of hours at the same rate of pay. This might be possible if their kids have moved out, if they downsize their house, or if they pay off their mortgage.

In the 20th century, the standard career path involved continuously earning raises and assuming more responsibility throughout your working life, then retiring at your peak to full-time retirement. Your career trajectory might have looked like this:

The 20th century career trajectory

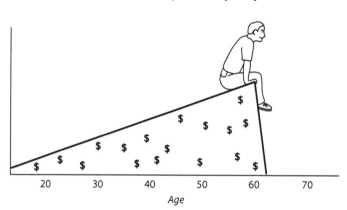

But perhaps it's more realistic and healthy to consider a career trajectory where you continue working longer but with reduced responsibility and pay in your later years. This type of career trajectory might look like this:

The 21st century career trajectory

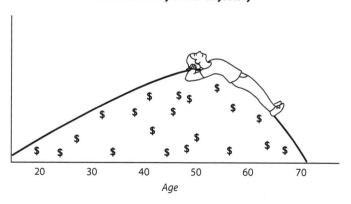

As we continue to dive into retirement planning, you'll learn that effective planning involves making choices in a series of informed trade-offs. One significant trade-off is how much spending power you're willing to give up in exchange for your freedom from work. It's a decision many people can't avoid if they want to make ends meet in their retirement years. If you're like many older workers, then you'll either need to work longer than you'd originally planned, reduce your living expenses to match your income, or develop some combination of these two strategies that works best for you.

> *"The old retirement dream was freedom from work. Perhaps the new retirement dream is freedom to work in new ways, to new ends, in a manner that's personally meaningful."*

—Marc Freedman, founder of Encore.org

When it comes to working, your goal is to make conscious choices that enable you to enjoy your retirement years. To do that, you'll want to understand the reasons you might want to work in your retirement years, explore various ways to continue working, find work that's right for your circumstances, and take action steps that enable you to continue working. Be open and creative about how you can continue to add value and be productive.

Before we talk about finding work, let's explore the various issues involved with extending your earning years.

Understand the reasons for working in your retirement years

"It's important to be clear about the reasons for wanting or needing to work in your retirement years. Your reasons for working can help you find the path to the type of work you might seek." This is critical advice for anyone considering working in their retirement years, and is offered by Helen Dennis, who was an instructor and researcher for many years at USC's Andrus Gerontology Center and is the co-author of *Project Renewment: The First Retirement Model for Career Women.*

Think about which of these six reasons might apply to you:

1. **You need money to pay your bills.** This will depend largely on your spending habits and how much income you'll receive from your financial resources in retirement.

2. **You have a purposeful strategy to cover your living expenses while you let your financial resources grow.** For many people, delaying the start of Social Security is a smart strategy, as I described in Chapter 5. Waiting to start drawing down your retirement savings, as described in Chapters 6 and 7, is also a wise move. As a result, you may want to work just enough to cover most or all of your living expenses until you begin drawing down your retirement resources.

3. **You want some extra spending money.** In this case, you might have enough lifetime retirement income to pay the basic bills, but you want some extra money for travel, gifts, or hobbies, or simply to have a cushion.

4. **You might need affordable health insurance from an employer.** This reason for continuing to work is often critical if you want to retire before age 65, the eligibility age for Medicare.

5. **You like your work.** Some people simply enjoy the work they do, they're working at something they believe in, or they still have goals they want to achieve before they stop working.

6. **You like the social contacts and fulfillment you get from work.** Many people like being productive and useful to society, and they enjoy the social interaction they have with people at work.

If you're like most people, there's not a single reason to continue working — it's more likely a handful of factors that makes you decide not to retire when you'd first planned. In earlier chapters, you learned about Social Security and some smart strategies for deploying your financial resources. You also read about ideas for managing your living expenses and the cost of health insurance. Once you've had a chance to read and absorb this key information, working longer may not sound like such a bad idea.

Earning longer can substantially improve your financial security

One important reason to work longer is to address the following harsh reality: It's very hard to save enough money in your 30s, 40s, and 50s so you can have a long retirement that starts in your 60s. A more realistic plan is to earn enough money in your 60s or even early 70s to cover your living expenses. This allows you to delay starting Social Security for as long as possible to ensure you get the largest benefit check and postpone drawing down your retirement savings.

"It's very difficult to finance a 25- to 30-year retirement over a 40-year career. The math just doesn't work."

—John Shoven, PhD, former director of the Stanford Institute for Economic Policy Research

For example, in a report I co-authored for the Stanford Center on Longevity, we conservatively estimated that retirees could increase their ultimate retirement income by 25% to 34% by delaying their retirement from age 65 to age 70.[1] To translate this example into dollars, if your total income from Social Security and retirement savings is $50,000 per year at age 65, by waiting to draw benefits until age 70, the amount you'd receive would grow to between $62,500 and $67,000 per year.* This extra income can make a big difference in your financial security when you're planning for the rest of your life.

Is 70 the new 65?

Working longer doesn't need to be a life sentence. A good target retirement age might be 70, at which point you'll have maxed out your Social Security benefits and are required to begin withdrawing from your 401(k) and deductible IRAs. Choosing to wait until age 70 might still mean you'll end up being retired for as many years as your parents, who most likely had shorter lifespans than you could potentially have.

Working longer might improve your health and well-being

Here's another fascinating reason to consider working longer: There's provocative evidence accumulating from several studies that correlates working longer with living longer, staying healthier, and keeping your wits longer.[2,3]

This evidence begs two questions: Is this causation, meaning does working actually cause or enable you to live longer? Or is it correlation — that is, is it more of a coincidence and working doesn't really cause you to live longer?

It's possible that there's only a correlation between working longer and living longer, staying healthier, and keeping your wits longer; however, various studies and anecdotal evidence are weighing in on the causation side. (For excellent summaries of this evidence, read John Rowe's groundbreaking book *Successful Aging* or George Vaillant's insightful book *Aging Well*.)

---

*For this example, we assumed that between ages 65 and 70, workers would not make additional contributions to their savings and that their savings wouldn't grow for investment earnings.

Actually, it seems that *engagement* with life is what helps *prolong* life. And while you can find engagement with life from working, you can also benefit from volunteering, getting involved in causes you believe in, participating in hobbies, and contributing to your family and community.

Here's the takeaway for me: Whether or not working longer *causes* you to be healthier and live longer is a theory that won't be proved conclusively in our lifetime. We'll have to make decisions based on the most recent scientific evidence and what makes sense to each one of us. Most likely, the type of work you find in your later years will make a significant impact on your health and longevity.

Based on the research I've seen, I believe that finding powerful reasons for getting up in the morning in my retirement years is just as important as the financial planning I'm doing. I don't want to just be on vacation for the rest of my life — I want to feel like I'm making a difference in my community and society.

Whether or not working is a cause of your health and happiness, the fact is, working at a job you like is an excellent way to stay engaged and earn some spending money. And doing so allows your financial resources to grow until you really need them, when you're no longer able to work.

Explore the many ways to continue working

Once you're clear about the reasons you should continue working, you'll want to investigate the many ways you can work in your retirement years to see which might be best for you. Here are the most common options:

- Continue at your current job, full time or part time, as long as it meets your needs and your employer is satisfied with your performance.

- Do the downshift: Work just enough to cover your living expenses, keep up your social contacts with fellow employees, and possibly continue health insurance at work. This would free up some time to enjoy your life more and enable your financial resources to grow as long as possible.

- Find a bridge job, where you work for a few years between a full-time job and full retirement.

- Pursue an encore career, where you work at a new career for several years, often giving back to society, working for a nonprofit, or pursuing a keen interest. Encore careers often build on the skills and contacts you've made during your career years.

- Create or expand on a "slash" career that combines making money with pursuing your interests. For example, someone who calls herself an "accountant/yoga instructor" might still work both jobs but perhaps do more yoga and less accounting to fully enjoy her work.

- Volunteer for a cause you believe in, or sign up for an internship, either of which might lead to paid work.

- Start your own business, preferably without spending a lot of money to get it going. Be open to creative service opportunities to earn income in your community. For example, shared living communities such as townhome developments often provide paid and unpaid opportunities to be of service to your neighbors, such as handyman projects or looking after a neighbor's house when they're away.

- Become self-employed as part of the gig economy. This often involves doing projects or contract work. Many employers, particularly small employers, might be interested in a contingent workforce that will fill in when full-time workers go on vacation; work on special, one-time projects; or help during busy seasons.

- Be aware of the natural opportunities for some types of workers. For example, teachers can become substitute teachers, and nurses can participate in on-call pools.

As you can see, working vs. retiring doesn't need to be an all-or-nothing decision. If you'd like to pursue any of these approaches, you should look for situations that give you more control over your schedule, with time to travel and pursue your interests.

Businesses with significant financial investments: A trap for the unwary

Some people start a business that requires substantial upfront financial investments, and they tap all their retirement savings to launch the enterprise of their dreams. If it doesn't pan out, they end up going broke and having to look for work. I knew one person who sank a lot of money into buying a bed-and-breakfast inn but had to throw in the towel after one year. Instead of risking your retirement savings, consider starting a business that has low capital requirements and little financial risk. Often these are service businesses that you can run from your home.

Next up: practical tips on finding work.

Be resilient, creative, and persistent

How often have you heard well-meaning advice to "find your passion" or "do work that you love"? This advice might fall on deaf ears or may even sound cruel for people who've been laid off or who work in a stagnant industry. And even during the typical retirement years, many people need to work to pay their bills. The reality for many older workers, however, is that it may not be easy to find any kind of reasonable work — work that pays well and isn't physically demanding.

Ageism is another significant barrier: Many companies don't want to hire older workers for a variety of *perceived* fears — that they're not as productive as younger workers, their skills aren't up-to-date, they get sick more often, they cost more, and so on.

If you're hoping to continue working in your 60s and 70s, it's important to understand that it might take a long time to find any kind of work, let alone your ideal encore career or a job you really love. There's a very good chance you may not find or be hired for the right job right away, and in that case, you'll have to get creative and investigate less well-known options.

But all the news is not dire: There are employment opportunities out there for people in their 60s or 70s who are looking for them, though they may not be your dream jobs. To help you in your search, I asked several experts and authors — Helen Dennis, Chris Farrell, Kerry Hannon, and Mark Miller — for tips on finding work in your retirement years. These authors' books are all listed in the "Helpful Resources" section at the end of this chapter.

After speaking extensively with each of these experts, I found that they all had remarkably similar suggestions, which amplifies the relevance of their advice. Here's a synopsis:

- There's a good chance you won't land a job just by submitting your resume to a company's human resources department or by applying for jobs online (although you shouldn't skip this step).

- Most positions are filled by people employers know. As a result, you'll want to be a relentless networker. Connect with family, friends, neighbors, colleagues, suppliers, vendors, competitors — anybody you know who might have useful connections.

- Build a list of references. Ideally, you'd start networking while you're still working at your career job, a few years before you make your transition. If you're a professional, your professional organizations can be very helpful for networking purposes.

- Imagine yourself as a recent college graduate who's just starting out on their job search — but with the advantage of decades of life experience and contacts. Go on many informational interviews, volunteer, and attend conferences and meetings.

- If you're exploring a new area of interest, be willing to start fresh or lower on the totem pole, possibly with reduced pay. This suggestion may only be possible if you've managed your spending, debt, and income such that you can afford to take a pay cut, which may be applicable to older workers who don't have dependent children and who have a savings cushion on hand.

"Networking is one letter away from 'not working.'"

—Kerry Hannon, author of *Great Jobs for Everyone 50 +: Finding Work That Keeps You Happy and Healthy ...and Pays the Bills*

Hannon also offers this invaluable advice: "Take steps to counter common perceptions about older workers. Keep your skills up to date. This is non-negotiable. Employers worry that you're set in your ways and not willing to try new ways of doing things. They're concerned that you're not up to speed with technology."

Hannon goes on to add: "Stay fit and trim — look healthy. When you're physically fit, you give off a positive vibe, a can-do spirit, that will help reassure employers that you're up to the task. People want to work with you and be around your energy. Potential employers, even clients, do judge a book by its cover. When it comes to fighting ageism, being physically fit is better than Botox or dying your hair."

Hannon has one more helpful tip: "Looking for work can be stressful. Find ways to take care of yourself and find peace of mind, such as yoga, tai chi, meditation, or exercise." As you saw in Chapter 11, this is good advice for your health as well.

Inventory your earning skills

A key part of any job search is to inventory your relevant skills and experience, according to author Kerry Hannon. To help you get started on this task, here's a simple three-part inventory of your earning abilities:

1. **Specific job skills and credentials**. What are the specific tasks you've completed over your career that might be useful to a potential employer? What skills did you learn that you can use in future jobs? What credentials, degrees, and certifications do you hold?

2. **Your work experience**. List all the jobs you've had and the relevant experience they've provided. For example, note where you've supervised other workers, managed groups of workers, interacted with the public, dealt with difficult situations, been a troubleshooter, been active with public speaking tasks, and so on.

3. **Your network of contacts**. Over the years, you've met many people who might help you find work in your retirement years or can suggest where to look. Make a list that includes friends, neighbors, work colleagues, vendors, and customers.

Hannon's book *Getting the Job You Want After 50 for Dummies* has an entire chapter devoted to this topic to help you create a more detailed inventory.

Find work you enjoy

While some people just need to find *any* work to pay the bills, others may have some breathing room to look for work that better fits their life. If you're part of this fortunate group, how can you find work that offers satisfaction instead of frustration?

"What's kept you at your current job for so long?" Helen Dennis suggests you ask yourself this question to get clues about the type of work you'd most enjoy during retirement. Typical answers from her retirement planning workshop participants include:

- Stimulating intellectual environment
- Working in a collegial atmosphere with interesting people
- A feeling of respect
- The sense that you're helping people and society in general
- Good pay and benefits
- Doing what you're good at — using your skills and experience in a productive way

Occasionally, one of Dennis' workshop participants will ask, "If we have these features at our current job, why retire?" I couldn't have put it better myself. The fact is, if you like your current work, there's no need to give in to cultural expectations to retire.

But there may come a time when your job no longer fits your lifestyle or needs, or you get laid off, and you find yourself seeking other work. In that case, to help you figure out what type of work would be best for you, Dennis counsels, "Use your work experience as a guide to the future. People don't change that much. If that's what you like at work now, then look for these characteristics in a retirement job."

A good first step, Dennis suggests, is to make a list of the features you like about your current job or career. Then look for these features in a retirement job.

Of course, life isn't always black and white, and with many jobs, there are features you both like and dislike. So I'd add to Dennis' advice: Also make a list of the features you *don't* like about your current job. Then, when you're looking for retirement work, try to avoid anything on that list, if possible.

Learn to love your current job

Remember Dennis' suggestion to make a list of things you like about your current job as a guide to potential retirement work? Try going through this exercise now, while you're still employed, and see how your current job stacks up. If the pros outweigh the cons, you might try reducing or eliminating the things you don't like so you can keep doing your current work for as long as possible. For many people who work during their retirement years, this can simply mean reducing the number of hours they work. It could also mean reducing your management responsibilities and seeking out just the tasks that you like and are good at.

Kerry Hannon contends that while many people may say they hate their job, they're really just bored. If that's the case with you, she suggests looking for ways to renew your interest in your current job. "Build relationships with colleagues in other departments, raise your hand for special projects, sign up for training in new skills, check out your company's volunteer program," she suggests. "There are many ways to breathe fresh air into your current position."

Great advice! I'd add that you might want to ask about "downshifting" opportunities at your current employer. Many employers want to hang onto skilled employees who have extensive institutional history and are willing to be flexible when it comes to reducing your hours or your responsibilities. Whatever you do, don't assume your current employer won't accommodate your desires to downshift. Instead, ask — you might be surprised at the answer.

Consider the gig economy

In spite of your best efforts to find a job, you might still come up short. In that case, the gig economy can be particularly attractive to seniors because it permits flexible work hours and allows people to be their own boss.

According to Dictionary.com, the gig economy is "a labor market characterized by the prevalence of short-term contracts or freelance work as opposed to permanent jobs." While the types of jobs may vary, the way a worker earns money — no matter the "gig" — is similar. Gigs are all short term — from a task that might take just a few hours to projects that can last for months. When the gig is over, workers must find another.

Here's a brief tour of possibilities that can help you earn some spending money in the gig economy:

- Uber and Lyft match drivers with people who need rides.

- Airbnb enables you to rent out a spare bedroom or two, or start your own short-term rental business.

- Roommates can help you find a long-term renter for that spare bedroom or two.

- Urbansitter matches parents with baby sitters (think Grandmas-R-Us).

- Rover matches dog owners with dog walkers, with the important side benefit that you'll get plenty of exercise.

- TaskRabbit matches homeowners with nearby people who are handy and can fix things.

- eBay matches buyers and sellers, for people who want to start a business selling stuff.

- Fiverr and Upwork match freelancers with businesses that have projects in many areas, including graphic design, marketing, coding, or translating.

- Wyzant enables people to find a nearby expert or tutor on a variety of topics.

- DoorDash lets you deliver restaurant food to people's homes.

- Etsy allows crafty people to sell their wares worldwide.

- Honor and Care.com match people who have long-term care needs with qualified care providers.

Most of these gig economy services have a common business model. They have a vetting process to qualify providers, because they don't want just anybody signing up to find work, rent their place, or start selling things. Their websites often rate both customers and providers, so buyers and sellers can check each other out. They facilitate the payment process, with buyers usually paying online or through their mobile device, and providers receiving compensation the same way. And of course, the websites take their cut.

While online platforms are very useful for connecting people, you don't necessarily need to resort to this new technology to make money — you can use old-fashioned networking and referrals. For example, a retiree I know (who was recommended by neighbors) takes care of our plants when my wife and I travel. And we know several freelancers and consultants who find their work through old-fashioned personal connections or even by posting flyers.

How are seniors faring in the gig economy? Not bad, according to a few sources:

- Airbnb identifies women age 60-plus as their most successful hosts and the fastest-growing community of providers.

- Uber reports that almost one-fourth of its drivers are over 50.

- DogVacay, which merged with Rover.com in 2017, reports that people over 50 constitute one-fourth of their providers.

- According to a 2016 study by the JPMorgan Chase Institute, more than 400,000 seniors are earning money in the gig economy.[4]

Earning income in the gig economy does have some challenges, however:

- Income can be unpredictable.

- Workers, also known as providers, are usually considered contractors and are responsible for keeping track of and paying their own taxes.

- Employee benefits that often come with a W-2 job — such as health insurance — aren't part of the package, so you'll need to find other sources of insurance.

For some retirees, these drawbacks may be an acceptable trade-off for earning additional spending money to supplement their Social Security and other regular retirement income. And a lack of employer-provided health care might not be a big deal for seniors who get medical insurance through Medicare, retiree medical insurance, or COBRA.

The gig economy also addresses an important barrier facing older workers: age discrimination. While age discrimination is formally illegal and many large corporations take steps to address it, many older job-seekers still report they feel they're being passed over for younger workers. With the gig economy, however, you're the boss, so you can decide to give yourself priority.

All the service examples included here share a common theme: seniors taking advantage of lifelong skills, connections, and assets to earn extra spending money in their retirement years. In the process, they're staying engaged, meeting people, and hopefully having fun. The gig economy represents another game-changing opportunity that wasn't available to prior generations.

Consider taking a break

An excellent study by Merrill Lynch/Age Wave examined how older workers and retirees made the transition from their career employment.[5] The researchers found that more than half of workers took a career intermission — they took a break from working when they first retired that lasted two years on average. This break allowed them to recharge their batteries, take care of their health, refresh their skills, and reflect on the best way to live their remaining decades. Some people find that the intermission to recharge and reflect on their lives allows them to extend their earning years longer, compared to just "sticking it out" at their current situation for as long as they could tolerate.

Now that I've given you some ideas for work you might want to do and be able to do during your 60s and 70s, let's talk about the work you'll need to do as part of your retirement planning to ensure that you'll be able to find and keep a job during your retirement years.

Earning in retirement will require planning

Once you're determined that you'll want to continue to work in your 60s and 70s, it's likely that you'll need to do more than just decide you want to work longer and start your job search. A few surveys give us insight into the reasons. A recent study from the Transamerica Center for Retirement Studies, for instance, indicates that two-thirds of workers over age 50 plan to work past age 65 or don't plan to retire at all.[6] They report the median age at which they'd like to retire as 67.

But if the experience of the people surveyed is the same as current retirees, they won't be working that long. Current retirees surveyed by Transamerica reported a median retirement age of 62, and nearly two-thirds retired before age 65.

"In survey after survey, we find that over two-thirds of people plan to work in retirement."

—Debra Whitman, chief public policy officer at AARP

Why exactly do workers retire before they planned? A recent study from the Boston College Center for Retirement Research (CRR) examined the reasons older workers retired early.[7] Poor health of the worker or spouse is the most common cause, followed by layoffs or business closings. Next come family factors, such as the need to care for dependent parents or a spouse retiring sooner than planned.

The CRR report shows that the "shocks" that can cause early retirement are quite common. When you add up the odds, the chances are good that you'll experience at least one of these shocks in your remaining working years.

The 2017 Retirement Confidence Survey (RCS) conducted by the Employee Benefit Research Institute provides confirming evidence.[8] According to the RCS, almost half of retirees left the workforce earlier than they'd planned. Many said they did so because of a hardship, such as a health problem or disability.

The results of these studies show that if you're counting on working in your retirement years, you'll need a smart plan to help achieve your goal. Here's one such plan from the Transamerica Center for Retirement Studies:

- Stay healthy so you can continue working.

- Perform well at your current job.

- Keep your skills up to date.

- Network and meet new people.

- Scope out the employment market and opportunities available.

- Go back to school and learn new skills.

Here are a few more steps to help you keep working:

- **Make sure you'll be physically or cognitively able to continue working at your current occupation.** If you won't be, then be prepared to retrain or assume less demanding work that will most likely be lower-paid.

- **Look for ways to decrease your living expenses**, such as cutting your housing or commuting expenses. A day may come when you're no longer able to earn your current salary, so you'll want to be prepared to afford your life at that point.

- **Have a "plan B" in case you experience one of the shocks described earlier by the CRR.** Don't blow off planning for retirement and justify it by thinking you'll just keep working at the same employer you're at now.

- **Learn how to squeeze the most from your financial resources**, so you can afford to assume a lower-paying job if necessary and to plan for the day when you're no longer able to work at all.

Don't count on working longer as a retirement plan

It's important to realize that however long you might *want* to work, the time will come when you're no longer *able* to work, either for health and frailty reasons, or because you might not be able to find work you can do. As a result, you'll want to plan for that eventuality by making sure your income, when you eventually fully retire, will cover your living expenses.

> *"Working longer by itself is a great aspiration for improving your retirement security — but it's not something you can rely on as a retirement plan."*

> **—Mark Miller, editor of RetirementRevised.com and author of *The Hard Times Guide to Retirement Security***

Several surveys show that some people assume they'll never retire or that they plan to keep working into their late 70s or 80s. I suspect that many of these people might have little or no retirement savings, so they're just throwing up their hands in frustration, saying that they'll just keep working.

Navigate the transition

The fact is, our U.S. society is in a transition phase as we try to figure out how to deal with the many older workers who are trying to finance longer lives. To successfully navigate this transition, we'll need to negotiate some conflicting points of view:

- Some people will enjoy continuing to work and contributing to society in their older years, while others already hate working and can't wait to retire.

- Many retirees report they're very happy and busy, yet others say they're bored and lonely.

- Many people are physically able to continue working into their 70s, while others have had physically demanding jobs or debilitating medical issues, which will prevent them from working into their later years.

- Many older workers worry that they don't have the financial resources needed to generate a retirement income that's similar to their preretirement income, yet many retirees also report that they're happy living on less income.

Fortunately, resolving these issues doesn't have to come down to a "one size fits all" answer. Instead, we'll have to embrace some ideas that will help us work through the transition, despite the fact that some of the ideas might appear to be contradictory and will be "easier said than done."

We'll also need to recognize that there are many solutions to the challenges of an aging society. For instance, some people will want to retire completely from their primary job and not work again, others will want to continue working full time at their primary career, and still others will want to transition into part-time or bridge jobs, or embark on encore careers.

To some people, it might seem unfair that many older people will need to continue working after a lifetime of punching the time clock and that it might be hard for them to find work. But consider the alternative: As we saw in the first chapter, the average life expectancy in the U.S. increased by 30 years during the 20th century, an amazing accomplishment when you think about it.

Because of that increase, we now have many, many more people today surviving to old age compared to 100 years ago. If not for this significant achievement, many of the older workers and retirees we're wringing our hands over would be dead. That means we have a nice problem to solve. Somehow, we'll collectively figure it out, and you will, too. It's just going to take some planning by all of us to make it work, both collectively and as individuals.

 **ACTION STEPS:**

- Identify the reasons you may want or need to work in your retirement years.

- Determine how much money you might need to make to cover your living expenses, so that you can delay starting Social Security and drawing down your retirement savings.

- Inventory your experience, skills, and personality. Consider taking a formal detailed inventory, such as one of the inventories available in some of the books or websites listed here.

- Determine whether you need to update or refresh your skills.

- Think about how your skills can add value to different businesses and customers, and what will be the most useful to them. Look for matches with what you like and what creates value.

- Make a list of what you like and don't like about your current work situation. See if it's possible to continue working at your current place of employment, perhaps with reduced hours.

- Investigate whether there are any options for project work from your prior employers or through your contacts.

- Start networking.

 **HELPFUL RESOURCES:**

Books

- *Aging Well: Surprising Guideposts to a Happier Life from the Landmark Harvard Study of Adult Development*, by George Vaillant. Hachette Book Group, 2002.

- *The Encore Career Handbook: How to Make a Living and a Difference in the Second Half of Life*, by Marci Alboher. Workman Publishing, 2012.

- *Getting the Job You Want After 50 for Dummies*, by Kerry Hannon. Wiley, 2015.

- *Great Jobs for Everyone 50 +: Finding Work That Keeps You Happy and Healthy...and Pays the Bills*, by Kerry Hannon. Wiley, 2018.

- *The Hard Times Guide to Retirement Security*, by Mark Miller. Bloomberg Press, 2010.

- *Project Renewment: The First Retirement Model for Career Women*, by Helen Dennis and Bernice Bratter. Scribner, 2008.

- *Successful Aging*, by John W. Rowe, MD and Robert L. Kahn, PhD. Dell Publishing, 1998.

- *Unretirement: How Baby Boomers are Changing the Way We Think About Work, Community, and the Good Life*, by Chris Farrell. Bloomsbury Press, 2015.

Websites

The following websites can help you find work as well as employers who are receptive to employing older workers:

- *AARP Real Possibilities.* This website contains helpful videos and online courses:
  - Age-proof your resume: https://aarptek.aarp.org/age-proof-your-resume
  - Elevator pitch: https://aarptek.aarp.org/elevatorpitch
  - Interview tips: https://aarptek.aarp.org/workandjobs/
  - Job search courses: https://elearning.aarp.org/Pages/Catalog/coursecatalog.aspx?subject=18

- *AARP Work & Jobs.* This website enables members to find appropriate and fulfilling work as they lead longer lives. Highlights include a list of companies that value experienced workers; tips for job-seekers, including pros and cons of part-time flexible and work-from-home jobs; career change guidance; peer networks; and empowerment tools: https://www.aarp.org/work/

- *Encore.org.* This website provides inspiration and resources for older workers looking for an encore career: https://encore.org

- *The Gig Economy: 100+ Creative Ways to Make Extra Money,* by Kyle Pearce. DIY Genius, August 2016.

- *Next Avenue.* The "Work & Purpose" page on this website contains a number of useful articles: https://www.nextavenue.org/channel/work-and-purpose/

- *RetirementJobs.com.* This website provides resources and advice to help people over 50 find work in their area: http://retirementjobs.com

- *RetirementRevised.com.* This website is maintained by author and journalist Mark Miller. It has a number of insightful articles on career planning: https://retirementrevised.com/category/career/

- *SideHusl.com.* This useful website helps older workers investigate jobs in the gig economy: https://sidehusl.com

CHAPTER 13

CHOOSE THE BEST PLACE TO LIVE

DON'T MAKE THESE MISTAKES:

⊘ Fail to anticipate your living needs as your life circumstances change.

⊘ Forget to consider where you'll live during your frail years, when you might rely more on family and close friends for socioemotional and instrumental support.

TRY THESE GAME-CHANGING STRATEGIES:

➜ Make a conscious decision about the best place for you to live in your retirement years.

➜ Make any moves or modifications before you're too old or frail to make those changes easily.

➜ Coordinate your housing decision with the best use of your home equity, if your financial resources need a boost.

Choose the best life for you

Many people in their first middle age — as defined in Chapter 1 — built their life around working and raising their family. But this situation often changes as you transition into your second middle age or retirement. For instance, you may not need or want as big of a house as you have now. Or maybe your children don't live near you and you'd like to be closer to them geographically. You may be working or volunteering in a different way compared to the earlier years of your career. Or maybe your lifestyle will be just different enough that you'd like to live in a different type of community, or even in a different city or state.

If you haven't done so already, now's the time to consider how your situation and resources could change after you retire, to rethink your living situation to better fit your needs and lifestyle, and then choose the best place to live.

> *"Think about how much your living needs changed between your 20s, 30s, and 40s. That's how much your living needs might change between your 70s, 80s, and 90s. Don't become trapped in the suburbs or be held 'hostage' by the stuff you've accumulated!"*

> **—Phyllis Mitzen, active citizen in the Villages Movement**

This is definitely one step you'll want to think about sooner rather than later. Because you'll have the most energy to move in your 60s and 70s, you don't want to wait until you're forced to move by life's circumstances in your 80s, when you're less able to make a big move. The following three stories illustrate the possibilities you might consider.

My mother, Mary, lived alone for eight years after my father passed away. She became increasingly isolated in the suburbs, particularly after she couldn't drive on her own. All our family suggested she move to an assisted living facility where she could interact with other people and have her needs taken care of. But she refused, saying she had too many memories and didn't want to leave her home. As a result, she stayed in the family home, and when the time came, we arranged for home care during her last year. She passed away in the bedroom she had shared with my father for 59 years.

Mine is a different story. Once my kids grew up and moved out, I couldn't wait to leave the suburbs that were designed for raising children and driving everywhere you needed to go. My wife and I downsized and moved to a townhome away from the city, with cleaner air and less congestion. Somebody else does the yard work, and we're able to use the community pool and facilities. We've made many good friends and attend social activities at the clubhouse. Our neighbors look out for each other, providing rides for shopping and doctor visits when someone gets sick. Many residents walk for both social and shopping needs.

My daughter's situation illustrates a third possibility. Right after she graduated from college, she rented a room from a retired couple who had a four-bedroom house. Their kids had moved out, but they didn't want to move because they loved their home and community. But they needed the extra income, so they rented out two spare bedrooms to two different renters. They enjoyed having young people in the house, and since she lived far from us, we appreciated the adult presence our daughter had in her life.

What are the lessons you might take from these diverse stories? First, choosing where to live in your retirement years is a highly personal decision. It's essential that you think about the best life for *you*, not what's best for your friends or relatives. And don't blindly choose one of those locations you read about in magazines that tout "The Best Places to Retire" — they may be great places to live for some people, but will they be great for *you*?

Second, it's important that you make a conscious choice about the best place to live for the rest of your life. If your retirement resources are tight, you may also want to consider the best use of your home equity, as discussed in Chapters 6 and 15. Don't stick with the default decision — staying where you are — without at least considering other options.

Like many of the decisions this book suggests you consider, this one will take some time and effort as you explore your options and implement your strategy. There are many new, game-changing living opportunities that weren't available a few decades ago, and you should spend some time carefully considering all the possibilities.

Ideally, you should start exploring your options in the years leading up to your transition to retirement. You'll want to judiciously coordinate your housing decision with your income and expense budgets, think carefully about your needs and preferences, explore all your options, and discuss those options with your spouse or partner. You'll also want to plan for your frail years. And be aware that your needs and situation can evolve as you age, so if you decide to move, you may need to do so more than once.

Consider both sides of the I > E formula

Many older Americans have modest retirement savings that might not be enough to fund the life they truly want in retirement. As a result, when choosing where to live, you'll want to consider both sides of the magic formula for retirement income security ($I > E$) to make the most of the funds you have.

Let's start with the obvious: For most American retirees, the cost of housing is the largest item in their monthly budget. (Many people mistakenly think that medical costs will be their largest budget item in retirement, but that's usually not the case.) If your "I" isn't enough to pay for your "E," it simply makes sense to explore how you can reduce the largest item in your budget.

> *"Many retirees take into account the regular expenses they pay for housing, but they don't address predictable but irregular expenses, such as home repairs, increases in taxes and utility bills, and upgrades. And those who live in condos think about their regular monthly payments, but may forget that condos may require special assessments if there is a major repair needed. It is important not to get blindsided by predictable but irregular expenses."*

—Anna Rappaport, chair of Society of Actuaries' Committee on Post-Retirement Needs and Risks

On the flip side, home equity is often greater than retirement savings, so it makes sense to enhance your "I" by exploring methods to carefully deploy your home equity in order to improve your retirement security.[1,2] Chapter 6 discussed how to use reverse mortgages to enhance your "I," and Chapter 15 discusses possible uses of home equity for addressing the risk of long-term care expenses.

To make the best decision about where you'll live in your retirement years, you'll want to consider *all* of the following factors:

- General geographic location
- Specific house and community
- Best use of home equity

Of course, there's probably no one best choice for anyone when it comes to deciding where to live. Instead, you'll need to make a series of trade-offs that reflect your priorities, circumstances, and needs; remember, these might be different from those of your friends and family, so don't let their decisions influence your choices. And in the end, after careful thought, you might make the decision that my mother, along with many other retirees, make: "I love my home, and I'm not moving."

To help you make the best decision for you, the next two sections contain checklists so you can systematically explore your options for finding the best place to live.

Complete the checklist for the general location you want

Here's a checklist of possible goals that might be important to you when it comes to choosing the general location that best meets your needs. If you're the type who systematically explores your options, rate the priority for each item on a scale of 1 to 3, with 1 being the highest priority.

_____ You want to be near family.

_____ You want to be close to friends.

_____ You need to live close to dependent parents or grandchildren to provide care to them.

_____ You need to be close to work or volunteer opportunities.

_____ You have specific activities or interests in your general location.

_____ You need to reduce housing expenses by moving to a less-expensive residence or an area with lower real estate costs.

_____ You want to reduce state and local taxes.

_____ You have specific health care needs that dictate location.

_____ You want better weather.

_____ You want to take advantage of regional public transportation (such as major subway systems).

_____ Other reasons? List them here.

Once you're done reviewing this list, review the ones, twos, and threes, and reflect on which items came out on top. Prioritizing this checklist can help you make the trade-offs that are inevitable: It's very likely you won't get all your needs met by any one location, so you've got to choose the location that seems to fill most of your essential needs. Be sure to rate your current location based on this list, and compare it with other locales you're considering.

One thing that's interesting to note: Even after evaluating other locales, many people end up staying in their same general location, since that's where their family and friends live. However, they often pick a specific house and community that better meets their needs.

Complete the checklist for the specific house and community you want

The following checklist includes the possible goals that might be important to you when choosing the specific house and community that best meets your needs. Once again, if you want to address this issue systematically, rate the priority for each item on a scale of 1 to 3, with 1 being the highest priority.

_____ You want a safe, walkable, or bike-friendly neighborhood within a short distance of stores, health care providers, and social activities.

_____ You want to be close to friends and family for social engagement and support.

_____ You want to be close to your favorite activities.

_____ You have specific needs that are best served by local health providers, businesses, or public agencies.

_____ You prefer to be close to parks, walking paths, and open spaces.

_____ You want to live in a diverse community.

_____ You want to take advantage of local public transportation, such as trams and buses.

_____ You want a house that meets your basic living and social needs, such as having a home office or room for guests.

_____ You want to reduce your housing expenses, such as utilities, maintenance, and taxes.

_____ You want maintenance obligations and yard work that are manageable.

_____ You need a house with no stairs.

_____ You need a house to accommodate possible physical limitations — for example, one that allows wheelchair access.

_____ You want to age in place into your frail years (see the following section titled "Imagine what you'll be like in the future" for more about this topic).

_____ Other reasons? List them here.

Once again, when you're done reviewing this list, consider the ones, twos, and threes, and reflect on which items came out on top. Prioritizing this second checklist can also help you make the inevitable trade-offs. Don't forget to rate your current home and community with other houses and communities you're considering.

Use the "Best Places to Retire" articles just for ideas

If you're like me, it may seem as if every time you go online or open a magazine, there's a new ranking of the ideal places to live after you retire, either in the U.S. or in another country. There's certainly no shortage of lists you can review. Google these publications — *Money* magazine, *Forbes*, AARP, Milken Institute, Topretirements.com, and *International Living*, just to name a few — and you'll be reading for hours.

After quickly reading through some recent lists, I've counted more than 200 "Best Places to Retire" — there's at least one in every state. There are a few powerful reasons why you see so many of these lists. For one thing, readers love them, and the rankings help sell magazines and attract online readers. But can they really tell you where you should retire? I'm skeptical.

"You won't want to move to any place in retirement just because it's on a Best Places list, of course. And no ranking can account for a key retirement location criteria for many people: proximity to family members. Still, Best Places to Retire rankings can be a useful part of your research as long as you closely read their methodology, so you understand what the raters were rating."

—Richard Eisenberg, managing editor of *Next Avenue* and creator of *Money* magazine's "The Best Places to Live in America" list

The problem with these lists is, they're typically based on broad geographic statistics, such as home prices, cost of living, state and local taxes, the availability of medical care, public transportation, cultural activities, weather, and crime rates. These lists might measure factors that are important for you to consider when choosing a place to retire, and they can certainly give you ideas to think about. However, other criteria might well be more important to you, such as the ones in the two checklists outlined earlier in this chapter. Often these types of criteria can't be quantified in a "Best Places to Retire" article.

The best way to decide where you should retire is to find the place that best meets your needs and circumstances — however you define them — using the checklists shown previously.

Consider creative alternatives

Once you've completed the two checklists in this chapter, you're ready to consider and compare your options. In addition to the standard single-family-home housing option, there are many creative living solutions and situations that might be affordable and a good fit for boomers in their retirement years, even those with modest resources.

The following solutions are true examples of the old saying "Necessity is the mother of invention." While they won't be for everybody, they might give you some ideas and insights for your own future living situation. Let's take a brief tour:

- Townhome and condominium communities often provide lower-cost housing than single-family homes. They share maintenance and insurance costs, they might provide opportunities for social activities, and you might make friends with your neighbors.

- Intentional communities go one step beyond townhome and condominium developments by organizing themselves around certain goals or criteria, such as co-housing, collective living, eco-living, spiritual or religious beliefs, or active senior living. Consider exploring these numerous senior community options.

- AARP's *Livable Communities* initiative supports the efforts of neighborhoods, towns, cities, and rural areas to become great places for people of all ages. If you want to remain in your community, their initiative can help improve your hometown by advocating and providing tools for designing safe, walkable streets; age-friendly housing and transportation options; access to needed services; and opportunities for residents of all ages to participate in community life.

- The Village to Village Movement is an association of grassroots villages across the U.S. that supports groups of households in an immediate geographic community to meet the specific needs of seniors in the area. Residents in each area determine the services they want to share, which typically include transportation, shopping, home cleaning and light maintenance, social activities, and educational opportunities. It's a great way to make social contacts and age in place.

- A related phenomenon is "naturally occurring retirement communities," often referred to by the acronym NORC. NORCs are housing complexes that usually have half or more of their residents over age 60. They are supported by public and\or private organizations that recognize and respond to the social and health needs of their aging residents.

- Roommates.com allows you to search for roommates to share living expenses. Home-sharing might be essential for singles living on a low budget. For example, several years ago, I wrote a blog post for CBS *MoneyWatch* that showed how the "Golden Girls" solution could work for four divorced and widowed older women who just had Social Security benefits.

- Your local Area Agency on Aging might help you find roommates or other affordable housing options.

See the "Helpful Resources" section at the end of this chapter for a list of links and other helpful sources that can help you learn more about these possibilities.

Imagine what you'll be like in the future

When thinking about where you'd want to retire, it might help to put yourself in your own shoes 20 years from now — the results could be eye-opening. You may well find that your house and town might not be suitable when you're less mobile years from now, or you may be relieved to find they'll still be a perfect fit.

Start by thinking about the physical structure of your house. Do you still need as much space as you had during your career or family years? As you get older, smaller spaces are easier to maintain. Consider whether your current home is designed to make life easier for you (and your visitors) as you age. Features to consider include single-story residences, wide hallways, lever doorknobs, comfort height toilets, wheelchair access to appliances and work areas, and curbless showers with attractive grab bars.

An emerging architectural concept is "universal design" that makes living easier for people of all ages. For example, a wide door with lever handles is not only easier for the elderly, but it's also helpful for a young mother with two toddlers and a bag of groceries in her hand. In some cases, a traditional home can be remodeled using universal design concepts. On the other hand, it might be easier to relocate to a newer home that already includes these features.

Also consider the maintenance that might be needed for your home. When you reach your 70s or 80s, you may be less able to complete routine maintenance or repairs, or even arrange and pay for somebody else to make necessary repairs.

One goal of some of the creative living alternatives described here is to reduce maintenance demands on individuals.

As you age, you'll probably want to look for a community that's less dependent on cars. Try going a week or two without using a car to see how you'd fare in your current community. Is there a mass transit system in place? Do you already live within walking distance of stores, doctors, and other essential providers?

Your future community should also be able to easily accommodate the delivery of health care and long-term care as well as encourage social interaction. Since isolation is a serious risk for seniors, look for opportunities for convenient social activities. Many people also want to live in a multigenerational community and not be surrounded exclusively by older people. If that's important to you, be sure to keep that in mind.

AARP's *Livable Communities* website provides a wealth of useful information for assessing specific communities, as well as tools for improving your hometown's ability to allow citizens to age in place. Be sure to look for the link in the "Helpful Resources" section at the end of this chapter.

Be aware of alternatives for your frail years

As you age, you might have heightened needs for your home and community for your no-go years, compared to your go-go and slow-go years. Many of the creative ideas discussed here might work well for you during your second middle age, but then you might end up having to move again to accommodate your needs as you — or your spouse — become increasingly frail.

Here's a brief overview of possibilities:

- Assisted living facilities are usually small apartments in buildings for residents who need some help but still want to remain as independent as possible. These facilities usually offer help with the standard activities of daily living, meals, personal care, support services, and social activities.

- Continuing care retirement communities (CCRCs) are living arrangements that offer a continuum of care as residents' health changes; they also offer social, recreational, and cultural activities. Residents typically start in the independent living area and move as necessary to the assisted living section and later to the community nursing home.

- Nursing homes/skilled nursing facilities involve living arrangements that serve older adults who need nursing care, speech and physical therapy, supervision, and medical monitoring and intervention.

All of these possibilities can be very expensive and have different terms and conditions. For example, most CCRCs require a large upfront financial investment as well as ongoing monthly fees. Some allow a choice of renting as opposed to purchasing housing. Most CCRCs provide a transition from early old age through end-of-life care. Thus, CCRCs can function as a type of long-term care insurance, as you'll read more about in Chapter 15.

It's important to understand not only the benefits and services being purchased with a CCRC, but also the long-term financial stability of the community itself. You'll want to understand the fees for various services, and the circumstances under which they can be increased. Be careful whenever there's a large upfront fee involved. Some older people sell their homes and use most of that money or their savings to pay CCRC upfront costs and fees. In this situation, they may have little money left over if they want to leave a CCRC, if the ongoing fees become unaffordable, or if the CCRC becomes insolvent, as sometimes happens.

In spite of these cautions, you might find that you'll need some type of assisted living, CCRC, or nursing home facility for your frail years. Shop carefully — thousands of dollars, as well as your comfort and health in your frail years, are at stake. As a result, you'll want to spend time carefully investigating your options, and involve your spouse and family in your exploration and decision.

As they age, many people experience a gradual transition in their living needs; there isn't a warning light that comes on and says it's time to move into an assisted living facility. You may want to keep your radar out for such possibilities in your area so that as your living needs evolve in your frail years, you're aware of your options. Also, listen carefully when you hear about the experiences of your friends and relatives — you may learn about the pros and cons of these different facilities, which could affect your decisions down the road.

Deploy your home equity carefully

After reviewing your financial resources as discussed in Chapters 3 through 10, you might find that you don't have enough income to cover the necessary living expenses for the life you want. If you have substantial home equity, however, you might want to explore creative ways to use this asset to boost your "I" or reduce your "E."

Following are various ways to use home equity in retirement. You can:

- Sell your home and downsize to a less expensive house. Add any net gains from the sale of your house to your retirement savings, and then use this savings as a retirement income generator (see Chapters 6 and 7 for more details).

- Pay off your mortgage — either on schedule or accelerated on purpose — and enjoy living mortgage-free in your home after you retire.

- Rent a room or two for extra income.

- Reserve your home equity as a resource you can tap in the future if you have high long-term care costs (see Chapter 15 for more details).

- Take out a reverse mortgage to boost your monthly retirement income, or integrate it with your retirement income strategy to increase your available funds, as discussed in Chapter 6.

If you don't use your home equity during your retirement, it can serve as a legacy to your children or charities.

Choose the "best life," not the "best place"

Your housing decision is one of many decisions reviewed in this book — finances, health, and well-being — that all intertwine and reinforce each other. Choosing the place you're going to live when you retire is about much more than simply finding an area with inexpensive living costs, low taxes, delightful weather, and fun things to do. It's about living the best life you can for the rest of your life. No matter whether you plan to age in place or relocate, you'll want to find the best place to call home by determining what truly matters to *you*. For many people, it seems, the best place to retire is where the heart is.

 **ACTION STEPS:**

- Begin investigating your alternatives a few years before you need to make any big changes.

- If you're considering moving to a different area, spend some time there to investigate it as thoroughly as possible before making a commitment.

- Complete the checklist for your goals regarding the general location of your retirement home, and compare it to your current location.

- Complete the checklist for your goals regarding the specific house and community you'd like to live in when you're retired, and compare it to your current house.

- If your financial resources aren't sufficient to pay for your living expenses (because your "E" exceeds your "I"), consider how to best deploy your home equity to make ends meet.

- Coordinate any strategy to deploy your home equity with your strategy to address the threat of high long-term care expenses (see Chapter 15 for more details).

 **HELPFUL RESOURCES:**

Book
- *Where We Live: Communities for All Ages,* by Nancy LeaMond. AARP. 2017. https://www.aarp.org/livable-communities/tool-kits-resources/info-2016/where-we-live-communities-for-all-ages.html

Websites
- *AARP Livable Communities*, maintained by AARP: http://www.aarp.org/livable-communities/
- "Best places to retire" or "Best places to live" lists from *Money* magazine, *Forbes*, AARP, Milken Institute, Topretirements.com, or *International Living*

- *Fellowship for Intentional Community*, a website containing information on intentional communities including a directory: http://www.ic.org

- "Guide to Senior Housing and Care" is a good description of options and costs, maintained by *aPlaceforMom*: http://web28.streamhoster. com/apfmdev/apfm_ebook_guide-to-senior-housing_final.pdf

- Intentional communities: Wikipedia entry: https://en.wikipedia.org/ wiki/Intentional_community

- Kiplinger's state-by-state guide to taxes for retirees: http://www. kiplinger.com/tool/retirement/T055-S001-state-by-state-guide-to-taxes-on-retirees/index.php

- *Managing Retirement Decisions,* maintained by the Society of Actuaries.
  - o "Where to Live in Retirement" https://www.soa.org/research-reports/2012/research-managing-retirement-decisions/

- Naturally occurring retirement community (NORC) Wikipedia entry: https://en.wikipedia.org/wiki/Naturally_occurring_retirement_community

- *Roommates.com*. The name says it all: http://www.roommates.com

- U.S. State Department website on living abroad: https://travel.state.gov/content/passports/en/abroad/events-and-records/retirement-abroad.html

- *Village to Village Network*: http://www.vtvnetwork.org/content. aspx?page_id=0&club_id=691012#

CHAPTER 14

NURTURE YOUR WELL-BEING

DON'T MAKE THESE MISTAKES:

- ⊘ Discount or overlook the importance of nurturing your emotional well-being.
- ⊘ Become isolated and let your social network shrink.
- ⊘ Rely exclusively on one person for support, such as your spouse or partner.

TRY THESE GAME-CHANGING STRATEGIES:

- ➜ Tend to your emotional well-being and social network.
- ➜ Take steps to improve your inner state of mind.
- ➜ Actively build a diverse social portfolio with people of all ages.

Embrace the importance of your well-being

"I'm soooo happy I'm retired!"

"I was lost for a few years after I stopped working. I didn't know what to do with my life."

"In the years leading up to my retirement, I was really stressed about the critical financial decisions I needed to make — I didn't want to blow it. Now things seem to be working out OK."

"I'm busier now in retirement compared to when I was working. I'm having a blast!"

"Retirement planning is much more complicated than when my parents retired!"

"I miss the paycheck, but I miss my work friends even more."

"I don't set the alarm clock, and I can choose what I do each day. It's heaven!"

"My husband is miserable. He just watches TV all day. Now I have twice the husband and half the paycheck!"

"Now I have time to do all the things I've wanted to do most of my life."

I've heard all these expressions — and many more — from older relatives, friends, and participants in my retirement planning workshops. And when I ask them if they're working, I get answers that follow the wide range of what it means to be retired that were expressed in Chapter 1: Some are working part time in their career job or in a new field, some are enjoying an encore career, some are volunteering, and some aren't working at all. Clearly there's a wide variety of human experience — both positive and negative — in our retirement years.

For the most part, retirees who are surveyed report that they're happy. Most are glad to be free from the daily grind, the pressure of juggling family and work, alarm clocks, deadlines, and never-ending emails. For example, one survey conducted by Merrill Lynch reported that more than nine out of 10 retirees say their life is as good as or better than before retirement.[1] Nine out of 10 retirees also say retirement gives them the freedom and flexibility to do whatever they want, and on their own terms.

Of course, we should take such surveys with a grain of salt, since they're highly dependent on the characteristics of the group surveyed, their financial security, and how the survey defines happiness. However, we should also consider that many surveys and articles report consistent results.[2,3,4] Most retirees say life is better or at least the same in retirement, compared to before retirement — even if they've experienced a drop in their retirement income.

As a result of the stories I've heard and the surveys I've read, I've concluded that a successful retirement entails nurturing a positive state of mind in addition to planning for your financial security and physical health. A good sense of well-being might also influence your physical health, which then has implications for your financial security.

There's plenty of research that provides evidence for the importance of nurturing your well-being. For example, the *Sightlines* project from the Stanford Center on Longevity cites research that found that people who are socially isolated have a mortality risk that's equal to that of smokers, and twice the risk of people who are obese.[5]

In addition, a recent paper published by Stanford researchers finds that your state of mind can influence your physical health and longevity.[6] According to Alia Crum, PhD, "Our findings fall in line with a growing body of evidence that our mindsets ... can play a crucial role in our health." She adds, "Placebo effects are very robust in medicine. It's only logical to expect that they would play a role in shaping the benefits of behavioral health as well."

> *"There's a growing body of evidence that our mindsets*
> *can play a crucial role in our health."*

—Alia Crum, PhD, Stanford University

But as you'll see, nurturing your state of mind and your social portfolio can have many more benefits than simply avoiding health risks. For example, to face our significant retirement challenges, many of us might need to make critical lifestyle changes, something that's not always so easy to do. A positive state of mind and strong social support can help us make — and stick to — important and necessary decisions.

Earlier chapters discussed key strategies for improving your financial security, health, home, and community. Your perception of your quality of life in all these areas will also influence your sense of well-being, and making smart decisions gets you off to a good start. This chapter goes beyond these basics, however, to share ideas and strategies that can further enhance your sense of well-being.

Consider a two-part strategy to nurture your well-being

To start, let's acknowledge a basic challenge: Many new retirees experience a disruption in one or more of the following basic human needs:

- **Identity:** Many people identify themselves through their career or profession. "I'm an accountant/doctor/electrician/executive/manager/nurse/plumber/salesperson/teacher..." When they no longer have that job, they sometimes lose their sense of self.

- **Community:** For those who are employed, your community is often the people you see most frequently at work each day. When you leave the workforce, you often leave that community behind.

- **Sense of purpose:** It's critical to feel needed and be helpful to other people, and to contribute to your family/community/society. For some people, work provides that sense of purpose, and without it, they feel lost.

To make matters worse, parents in their 50s and 60s are hit by a double-whammy regarding these basic human needs when their kids move out of the house. For many people, being a parent is a key part of your identity and sense of purpose; many of you may have even built your social network around your children. So when your kids grow up and move on to college or out of the house, you may lose those social connections with other parents and feel you no longer have an essential role to play in your children's lives. Many people, especially mothers, often feel aimless.

I'll go out on a limb here, though, and assert that men in our society might have more trouble with the challenges of identity, community, and sense of purpose. And not realizing how essential they can be, they might dismiss these issues as not deserving of their time and attention when planning their retirement. *That would be a mistake!* By ignoring this critical element of retirement, they might be overlooking opportunities to enhance their enjoyment of life, financial security, and health.

To help you address these issues, there are many robust, scientific models of well-being.[7] But I like a simple two-part strategy to help guide your efforts to enhance your emotional well-being:

- **Tend to your self.** Enhance your own personal well-being or state of mind. For example, reduce your stress, stimulate your brain, and pursue activities that give your life meaning and purpose.

- **Invest in your social portfolio** with the same amount of importance and intention you gave to building your financial portfolio. Build meaningful and supportive relationships with your family, friends, and communities.

You don't have to address these strategies separately — they often overlap and work together to improve your well-being. And don't worry about how your friends and family are addressing these strategies: The appropriate balance between these two strategies will be different for each person and is influenced by your upbringing, culture, and environment.

Nurture your well-being!

Tend to your self   *Invest in your social portfolio*

In the book *Clash! How to Thrive in a Multicultural World,* authors Hazel Markus and Alana Conner describe two aspects of your persona that are similar to my two-part strategy. They assert that we all have two "selves": the "independent self" and the "interdependent self." The independent self values individualism, unique-ness, self-reliance, and the freedom to make their own choices. The interdependent self emphasizes relationships with others, the ability to adjust to situations, coop-eration with others, and honoring societal traditions and obligations. Markus and Conner advocate that it's best to find a healthy balance between these two aspects of yourself so you can more successfully navigate our modern world, something that becomes even more critical in our retirement years.

Although I'm offering a two-part strategy for *enhancing* your emotional well-being, there's no magic formula for *exactly* how to nurture your sense of well-being. In fact, the best strategies for *you* will be highly personal and specific to your unique circumstances. As a result, I'd like to share a few ideas and concepts in this chapter to get you started. I also encourage you to explore your own path of discovery to find what works for you.

To get started, let's begin with some potential steps you can take to tend to your self to enhance and maintain your emotional and mental health.

Tend to your self

It's become a tired cliché to see photos of smiling, healthy retirees taking cruises, fishing, golfing, traveling, and walking on the beach into the sunset. Advertisements and stories in the popular media typically only emphasize the fun and pleasurable aspects of retirement. These activities can certainly be an important part of your retirement years and may be particularly attractive for people who've worked hard all their lives and haven't played very much. However, they'll also make up just a small portion of your day-to-day life in retirement.

Your retirement should be much more than a 30-year vacation. It can be an opportunity to explore many aspects of your emotional well-being. You can investigate activities or interests that range from those that provide fun, pleasure, and happiness to those that give you a sense of satisfaction with life as well as a sense of purpose and meaning.

Retirement planning tip from your dog

Remain cheery and optimistic. Don't hold grudges, and be forgiving. These are common characteristics of dogs. If dogs were human, we'd say they have a "positive mental attitude," which, by the way, is something that can improve your physical health and longevity. Studies of centenarians have shown that consistent personal characteristics of these 100-plus-year-old folks are resiliency and resourcefulness.[8]

Here are a few practices and perspectives I've run across over the years that help me enjoy life, put loss into perspective, be satisfied with life, and be at peace as I get older. Hopefully, one or more of these will kick-start your thinking to help you nurture your own sense of well-being:

- Participate in activities that you enjoy and look forward to. The "fun" part of your retirement years will certainly add to your sense of well-being.

- Reduce your stress and cultivate peace of mind, which can come from such practices as meditation, mindfulness, prayer, forgiveness, yoga, tai chi, chi gung, and exercise.

- Achieve a sense of accomplishment or mastery, which can come from pursuing interests and hobbies. Not only will this give you pleasure, but by stimulating your brain, you might postpone or help mitigate dementia. For example, activities that provide a sense of accomplishment and are also associated with extending your brain health include learning a foreign language, playing a musical instrument, and ballroom dancing.

- Think about the personal characteristics you'd like others to use to describe you. Would you like to be considered helpful, friendly, patient, kind, strong, generous, thoughtful, caring, compassionate, creative, etc.? How can you nurture those characteristics in yourself?

- Look at the world with a sense of gratitude, wonder, humility, and empathy when processing events that can cause stress or be unsettling, or even for positive developments. My friend Tom Soma calls these four elements a compass for looking out at the world and for responding to anything that happens. Soma says, "Looking at my life's experience through one or more of these lenses helps me stay grounded and respond with compassion and love." Soma is an author and nonprofit executive who spent more than a year traveling throughout America, exploring Americans' spiritual beliefs and creating the website *Looking for God in America*.

Why not try one or two of these suggestions and see what happens? Keep an open mind, and you may be pleasantly surprised by the results.

Find your purpose and passion

"You need to find your passion and sense of purpose."

Many retirees, especially those for whom retirement may have been a disappointment, have likely heard this well-meaning advice from relatives, friends, and advisers. I've struggled with this suggestion myself. While it sounds uplifting and noble, as a practical matter, what does it really mean? And if your passion and purpose don't show up on your doorstep, how do you find them?

I like the simple definitions from Morten Hansen, PhD, a management professor at the University of California, Berkeley, and author of *Great at Work: How Top Performers Do Less, Work Better, and Achieve More*. He defines "passion" as the feeling of excitement and enthusiasm that comes from participating in activities that you look forward to. This could include social activities, hobbies, volunteering, and work.

Hansen defines "purpose" as the sense that you're part of something greater than yourself. You'll find this when you're helping others, contributing to your family, community, or society at large. And your actions don't have to be grandiose or something that will save the world, although that could be right for you, too. It can be as simple as making a positive difference in the lives of your family and friends, or volunteering in your community.

> *Having a sense of purpose might not just be a goal that feels good.*
> *Research suggests that people who have a sense of purpose*
> *experience better outcomes with their lives, both financially*
> *and with their health and sense of well-being.[9]*

Now let's explore some ideas for building your social portfolio.

Understand the importance of social connections

Amy Yotopoulos, the director of the Mind Division at the Stanford Center on Longevity, told me an insightful and delightful story about her 99-year-old grand-mother. "Grandma" has outlived her husband and most of her peers by many years and even decades. She's purposefully built a network of younger friends that she socializes with regularly. For example, she plays cards with a group of 60- and 70-year-olds, some of whom she babysat decades ago when they were children. According to Yotopoulos, Grandma credits her social activities with helping her to enjoy life for 99 years and counting! Her story illustrates the importance of social support for your health and longevity.

> *"Build a social portfolio with the same attention and intention*
> *you gave to building your financial portfolio. This will help*
> *increase your health, life enjoyment, and financial security."*

> **—Amy Yotopoulos, director of the Mind Division at the**
> **Stanford Center on Longevity**

As a result of both her research and her personal experience, Yotopoulos recommends that you purposefully build a social portfolio with the same atten-tion and intention you gave to building your financial portfolio. For instance, you'll want to diversify your social connections among people of all ages and interests just as you diversified your savings among a variety of investments.

You'll also want to keep in mind that as you age into your slow-go and no-go years, you'll want to be able to enjoy connections and activities that require less energy and mobility compared to your go-go years. Diversify your interests by participating in a variety of activities, some of which you may have to give up as you become less active, but also others that you'll be able to continue, such as a monthly book club or volunteering.

One other thing to keep in mind when building your social portfolio is the type of support you need as you get older. John W. Rowe and Robert L. Kahn's book, *Successful Aging*, describes two types of social support you'll need. Understanding these types of support can be particularly helpful for jump-starting your thinking about building a social portfolio:

- Instrumental support, such as hands-on help with household tasks, care when ill, and transportation

- Socioemotional support, which includes direct expressions of affection, love, esteem, and respect

Carefully think about the people in your life who can provide these two types of support, especially socioemotional support. While instrumental support can be important, Rowe and Kahn report that the frequency of emotional support someone gets is a more powerful predictor of their health and longevity.

> *"Just good-old fashioned talk therapy from friends and loved ones helps to keep the aging body vital."*

> **—From *Successful Aging*, by John W. Rowe, MD, and Robert L. Kahn, PhD**

Rowe and Kahn also use the term "convoy of social support" to describe helpful supportive relationships that you develop over the course of your life. These are the family members and friends of varying ages who can help you with both instrumental and emotional support. And while you're at the center of your own convoy, you're also most likely a member of other people's convoys, providing them with the type of support they need.

We've all experienced times in our lives when we feel down, and I'm sure you've appreciated it when family or friends come to your aid. Likewise, it feels good to be able to help others when they're feeling low. As we age, it's inevitable that we'll experience significant losses and will need support, and that close relatives and friends will have similar needs. It's part of being a human for a long life, so it only makes sense to be prepared to both give and receive help.

Consciously build your social portfolio

Whether you want to call it your "social portfolio" or your "convoy of support," let's take this idea one step further. Researchers who worked on the Stanford *Sightlines* project identified eight action steps that can enhance your well-being through social connections. They fall into two categories: meaningful relationships and group involvement.

Meaningful relationships

- Have deep interactions with a spouse or partner.
- Seek out frequent interactions with family.
- Get social support from family.
- Have frequent interactions with friends.
- Get social support from friends.

Group involvement

- Converse with your neighbors.
- Take part in activities such as volunteering in your community, or participate in your church or religious organization.
- Participate in the workforce.

The *Sightlines* project also identified people who are currently age 55 to 64 as particularly vulnerable in these areas, falling behind prior generations of people in the same age group as well as lagging behind other age groups today. As one of the researchers involved with the *Sightlines* project, I and my fellow researchers speculated that the reasons are tied to the challenges described at the beginning of this chapter: disruptions caused by leaving your career job, and children leaving the house and often living far away.

The next section shares a systematic way of thinking about your social portfolio or convoy to help you identify where some time and attention might help.

Retirement planning tip from your dog

Dogs are always happy to see you — they wag their tail and dance around a little to greet you. As a result, you're more than happy to take care of their needs. In our later years, we may become increasingly reliant on family and friends to help with our day-to-day household tasks and maybe even long-term care. It might help in your later years to think like a dog by doing your best to maintain positive, close relationships with your family, friends, and neighbors.

Inventory your social network

As we've discussed, your "social assets" can greatly help contribute to your comfort and enjoyment in your retirement years. In addition, it might be necessary for your financial well-being as well, particularly if your financial assets are modest or if you encounter unexpected setbacks.

The following tips can help you create a comprehensive list of your social assets:

✓ List the friends or relatives you can confide in and discuss important life decisions with.

✓ List the friends or relatives who live nearby and would come to your aid in an emergency.

✓ List the friends or relatives with whom you could share resources, such as a car, appliances, tools, etc.

✓ List the friends and relatives with whom you share regular activities that give you enjoyment and meaning in life. Are you "diversified," meaning that you have several close friends or relatives in addition to your spouse or partner?

✓ Identify any friends or relatives with whom you could share housing, if necessary. Could you move in with your children? Your grandchildren? Your sibling? A good friend?

✓ Identify any of your friends or relatives who would be able to take care of you if you need long-term care.

✓ Identify nearby community institutions that can help you and that provide social contacts, such as churches, social organizations, clubs, volunteer opportunities, and the like.

✓ Identify state and local government organizations or nonprofits that are available to provide potentially necessary services. Examples include the Area Agency on Aging and local institutions that serve seniors.

Be sure to shore up any areas now where you don't have the social assets you need. This can help you successfully transition through your go-go, slow-go, and no-go years.

Next, turn the inventory around, and think of all the people for whom you can play these roles. This reminds me of the sage advice from the American poet Ralph Waldo Emerson: "The only way to have a friend is to be a friend." This advice can also help you fill any shortcomings that you may perceive in your social network.

Accept that your priorities can change as you age

Laura Carstensen, PhD, the founder of the Stanford Center on Longevity, suggests that as people enter into the last half of their lives, their priorities change with respect to their social contacts and activities.[10] As they realize their remaining time on earth is limited, it becomes increasingly important for them to spend time with people they really love and enjoy being with, and pursue activities that provide them with joy and meaning. On the flip side, they have less patience for spending time on activities or with people who have low value to them.

In our early adulthood, we made decisions regarding career and family that strongly influenced the quality of our lives for the decades that followed, through our 50s and 60s. It's only natural that as our circumstances change when we age into our retirement years, we reexamine who we spend time with and how we spend our time.

Keep an open mind

Many of the strategies discussed in this book will entail some significant life changes. Examples include moving to a new home that better suits your needs, taking care of your health by exercising more or changing your eating habits, working longer or in new roles, and changing your spending habits, all topics I discussed in previous chapters. Unfortunately, many people have a hard time making changes. If you're one of those people, for the sake of your well-being, it would be a good idea to try to be open to making important yet potentially difficult life changes.

We've all met people who are open to trying new things; they often seem vibrant and healthy. They view the inevitable setbacks and mistakes as a learning opportunity and don't take them personally. On the other hand, we've also probably met close-minded people who reinforce the stereotype of older people who are grumpy and locked in their ways. These individuals view setbacks as criticism or negative judgments of their abilities or health.

A good place to start developing an open mindset is to acknowledge that we face significant and unprecedented challenges. We have nothing to lose — but a lot to gain — by being open to making significant changes in our lives. To help you successfully navigate the challenges of your older years, try remembering prior life challenges that you've faced successfully. They'll help remind you that you've been capable of making important life changes and can give you confidence to face the retirement challenges ahead.

"Having an open, growth mindset is essential for planning a successful retirement in today's challenging times."

—Carol Dweck, PhD, author of
Mindset: The New Psychology of Success

If you want to learn more about improving your mindset to help you succeed, read the excellent book *Mindset: The New Psychology of Success* by noted psychologist Carol Dweck, PhD. Her book shares research showing that people with open mindsets are more likely to be successful in all aspects of life compared to people with closed mindsets. It also offers a four-step strategy for encouraging a growth mindset.[11] I found her book to be very helpful.

For me, making important life changes starts with motivation. Remember the visualization technique I suggested from Chapter 2 that could inspire and motivate you? Here's one image that works for me: I imagine my 95th birthday party, surrounded by my caring wife, children, grandchildren, and possibly even some great-grandchildren. I look around with satisfaction and reflect that I've lived a good life, on purpose.

Congratulations on reading this far! You have two more goals to explore — preparing for your frail and final years, and designing the legacy you'll leave, both of which can contribute to your sense of well-being.

ACTION STEPS:

- Think about positive examples of older relatives and friends who have aged well into their 80s and 90s. Ask them what they attribute to their well-being.

- Identify activities or viewpoints that will help contribute to your inner sense of well-being.

- Inventory your social network and identify areas for improvement.

- Reflect on how you can keep an open mind about making important life changes.

HELPFUL RESOURCES:

Books

- *Clash! How to Thrive in a Multicultural World,* by Hazel Markus, PhD and Alana Connor, PhD. Plume Publishing, 2013.

- *Great at Work: How Top Performers Do Less, Work Better, and Achieve More,* by Morten T. Hansen. Simon & Schuster, 2018.

- *The Mature Mind: The Positive Power of the Aging Brain,* by Gene Cohen, MD, PhD. Basic Books, 2006.

- *Mindset: The New Psychology of Success,* by Carol S. Dweck, PhD. Ballantine Books, 2016.

- *The Power of Purpose: Find Meaning, Live Longer, Better,* by Richard Leider. Berrett-Koehler Publishers, 2015.

- *Successful Aging,* by John W. Rowe, MD and Robert L. Kahn, PhD. Dell Publishing, 1998.

Websites

- *Greater Good Magazine.* "How to Find Your Purpose in Life." https://greatergood.berkeley.edu/article/item/how_to_find_your_purpose_in_life

- *Looking for God in America.* This website is maintained by Tom Soma, author and nonprofit executive: http://www.lookingforgodinamerica.com/blog/

- *Next Avenue.* The "Living & Learning" page on this website contains a number of useful articles: https://www.nextavenue.org/channel/living-and-learning/

CHAPTER 15

PREPARE FOR YOUR FRAIL AND FINAL YEARS

DON'T MAKE THESE MISTAKES:

- ⊘ Be oblivious to the threat of potentially ruinous long-term care expenses.
- ⊘ Overlook steps to protect against elder fraud.
- ⊘ Forget to clarify your wishes for your final years with the people who matter.

TRY THESE GAME-CHANGING STRATEGIES:

- → Plan ahead. It helps smooth your transitions, makes the best use of your financial resources, and significantly reduces the stress of the people who love you.
- → Protect yourself against elder fraud and abuse.
- → Adopt a strategy to pay for long-term care expenses, and arrange for someone to manage your care.
- → Develop a plan to transition responsibility for important life decisions as you age.
- → Make sure your spouse or partner will be OK financially after you're gone.

Think beyond your go-go years

Many stories you'll hear about retirement describe a wonderful life of traveling, hanging out with grandkids, volunteering, and pursuing your interests. And indeed, it's well worth the effort to plan for this type of enjoyable life, including taking any steps needed to improve your health and well-being, as described in Chapters 11, 12, 13 and 14.

But no matter how healthy you might be in your 60s, 70s, and maybe some of your 80s, most people eventually slow down at some point in their lives. They transition from being free and independent to being dependent on others for daily necessities such as housecleaning, cooking, taking care of personal hygiene, and managing their finances. They may become much less mobile, and they'll settle down in their home and local community. And of course, we all share the same ultimate fate — medical science most likely won't cure death in our lifetime.

Welcome to your slow-go and no-go years. Here's when the challenges of living a long retirement can really kick in. But you can be prepared: Many of the decisions you make as you transition out of the workforce in your 50s and 60s will impact how well your life might turn out in your 70s and beyond. If you spend some time *now* planning for those later years, then you may just weather them with confidence and peace of mind.

We'll cover two important events that are distinct but related: your frail years, during which you might need help with the activities of daily living, and the time when you eventually pass away.

Understand the threat of long-term care expenses

Many older Americans are oblivious to the threat posed by potentially ruinous expenses for long-term care. They think somebody else will pay for it, but that's usually not the case.

> *Many older Americans and their families have their heads in the sand regarding the potential threat posed by long-term care expenses.*

How real is this threat? You can read the statistics, but if you want to truly understand how serious the problem is, ask your 50-something or 60-something friends if they've had to deal with long-term care for their parents. Chances are good that you'll find at least one who has had to either provide care themselves, arrange for it, or pay for it out of pocket.

Ask these friends about the financial burden and the strain it puts on their lives. You'll likely get an earful about careers put on hold, the lack of time for family and outside interests, arguments with siblings and spouses, and sleepless nights filled with anxiety about making the money last. Most likely, you'll also hear they were glad to make the effort to provide care that's both helpful and meaningful.

Both my wife and I helped our parents in their frail years. We both gladly pitched in to care for them — it was simply the right thing to do. However, our experience also motivated us to plan ahead to help reduce the resulting strain on our children when we reach that phase in our lives.

Now for some statistics: A recent survey of Americans age 40 and older conducted by the Associated Press-NORC Center for Public Affairs Research found that more than two-thirds of people age 65 and older will need at least some form of long-term care during their lives, and half will need extensive services. Yet two-thirds of survey respondents say they've completed little or no planning for their own long-term care needs.[1]

Before we go any further, let's make an important distinction and dispel a critical misconception: Long-term care shouldn't be confused with medical care — they're not the same thing.

- Medical care includes interventions by qualified health professionals and medical institutions to help patients recover from illnesses or injuries. Health insurance and Medicare pay for a large portion of older Americans' medical care costs.

- Long-term care helps frail and disabled people with common activities for which they need assistance. In their younger years, most people carry out these activities every day without needing any assistance, but these activities become difficult when people become frail. There are six basic "activities of daily living" that typically require specialized care: eating, bathing, dressing, using the toilet, transferring (walking), and continence. Another basic need can be remembering to take medicine. Most health insurance policies and Medicare don't pay for help with these activities of daily living, except in very limited situations.

Many Americans are mistaken about how they're going to pay for long-term care. More than half of Americans age 40 and older expect to rely on Medicare to pay for long-term care, even though it doesn't normally cover this type of care.[1] The exception is when a doctor prescribes that a patient should move directly from a hospital stay to a qualified skilled nursing facility to help the patient recover from the illness, surgery, or accident for which they were hospitalized.

Even in this situation, Medicare will only pay for the full cost of a skilled nursing facility for 20 days. For the next 80 days, Medicare requires a substantial copay, and it pays nothing for stays longer than 100 days. This is a sobering reality that people must seriously take into account.

In many states, Medicaid will pay for long-term care for people with low income and few assets. But don't assume you might be eligible! It's likely that Medicaid assistance won't be available to retirees whose income and assets exceed the modest thresholds specified by most Medicaid programs.

Here's another misguided belief: More than two-thirds of survey respondents report they'll rely on their family for support as they age.[1] Unfortunately, this overlooks the high costs that family members and informal caregivers incur for providing care, including lost income and increased stress. In addition, family members might live far away and could be unable to provide the type of assistance needed. When families and informal networks of friends fall short, paid long-term care services will be required to fill the gap.

The unfortunate reality is, most older Americans and their families will need to plan for and pay the costs of long-term care.

Here's something else to consider: If you can't rely on family or friends to help at all, then you might need to pay someone for a great deal of care. Paid services could include home health care aides, assisted-living communities, CCRCs (described in Chapter 13) and nursing homes. Unfortunately, about three-fourths of surveyed Americans have misconceptions about the cost of such care:[1]

- Only about a quarter of survey respondents could correctly estimate the national average monthly cost of a nursing home, which is $6,000 to $8,000.

- Only one-fourth could correctly estimate the average monthly cost of an assisted-living facility, which can be $3,000 to $4,000 or higher.

- Just 29% could correctly estimate the average monthly cost of hiring a part-time home health care aide, which is $1,000 to $2,000.

More than half of survey respondents believe that ideally, somebody else — either Medicare or health insurance companies — should be responsible for paying for their long-term care. But given the current political environment and the existing financial strain on Medicare, it's highly unlikely that the federal government will expand Medicare to cover long-term care expenses, or that Medicaid will be extended to cover middle-income citizens.

The unfortunate reality is, most older Americans and their families will need to plan for and pay the costs of long-term care. You might become a caregiver yourself, either for a spouse or close family member, which also creates significant challenges. While preparing for long-term care for yourself or a family member may be much easier said than done, it's nevertheless a crucial retirement planning task you shouldn't ignore.

Develop a strategy to pay for long-term care expenses

What can you do to prepare for this serious threat? First, don't ignore the problem or assume it can't happen to you. If you do nothing, you're simply hoping that your family or public assistance will take care of you if you ever need long-term care — and hope is *never* a good strategy.

No magic bullet will easily or cheaply address the threat of long-term-care expenses, but you *can* do things that will help. If you want to protect yourself and your family, consider taking one or more of the following steps:

- **Take care of your health to minimize the odds that you'll eventually need long-term care.** The tips and advice in Chapter 11 can help.

- **Shop for long-term care insurance**. If the premiums are too high for your budget, consider buying "catastrophic" insurance or a policy that will pay for some, but not all, of the potential expenses. After all, some insurance is better than none. Also, look for ways to reduce your premium costs. One possibility is buying a policy with a long "waiting period" during which you'll pay for care out-of-pocket. The insurance eventually kicks in if you incur a long period of care. Also, long-term care insurance costs less if you buy it at an early age, so it pays to shop for this insurance many years before you think you'll need it. In some cases, you might save money by participating in a group insurance policy if it's offered by your employer.

  In any case, shop carefully. There's a large variation in long-term care policies, and none is a "magic bullet." If you do end up buying long-term care insurance, you'll need to include the premiums in your budget for living expenses, since you'll most likely be paying them for the rest of your life. In addition, be aware of the fine print that can reduce or exclude reimbursement for care. For example, most insurance companies require a doctor to certify that your medical conditions prevent you from carrying out the activities of daily living before they'll approve paying for that care.

- **Maintain a reserve of savings that's dedicated to paying for long-term care and won't be used for generating retirement income.** For example, you could use a Health Savings Account for this purpose, as described in Chapter 10. Another strategy could be to just use interest and dividends for retirement income, and preserve your principal in case you need it for long-term care. Note that you'll need at least a few hundred thousand dollars of savings for these strategies in order to cover your financial needs in the event you need long-term care for an extended period.

- **Use your home equity as a reserve to pay for potential long-term care costs.** Another possibility is to keep your home debt-free and hold it in reserve until you need to sell it to pay for long-term care. Another option is to take out a reverse mortgage line of credit before you need it for long-term care and let it grow until you might need it. In this case, you won't want to use up your borrowing capacity with a monthly tenure reverse mortgage to generate retirement income, as described in Chapter 6.

- **Buy a longevity annuity, also known as a deferred income annuity (DIA) or qualified longevity annuity contract (QLAC).** This type of annuity pays an additional stream of monthly lifetime income starting at an advanced age, such as age 80 or 85, when you might need long-term care. You may be able to buy a QLAC through your 401(k) plan, or buy a deferred annuity through an online annuity bidding service as described in Chapter 6.

Be sure to include your spouse when developing your long-term care strategies, and tell your children and close relatives about your plans. This way, they'll know your objectives, can arrange for and monitor your care, and can carry out your wishes in the event you're unable to tell them later.

See the "Helpful Resources" section at the end of this chapter to learn more about strategies and resources to help pay for long-term care.

Arrange for elder care and support when needed

Suppose you've developed a strategy to pay for long-term care expenses and arranged for help with carrying out the daily living activities previously mentioned. You're still not finished planning! Most likely, somebody else will need to be involved with other important tasks that you may not be able to handle on your own in your later years. These activities include planning and arranging for your care, managing your finances, taking you to doctor's appointments, helping you manage your prescriptions, and providing general help with navigating the world. It might be your spouse, one or more of your adult children, or other close relatives. As a result, you'll want to stay on good terms with your close relatives and perhaps consider living nearby the people who'll be helping you out.

Another issue you may have to deal with is the fact that in today's world, many elders live far away from their adult children and relatives, or never had children. As a result, they've become "elder orphans" who don't have someone close by to look out for them. This is a serious issue for singles *and* married couples. If you're part of a married couple, it's inevitable that one of you will become widowed at some stage in your life, or it's possible that both of you might need help at the same time. If you think you could end up as an elder orphan, you'll want to carefully assess your living circumstances and social network to determine how you can get help with elder care in the years to come.

In addition to arranging and paying for help with the daily living activities associated with long-term care, you'll want someone close by to watch out for you. If you don't have close family or friends who can help in this way, you may want to hire an elder care manager.

In some cases, informal networks of relatives, neighbors, and friends can help, and this should probably be a consideration when planning where you'll live. You can also pay someone to manage your care; these individuals are often referred to as "elder care managers" or "geriatric managers." If you buy long-term care insurance, some insurance companies include coverage for the services of these people.

One more point: Long-term care is a very serious issue for women, more so than for men. When you visit an assisted living facility or nursing home, you'll see that most residents are women. That's because women typically outlive their husbands and then have no one to care for them. Also, the wife is often the primary caretaker if the husband needs long-term care, which can be quite a strain on both her health and well-being. This can push her into an assisted living facility soon after her husband passes away. If you're married or in a partnership, this is something you should seriously discuss and plan for so that you don't burden your spouse or partner. It's just one more compelling reason to take the time to plan for long-term care.

The "Helpful Resources" section at the end of this chapter identifies sources for elder orphans and geriatric care.

Protect yourself from elder fraud and abuse

My friends and colleagues at the Stanford Center on Longevity, Marti DeLiema, PhD, and Martha Deevy, are two of the nation's leading experts on financial fraud. They hear many heart-wrenching stories about regular folks who've been duped by criminals and lost their hard-earned savings.

Fraudsters target people of all ages, but older adults with retirement savings are particularly lucrative targets. They're also particularly vulnerable: The consequences of fraud can have a devastating impact on older adults who depend on their retirement savings after they leave the workforce.

> *"If you're an older worker or retiree, taking steps to protect against financial fraud and exploitation should be an important part of your retirement planning. Consider that you might reach an age when you're no longer interested or able to manage your financial affairs."*

—Marti DeLiema, PhD, Stanford Center on Longevity

What type of fraud or abuse is commonly targeted at older adults? It's often crooks posing as financial advisers, or salespeople who might not be breaking the law but who are pitching investments that aren't appropriate for retirees. DeLiema recommends six steps you can take to protect yourself and your loved ones from either type of exploitation:

Step 1: Leave your retirement savings with your employer's retirement plan, and elect to draw a lifetime monthly payment.

Most employers allow retired employees to keep their money invested in an employer-sponsored 401(k) or 403(b) plan. DeLiema recommends that you consider leaving your savings with your employer, because employers must operate under fiduciary standards. This means they're legally required to act in the best interest of their plan participants and their beneficiaries.

While most advisers and brokers act with integrity and have their clients' best interests in mind, some high-priced, predatory brokers encourage retirees to roll over their 401(k) or 403(b) funds into higher-cost investments that they'll manage for the investor. They may promise to beat investment returns offered by an employer-sponsored plan. Often they use emotional appeals to persuade retirees to invest their savings immediately instead of taking time to do research on other options.

But the options they're offering often have much higher investment fees and costs than your employer's retirement plan. This often leaves you with less money to spend in retirement, once you take into account these investment expenses.

Here's another situation that's not necessarily fraudulent but is ripe for exploitation: when a retiree is offered — and encouraged to take — a lump-sum payment from a traditional defined-benefit pension plan instead of the lifetime monthly paycheck. Retirees shouldn't trust overblown claims from advisers who say they can outperform effectively managed employer-sponsored plans. Such statements are typically too good to be true. As discussed in Chapter 6, it's hard to generate more monthly income for your lifetime if you elect a lump sum from a pension plan, compared to electing the monthly income from the plan.

Electing the monthly paycheck option instead of the lump sum can also protect your financial resources by reducing easy access to your funds (see Step 3 for more on this).

Step 2: Activate security features for your accounts.

DeLiema recommends activating the existing security features on all of your financial accounts. You should elect to receive fraud alerts and use two-step authentication to access the accounts online. Some firms also use voice authentication and other biometric security features to protect their clients' money from hackers and identity thieves. You should employ any options that are available to you in order to protect your financial assets.

You should also opt out of receiving paper statements in the mail because identity thieves can intercept these materials. Instead, choose to go paperless and get your statements emailed to you.

Step 3: Reduce liquidity and automate the payout process.

Financial exploiters — including greedy family members, friends, and hired care-givers — look for easy opportunities to take money from vulnerable elders. They'll often go after the money held in checking and savings accounts because it's easier to access these liquid funds than other investments. DeLiema suggests that reducing your asset liquidity is one way to keep your money protected. For example, leaving your savings in your employer's retirement plan is one way to reduce easy access to it.

Electing a monthly check from your employer's pension plan instead of a lump sum is another way to protect yourself from fraud. If you don't have a pension from an employer, then a low-cost, competitively bid payout annuity serves the same purpose, acting like a personal pension with disbursements administered monthly. Not only do pensions and payout annuities help people spend more carefully throughout retirement, as you read in Chapter 6, they also prevent financial opportunists from accessing retirees' savings and leaving them penniless. In addition, they're helpful when you reach an age when you're less able to manage your investments inde-pendently. Instead of having to worry about monitoring your investments yourself, you can simply wait for your monthly check to be deposited into your checking account.

And that leads me to our next piece of advice: Disbursements from annuities and other retirement accounts, including employer-sponsored retirement plans, should be done via electronic transfer into a bank account rather than deposited as a check. Similarly, you'll want to automate payment of your various utility and insurance bills. Not only does this prevent checks from being stolen out of the mail or even out of your home, it helps keep the bills paid if you get forgetful in your later years.

Step 4: Diversify your accounts.

When your entire retirement savings is held in a single account in a single financial institution, a successful hacking attempt or a bad financial decision can wipe out your retirement security in one fell swoop. That's why DeLiema recommends that retirees diversify where their accounts are held, just as they would diversify their investment portfolios.

By diversifying the number of institutions that have your money, even if one account or institution is compromised, the money held in the other accounts is still safe. This is especially important for retirees with significant assets — accounts with large balances are a major draw to fraudsters.

Step 5: Demand fiduciary standards from your financial adviser.

Large employers that sponsor retirement plans have a legal duty to act prudently on behalf of their plan participants, which is another reason to leave your accounts with your employer. By being legally responsible to act sensibly on your account, there's less chance that your money will be invested in expensive or fraudulent investments.

The U.S. Department of Labor recently instituted a rule requiring that advisers who provide investment advice to people with retirement accounts or IRAs must also comply with fiduciary standards. At the time of publication of this book, this rule was under review by the U.S. Department of Labor and certain members of Congress were trying to overturn these standards.

Even if these rules are repealed or revised, many advisers will still choose to act as a fiduciary on your behalf, so you'll want to seek out those types of advisers. In addition, you should ask your financial adviser to act as a fiduciary with *all* your accounts, regardless of whether they're for your retirement.

Step 6: Sign a "springing" power of attorney.

A power of attorney is a legal document that gives written authorization for one person to act on another's behalf in legal, financial, and health care matters. A "springing" power of attorney is available in some states and takes effect when a specified event occurs, such as when the individual, or "principal," loses the capacity to make independent financial decisions.

You can specify exactly how and under what circumstances the power of attorney springs into effect. You can also have control over what powers you give to your agents. It's a good idea to make it clear that your agents may not engage in activities that would alter your wealth transfer plan or affect your beneficiaries.

Social isolation is a big risk factor for exploitation, because isolated adults have less oversight from others who could potentially stop financial predators from taking control of or stealing their funds. So instead of giving just one person a power of attorney, older adults should consider naming joint agents. That way, both agents must agree on important financial actions, making exploitation more difficult.

Copies of signed powers of attorney, in addition to information about relatives and friends who are not to be trusted with financial decisions, should be provided to your financial advisers.

A final recommendation from DeLiema: She suggests that retirees engage trusted family members in their important financial decisions, including getting assistance with reading contracts that the elder is asked to sign. Not only will this help family members understand your financial goals, it will also prevent others from secretly exerting undue influence on you.

Spare your family, plan for transitions

There's usually a gradual decline from your slow-go to your no-go years, and there's rarely a clear event that alerts you and your family that it's time to transition responsibility for essential life responsibilities. Usually, an older person increasingly needs help with certain tasks as they're no longer able to do these tasks themselves. Key transitions should take place when you need help with the following routine tasks:

- Transportation, because you're no longer able to drive

- Shopping for food and other household essentials

- Cleaning, cooking, and managing the household

- Managing your finances, such as investments, a checking account, and credit cards

- Tasks that your eyesight or hearing can no longer manage

Living independently can be a source of pride for many people, who might resist transitioning responsibility to other family members even if they truly need help. This only makes the transitions more difficult and can result in creating investment losses and big household messes.

It's best if you plan for these possibilities well in advance of the day when they might occur. Tell your family the steps you'd like to take when it's necessary, if certain events happen. Think about setting up "tripwires" that indicate the need to transition responsibility for common daily tasks. Here are some examples, to get your thinking started:

- While you're still fit and in good health, you might tell your family: "When the day comes that my doctor says I'm no longer fit to drive, let's sell the car and cancel the car insurance. We can use the money we'll save to start paying for taxis, Uber, or Lyft to take me where I need to go." You might set up other tripwires that indicate a need to reduce or eliminate driving, such as incurring a higher number of traffic tickets or fender-benders.

- While you're still able to manage your finances, set up indicators that point to a need in the future to transition the management of your finances. For example, if you notice you've bounced some checks, missed paying some bills, or made some obvious mistakes with your finances, take that as a signal to turn over more of your finances to a trusted family member.

- You may want to ask for help managing your finances if you're no longer able to read important documents or hear financial instructions on the phone or in person.

In addition to handing over responsibility for daily tasks, preparing a medical directive and having clear conversations with your spouse and family about these transitions should be near the top of your retirement planning to-do list. It may be difficult to have these conversations, but if you take the initiative, you can significantly reduce the anxiety and stress your family might feel about arranging for your care.

Finally, you'll want to organize and store your important financial and health files where your family can find them, as discussed in Chapter 3. If you become unable to independently manage your finances, you'll want them to have all the information they need to help you make decisions and more easily manage your affairs.

Protect your spouse or partner

If you're married or in a committed relationship, it's certain that one of you will die before the other. In fact, there's a good chance that the survivor might live for several more years after their spouse or partner passes away. In America, more often than not, the wife outlives her husband by many years, since men tend to marry younger women and women tend to outlive men. When you put these two facts together, married couples should plan for one spouse to have a five to 10-year period of widowhood at the end of their lives, and possibly even longer.

My parents provide a typical example of this situation. After my father passed away, my mother lived for another eight years. Fortunately, she and my father had made wise choices when my father retired, so my mother never worried about running out of money. Sadly, for many couples, this isn't always the case.

Making smart choices regarding the important decisions described in this book will go a long way toward protecting your spouse. For example:

- Optimizing Social Security benefits by delaying the start of benefits for the primary wage-earner as long as possible will help increase the income to the surviving spouse.

- If you're eligible for a traditional pension, select the joint and survivor annuity to continue the pension to the surviving spouse after the other spouse dies.

- When deploying your retirement savings, design a retirement income strategy that will generate income as long as either spouse is alive.

- Choose the community and house that will best support the logistical and social needs of the surviving spouse. Be sure to consider the location of both family and friends.

- Develop a strategy that will address the threat of long-term care, so that financial resources aren't drained by the long-term care needs of the first spouse to die.

- Make joint decisions when working with financial planners, attorneys, and other professional support, so that the surviving spouse is familiar with the plans and the planner.

One actuary friend of mine, Richard, summed up these actions quite succinctly. "I made all these smart choices to show my wife that I love her."

Prepare for the end

Dying ranks up there as one of your most important life events, including meeting your life partner, getting married, and having children. It only makes sense to put some time and effort into planning your passing so that it's not a traumatic experience for both you and your family.

Most Americans say that they would prefer to die at home, in familiar surroundings, and cared for by their loved ones. Yet more than 75% of Americans die in a hospital or nursing home, where they're often alone at a time when their need for comfort and emotional support may be very great. Of those who die in hospitals, nearly half spend their last days in intensive care units, hooked up to machines and feeding tubes, unable to communicate with their families.[2] It costs a lot of money to die this way, a cost borne not just by Medicare and the insurance companies but by families as well, families who will most likely incur substantial out-of-pocket expenditures.

If you're serious about dying at home, it's going to take a concerted effort to do so. The hardest thing you'll have to do may be to overcome a strong cultural bias and medical preference to prevent death and prolong your life at any cost, in spite of overwhelming evidence that eventually everybody dies. The automatic reaction in most end-of-life situations is for medical caregivers to do something, anything, to keep you going.

My mother's story is quite typical of someone who grows old and frail before they pass away as opposed to dying from some traumatic event. After my father passed away, she lived another eight years — into her 90s — yet she had no life-threatening diseases. Eventually she became very weak, yet she repeatedly stated a strong preference to stay at home. Three months before she died, she had spent more than a week in a hospital, and in her fragile state, she was nearly killed by the lack of sleep, bad food, and constant testing and interruptions from well-meaning medical professionals. Our family was convinced that another trip to the hospital would be her last, so we hired in-home caregivers.

My sister, brother, and I all agreed to honor her wishes to stay at home. Fortunately, she wasn't hooked up to life support or any other medical intervention that would prevent her from being at home. When the end was near, her doctor and caregivers repeatedly asked us to admit her to the hospital "for observation." We asked my mother again and again if she wanted to go to the hospital, just to be sure, and she was adamant that she wanted to stay at home where she was comfortable and cared for by her family.

The lesson here is that you need to express your desires clearly, repeatedly, and in writing with an advance medical directive. You also need to have all your close relatives on board with this decision; it can take just one strong-minded relative to disagree and override your wishes, even if you've put them in writing. Your family needs to present a united front to the doctors and caregivers so there's no doubt they're carrying out your wishes.

This is not to say that the doctors and caregivers are the bad guys in this situation. Over the past two decades of my mother's life, modern medicine intervened at key times to keep her alive and well, enabling her to be around longer to enjoy her children and grandchildren.

But medical professionals are trained to preserve and prolong life; it's ingrained in their DNA. It just so happens that their training may be at odds with your desires at the end of your life and that you'll need a concerted effort to carry out your preferences.

Hospice care, which is intended to make you comfortable without trying to cure your terminal condition, was a godsend for my mother. Her hospice workers managed her pain, which is a critical component of hospice care.

If you don't want to stay at home but aren't sure you want to be in a hospital, you might qualify for a hospice facility. My father died at a hospice facility that was peaceful and comfortable, and allowed our extended family to be at his side when he passed away. In both my mother's and father's situations, the hospice doctors and nurses provided needed care to make them both comfortable and offered valuable guidance to our family. In my mother's situation, the hospice doctor and nurses went to her house to administer their care. And hospice care is an allowable expense that's reimbursed by Medicare, when prescribed by a doctor.

My mother died in the bed and bedroom that she had shared with my father for more than 50 years, surrounded by her family. Her room was a peaceful haven, a shrine to what mattered most to her — dozens of pictures of her children, grand-children and great-grandchildren hung on the walls and sat on her dresser. In the end, she simply stopped breathing without any visible distress.

They say that hearing is the last sense you'll lose when you pass. I choose to believe that the last things my mother heard as she left us were all of us calling out to her "Godspeed," "Say hi to Dad," and "We love you." It can't get any better than that.

Plan for peace of mind

Unfortunately, it's not a matter of *if* you'll experience the events discussed in this chapter, but *when* they'll happen to you. And when they do, you'll be thankful you spent the time to consider these matters carefully, not only to protect yourself and your family but also to leave this world in a way that makes the most sense for you.

Planning for your frail and final years may be the least exciting part of your retirement strategy, but it's something you can't afford to ignore. If you address these very real and serious issues, you'll give yourself peace of mind about the future, which will allow you to enjoy what you really want to do in your retirement years.

 **ACTION STEPS:**

- Decide on a strategy for paying for any potential long-term care expenses.

- Take steps to protect yourself and family against elder fraud and abuse, and coordinate those steps with your strategies to build your portfolio of retirement income.

- If you're married or in a committed partnership, make sure your spouse or partner's financial, medical, and household needs can be met either for long-term care or if you should die first. Coordinate these decisions with your strategies for retirement income and long-term care.

- Plan for a period when you might be very dependent on your family for elder care. Talk to your family about what you want and confirm who will be able to help.

- Prepare a medical directive for your care if you become unable to make these decisions. Be sure to discuss your choices with your family so they all know your wishes.

- Document and identify all your health care providers and prescription drugs, so that a family member can help manage your care.

 **HELPFUL RESOURCES:**

Books

- *Being Mortal: Medicine and What Matters in the End,* by Atul Gwande, MD. Picador Publishing, 2017.

- *The Best Care Possible: A Physician's Quest to Transform Care Through the End of Life,* by Ira Byock, MD. Avery Publishing, 2013.

- *Ethical Wills: Putting Your Values on Paper,* by Barry K. Baines, MD. Da Capo Press, 2006.

Websites

- Agencies to help navigate Medicare, Medicaid, and long-term care:
  - Area Agencies on Aging: https://www.n4a.org
  - SeniorCare.com: https://www.seniorcare.com
- American Association for Long-Term Care Insurance. This website contains helpful background information on insurance and a directory of agents who sell long-term care insurance: http://www.aaltci.org
- Annuity bidding services to buy online a longevity annuity or QLAC:
  - *ImmediateAnnuities.com*: https://www.immediateannuities.com
  - *Income Solutions*: https://www.incomesolutions.com
  - Websites of Fidelity, Schwab, or Vanguard
- *The Caregiving Journey.* This helpful guide from the Metlife Mature Market Institute and National Alliance for Caregivers covers issues and information to help families make necessary decisions about caregiving: https://www.metlife.com/assets/cao/mmi/publications/Guides/mmi-caregiving-journey.pdf
- Elder orphan resources:
  - *AgingCare.com*: https://www.agingcare.com/local/geriatric-care-managers
  - Carol Marak, elder orphan expert: http://www.carolmarak.com
  - Elder orphan Facebook page: https://www.facebook.com/groups/elderorphans/
  - *Elderorphan*: http://elderorphan.org
  - *National Care Planning Council*: https://www.longtermcarelink.net/eldercare/using_a_care_manager.htm
- Hospice care resources:
  - Medical definition of hospice: http://www.medicinenet.com/script/main/art.asp?articlekey=24267
  - Medicare's provisions on hospice: https://www.medicare.gov/coverage/hospice-and-respite-care.html

- "Improving Retirement by Integrating Family, Friends, Housing and Support: Lessons Learned from Personal Experience," by Anna Rappaport, FSA. https://www.soa.org/essays-monographs/mono-2014-managing-ltc/
- *Life Review Letter:* https://med.stanford.edu/letter/friendsandfamily.html
- Long-term care services:
  - *AgingCare.com*: https://www.agingcare.com
  - *Care.com*: https://www.care.com
  - *Honor*: https://www.joinhonor.com
- *Managing Retirement Decisions,* a very helpful series of short briefs prepared by the Society of Actuaries: https://www.soa.org/research-reports/2012/research-managing-retirement-decisions
  - "Taking the Long-Term Care Journey"
  - "Estate Planning: Preparing for End of Life"
- *Next Avenue.* The "Caregiving" page on this website contains a number of useful articles: https://www.nextavenue.org/channel/caregiving/

CHAPTER 16

LEAVE YOUR LEGACY

DON'T MAKE THESE MISTAKES:

- ⊘ Jeopardize your basic financial security by giving too much money to children and grandchildren while you're still alive.

- ⊘ Fail to make your wishes known in writing for how you want your assets distributed after you're gone.

- ⊘ Restrict your legacy to financial assets.

TRY THESE GAME-CHANGING STRATEGIES:

- ➜ Fund your financial giving from your lifetime retirement paychecks and bonuses so that you don't run out of money.

- ➜ Look for ways beyond money to give to your family, community, and society at large.

Plan your giving

"I don't want to be a burden on my children. The last thing I want is to end up broke and have to move in with my kids because I need them to take care of me."

"I want to help my children and grandchildren. It's only natural that parents should sacrifice to help their family."

"I won't have enough money to leave to anyone. I'm spending my children's inheritance now."

At my retirement planning workshops, I hear a wide range of perspectives regarding giving back to families, communities, and society at large. The quotes above represent just a few of the ways people feel about their money and what they plan to do with it. How you spend your money is clearly a personal choice.

Two-thirds of retirees say retirement is the best time in life to give back to family and society, according to a recent report by Merrill Lynch and Age Wave.[1] They estimate that over the next 20 years, America could receive a "longevity bonus" of donations and time from retirees worth an estimated $8 trillion.

Merrill Lynch and Age Wave identify the three M's of giving:

- *Money: charitable donations*
- *Minutes: volunteering*
- *Meaning: passing along values and life lessons*

But money isn't the only thing you can give. With more time on your hands after you retire, one way to consider spending some of that time is to volunteer. For example, more than one in four Americans age 65 to 74 volunteers an average of 183 hours per year, according to the *Sightlines* report from the Stanford Center on Longevity.[2]

Planning your giving, whether it's time or money, is an important part of your retirement planning. This chapter shares a few ideas to help you decide how to give your money, minutes, and meaning in a responsible and realistic way that's consistent with your values.

Spend just your retirement paychecks and bonuses

I've heard horror stories about well-intentioned parents who freely gave money to help their adult children and grandchildren, even sacrificing their own retirement security. A few years later, they no longer had enough money to live independently and had to ask for help from their kids or even needed to move in with them.

If your children or grandchildren need help, what's the best way to assist them without going broke? Adhere to the magic formula for retirement income security: *I > E*. By treating your financial giving as a budget item in your living expenses (your "E") that's paid from your lifetime retirement income (your "I"), you can feel confident that you're helping within your means and won't jeopardize your long-term financial security by outliving your savings.

If your retirement income is modest and you have a strong desire to help, you might need to reprioritize your budget for living expenses. Just keep your total "E" less than your total "I." I know that might be easier said than done, but nevertheless, it should be your goal in order to maintain the level of savings you need for your own expenses. And look for ways to help that don't involve money, such as giving your time or sharing helpful insights from your life experience.

Coordinate your money legacy with your retirement security

If you want to leave money to your children and to charities after you're gone, there are at least two ways to do this:

- Use just the interest and dividends from your invested retirement savings to generate your retirement bonuses, and leave the principal intact, as discussed in Chapter 7. This principal will then be available for monetary legacies after you die.

- Preserve your home equity by not taking out a reverse mortgage. If you don't need to draw on your home equity to pay for long-term care expenses, it can serve as a legacy after you're gone.

Of course, these methods of setting aside funds for a monetary legacy can only work for retirees who've accumulated sufficient financial resources. Many older workers and retirees will need to do all they can to squeeze the most income from their savings and possibly from their home equity, and they may not be in the position to leave much of a financial legacy. In this case, leaving a legacy of "minutes and meaning" is their best option, which can end up being pretty darned good!

Spell out your legacy in writing

Simply put, if you don't create a will to express your wishes in writing for distributing your assets upon your death, somebody else will do it for you — and it'll most likely be the state you live in. People who die intestate, or without a will, will have their assets distributed as indicated by the laws in their state. In this case, your assets may be distributed to relatives whom you don't want to leave a legacy.

As a result, it pays to spend time to specify exactly how you want to take care of your spouse, family, and friends with any money or assets you have left. In addition to assets that have financial value, you'll also want to specify how to distribute personal items that have meaning to your family and friends. Estate lawyers can tell you horror stories about relatives who didn't care how the money was distributed but fought over Dad's favorite rocking chair or Mom's favorite dishes.

Further details about wills and trusts are well beyond the scope of this book, but there are plenty of lawyers who can help you work through this issue. If you have a relatively simple situation and are a motivated do-it-yourselfer, books and online software are also good resources. Just don't neglect this essential task: Preparing your will should be a priority on your retirement planning to-do list, no matter how old you are.

Volunteer to change the world

Many of us started our adult lives wanting to change the world. Living through the turbulent '60s motivated us to take up important causes like the peace movement, equality and ending discrimination, saving the environment, promoting social justice, educating the next generation, and helping the disadvantaged, as well as favorite personal or community causes. Then we got distracted by raising families and pursuing careers, which was certainly understandable. The next few decades, however, represent our remaining best chance to pick up where we left off or to focus on new causes that we're passionate about now.

For many of us, there would be nothing better than to be able to leave the world a better place for our adult children, grandchildren, and great-grandchildren. Volunteering might be a feel-good activity in more ways than one. Evidence is accumulating that volunteering can improve your health and well-being by providing valuable social connections and purpose in life.[3,4,5] And for some people, volunteering can lead to paid work opportunities, which can help boost their finances.

> *"Older adults are the only natural resource that*
> *is actually growing."*

—Laura Carstensen, PhD, founder of the
Stanford Center on Longevity

People who find volunteer causes in their last few years at work are much more likely to continue volunteering when they retire, compared to people who didn't volunteer while they were working, according to recent research.[6] Furthermore, many employers are facilitating volunteer opportunities for their employees as part of their community outreach programs and philanthropic initiatives, including offering paid time off for qualified activities. If this opportunity is available to you, it might be a smart way to boost your engagement with your current job as well as help ease your transition into retirement.

Join the millions of older Americans who are using some of their newfound freedom to help change the world for the better. See the "Helpful Resources" section at the end of this chapter for websites that can help connect you with the causes that resonate most with you.

Pass down your values

Throughout the ages, the elders of our societies have been the keepers of wisdom and culture, passing values along to the next generation. Of course, by taking care of your own financial security, health, and well-being, you're setting a good example that will positively influence the lives of your close family and friends. And by being actively involved in the well-being of your family and community, you're sending powerful messages that caring and volunteering is a good way to use your time.

But there are other ways to share your values with the younger generations of your family. One interesting recent trend has been to pass along your values and life experience to close family and friends through an "ethical will," which can be done in writing or videotaped. For example, you might want to tell stories about your life experiences that shaped your values and decisions. Maybe you want to share the steps you took that helped your health, financial security, and well-being, or the regrets you feel about times when you might have done better. You can create a special moment by sharing your ethical will with your loved ones before you pass away.

Leave the world a better place

What will you leave behind when you're gone? Many people think it's just wealthy people who worry about this question. As you can see, however, there's a lot more you can do in your retirement years to make the world a better place, leaving behind a legacy that's just as important as money.

If you're still not sure what you'd like to do to help your family, community, and the world at large, try the visualization strategy mentioned in Chapter 2. Picturing your future may help you decide what to do in your present.

Here's a visualization message that helps motivate me: I'm in my final days, reviewing my life and receiving visits from cherished friends and family. I'm satisfied that, given my circumstances and abilities, I did the best I could throughout my life to help my family, community, and the world. I have no regrets.

Sharing ideas about leaving your legacy is a fitting way to wrap up the strategies, ideas, and action steps in this book. The last chapter provides a checklist to evaluate your progress on the action steps that I shared in this book.

It's my sincere hope that we can band together to build our financial security, maintain our health as long as possible, and nurture our well-being, so that we all can leave this world a better place. Best wishes, and good luck!

 **ACTION STEPS:**

- Devise a thoughtful strategy for giving money to children or charities while you're alive that won't jeopardize your long-term financial security.
- Explore volunteer opportunities while you're still working.
- Think about the values you want to pass along to close family and friends.
- Prepare your will.

 HELPFUL RESOURCES:

Websites

- *Celebrations of Life* website includes helpful resources on ethical wills, including the highly rated book *Ethical Wills: Putting Your Values on Paper*: http://celebrationsoflife.net/ethicalwill-com/
- Here are websites that help match your cause preferences, skills, and availability with local volunteer opportunities, based on a series of questions that you answer:
  - AARP's *Volunteer Wizard*: http://sweeps.aarp.org/volunteerwizard/
  - *Volunteer Match*: https://www.volunteermatch.org
- *Hidden in Plain Sight: How Intergenerational Relationships Can Transform Our Future,* by the Stanford Center on Longevity, is an excellent summary on the various benefits of volunteering: http://longevity.stanford.edu/wp-content/uploads/2017/04/Monograph_web_07_11_2016.pdf
- *Life Review Letter:* https://med.stanford.edu/letter/friendsandfamily.html
- *Managing Retirement Decisions,* a very helpful series of short briefs prepared by the Society of Actuaries.
  - "Estate Planning: Preparing for End of Life" https://www.soa.org/research-reports/2012/research-managing-retirement-decisions

IV.

EVALUATE

Retirement Game-Changers is chock-full of ideas and strategies to improve your financial security, health, and enjoyment of life. To help you put it all together, you can track your progress with the Retirement Reality Check. You'll want to periodically review this list to make sure you keep on track over the next few years.

Completing this list will give you the confidence that you're not forgetting important steps for your planning.

CHAPTER 17

TRACK YOUR PROGRESS WITH THE RETIREMENT REALITY CHECK

DON'T MAKE THESE MISTAKES:

⊘ Retire before realistically assessing your situation (in other words, winging it).

TRY THESE GAME-CHANGING STRATEGIES:

→ Track your progress regarding the important action steps in this book.

Be brave — don't put your head in the sand

Remember Elaine's story in Chapter 3? She was brave and faced up to the reality of her situation, and then made some smart life choices in order to improve her chances of experiencing a successful and enjoyable retirement.

Unfortunately, I've seen too many people in their 50s and 60s shy away from assessing their retirement resources, either because they don't know how or are too scared to face their reality. Then something happens and they end up retiring sooner than they'd expected to — either because they get laid off, poor health forces them to stop working, or they experience a frustrating "I'm outta here" incident at work and retire impulsively. Years later, when money gets tight, they regret that earlier decision to avoid planning their retirement.

Don't be a victim of retirement delusion! By finding out when it's actually realistic for you to retire, you'll enjoy a more secure "rest-of-life." The Retirement Reality Check in this final chapter puts together all the action steps described in this book and gives you a checklist to track your progress.

Start by laying the basic foundation to attain financial security in your retirement years. Then build on this foundation by taking steps to further enhance your finances, improve your health, and nurture your social network. Finish the job by planning for the best possible life in retirement and preparing for your frail and final years.

Make the Retirement Reality Check work for you

I've seen many positive results from people who review and follow the Retirement Reality Check. Here's one common situation: Many people in their 50s and 60s get tired of working for various reasons, and they think retirement will make their lives better. But instead of just quitting, they do their homework and analyze the magic formula for retirement income security from Chapter 4 by estimating their retirement income and living expenses.

Once they see the results, it's not uncommon for them to discover they aren't even close to making ends meet for a long retirement. That convinces them to work longer, but they also know they can't stomach the thought of continuing to work in the same way they've been working for so long. As a result, they investigate how they can make their work more fulfilling and enjoyable, or they look for creative ways to reduce their living expenses and still be happy.

The Retirement Reality Check forced them to dig deeper for solutions that would make their life better, and now they're making real progress!

I highly recommend you complete the Retirement Reality Check outlined in this chapter in your late 50s or early 60s. Think of age 60 as the milestone age for assessing your retirement situation, much like the medical tests you're supposed to take at age 50. Don't worry if you're older than age 60 now, though — it's never too late to take charge of your life.

The Retirement Reality Check reviews the strategies
and action steps in this book. Use it as a checklist
to mark your progress with your planning.

Don't wing it: Build a foundation for your financial security

As a minimum goal, you'll want to assess the resources you have that will help you build a financial foundation for your retirement years. Simply put, if you haven't completed these tasks yet, you're not ready to retire.

Here are five steps you should take to make sure you're not winging it with your retirement planning:

- Take inventory of all your financial assets. Chapter 3 contains a checklist.

- Estimate the total of your retirement paychecks and bonuses from all sources: Social Security, a pension if you have one, work, investment income, and payouts from your savings. Be sure to distinguish between:

  o Secure "paychecks" that will last for the rest of your life, such as Social Security, pensions, and annuities, and

  o Variable "bonuses" that can fluctuate in amount or might not last for life, such as earnings from work or withdrawals from invested assets.

  Chapters 4 through 8 provide the details you need to complete this task.

- Complete a budget for your living expenses that includes housing, transportation, food, utilities, medical expenses, and taxes. Be sure to distinguish between basic living expenses and discretionary expenditures. Then estimate how these numbers might change in your retirement years. See Chapter 9 for details and resources to help you with this task.

- Know where you'll be obtaining health and dental insurance, and how much it will cost both before and after eligibility for Medicare at age 65. Also, guesstimate how much money you might spend out-of-pocket for medical expenses, including copayments, deductibles, and coinsurance. Many people are surprised to learn that out-of-pocket costs for medical insurance premiums, deductibles, and copayments increase substantially when they leave their career job. See Chapter 10 for details on this step.

- Estimate how you'll address the magic formula for retirement income security ($I > E$), both in the immediate future and for the rest of your life. Make sure the formula will work for your spouse or partner, if applicable, after you're gone. Chapters 2 through 10 provide ideas and resources to help you complete this critical step.

For this last step, you don't necessarily need to work out every last detail about your retirement income (your "I") and expenses (your "E") for the next 20 to 30 years. That's unrealistic. What you will want to do is see if it's reasonable that your income will cover your living expenses for a potentially long retirement. You'll also want to make sure you have enough margin with your income, expenses, and emergency savings to deal with surprises and shocks that could likely happen during your retirement years.

Congratulations! Complete these steps, and you've laid the financial foundation to live a good life in retirement. Now let's see how you can build on your efforts.

Make it better: Refine your financial strategies, improve your health, and nurture your social network

Let's move beyond the money basics of retirement to see how you can enhance your retirement planning:

- Line up encore/downshifting work or volunteering, or explore your work or volunteer opportunities. Take inventory of your relevant work skills and experience. See Chapter 12 for more details.

- Eliminate ongoing credit card debt and student debt, if applicable (either for yourself, children, or grandchildren). Or, work out a schedule to pay off these debts. Be sure to include these costs in your budget for living expenses. Plan to pay off your mortgage at some point before or during your retirement years.

- Identify professionals who have the skills to help you with your finances and health, and have your best interests at heart. For details, see the bonus chapter titled *Get Help* on the "Advanced Study" page of www.retirementgamechangers.com.

- Know your basic health indicators and measures as discussed in Chapter 11. Make sure you're satisfied with the steps you're taking to improve these numbers and your health with your nutrition, exercise, and lifestyle habits. If you have specific health conditions, develop a plan to manage or improve these conditions. If you haven't yet taken these steps, identify a path for improvement. See Chapter 11 for details on improving your health.

- Make sure you have or plan to create a diversified portfolio of social engagements beyond the activities you do with your spouse or partner. Complete the social inventory in Chapter 14, and see that chapter for details on nurturing your well-being.

Once again, you don't need to work out all the details of these steps. It's often enough to commit to learning and exploring more once you get some free time. And you'll want to be sure to discuss these steps with your spouse or partner, if you have one.

Finish the job: Plan for the best possible life, and prepare for your final years

Take the following steps so you can feel good that you're leaving no stone unturned when planning for your retirement years:

- Get on good terms with your spouse or partner, and close family and friends. Make sure you have no unfinished business with them or have important people you're estranged from. If you still have unfinished business, commit to a plan for making amends.

- Develop hobbies and interests that you'll look forward to on a daily or weekly basis, if you haven't already. By doing so, you'll find that you can fill most of your days with meaningful activities, beyond the "vacation" aspects of retirement.

- Give serious thought to where you'll live in your retirement years, both the community and the specific house. Make conscious choices about one or more of the following goals:

- ○ Relocating, perhaps to be near family, work, or activities, or to reduce living expenses

- ○ Downsizing, often to reduce your living expenses

- ○ Making improvements needed to age in place, as you prepare for your slow-go and no-go years

   See Chapter 6 for strategies on deploying your home equity and Chapter 13 for ideas on the best place to live.

- Create a strategy to address the possibility of needing long-term care in your frail years. This should include financial, health, and social strategies. See Chapter 15 for details about these strategies.

- Plan the legacy you'll leave, which can be strictly financial or can be a matter of passing along values that are important to you, as discussed in Chapter 16.

The Retirement Reality Check sums up all the action steps discussed in this book. It's a lot of work to put these steps into place, but it's well worth the effort to make the best of the years you have left.

Once you've completed the initial assessment, you'll want to periodically revisit the Retirement Reality Check in the months and years ahead to mark the progress you're making. Be sure to celebrate as you check off the tasks, knowing that you're on your way to a better life in retirement.

Best wishes for the rest of your life!

ACKNOWLEDGMENTS

Writing a book is a long and winding journey, where you gain valuable insights and perspectives by engaging with your existing colleagues and connections, meeting new people, and reconnecting with old friends. Along the way, you learn a lot about yourself, changing your mind and beliefs at times. Writing this book has been an extraordinary journey for which I feel very blessed.

Two people accompanied me every step of the way, from brainstorming the initial concept to final production: my wife, Melinda, who applied her experience and expertise from a 30-year career in book publishing, and Teresa Ciulla, my talented editor. Melinda and Teresa read and edited the entire manuscript several times and spent countless hours brainstorming the issues we wanted to cover. Both helped me consider the layperson's perspective, and their efforts made *Retirement Game-Changers* much easier to read and understand. I couldn't have written this book without them.

Marla Markman served as the Project Manager, helping bring the manuscript into its final form with her production services and expertise. Marla and her book designer, Gwyn Kennedy Snider of GKS Creative, were very helpful and patient as we worked to accomplish an important goal for the book: I wanted readers to relax and feel confident to tackle a potentially scary subject. Their book cover and design services helped achieve this goal. Our talented artist Richard Sheppard prepared the engaging and delightful illustrations. Thanks also to Allison Phillips, who proofread the entire manuscript and provided another set of eyes looking at the text.

I'm very grateful for the opportunity to work at the Stanford Center on Longevity, founded by Laura Carstensen, PhD, who's the author of *A Long Bright Future*. Laura helped with the overall framing of longevity issues during two interviews, as well as providing helpful insights and research citations on the importance of social connectedness and well-being. Working at the Center has enabled me to work on several projects that are discussed in this book. I also appreciate Martha Deevy, associate director of the Center, for hiring me and supporting my research and projects on retirement income, behavioral economics, and retirement decision-making.

Working at the Center has opened many doors to talented researchers and colleagues who are mentioned here.

I also appreciate my employer-clients that host the retirement planning workshops I conduct for their older workers as they approach retirement. I've gained valuable insights into how older working Americans make decisions by getting face-to-face with them and fielding their many questions. This understanding has driven home the need to simplify retirement planning strategies and communicate them so that ordinary workers can apply these strategies in their lives.

I've written a regular column for CBS *MoneyWatch* on retirement issues for many years, interacting with countless readers and answering their questions. The need to write up to eight columns per month for eight years has required me to conduct extensive research on many different retirement planning topics. In the process, I've been introduced to many other researchers and writers. Here's a big thank you to my CBS editors Glenn Coleman and Alain Sherter.

It's my belief that many problems experienced by older retirees result from not paying sufficient attention to the serious decisions they need to face on a variety of topics. Consequently, it was important that early in the book, I introduce concepts to help motivate and inspire people to spend the time that's needed to make effective decisions. I've benefited over the years from several conversations with Geoff Cohen, PhD, who was helpful with editing the section in Chapter 2 about his research on affirmations.

Sally Hass ran one of America's most comprehensive retirement readiness programs at corporate giant Weyerhaeuser for many years, and I've seen firsthand the value of her exercise on "hopes and dreams" and "fears and concerns." This exercise has proven to be very successful in my retirement planning workshops. I've also had many insightful conversations on motivational strategies with Tamara Sims, PhD, who is a research analyst at the Stanford Center on Longevity. Jeremy Bailenson, PhD, has also shared his intriguing research on the value of visualizing your future self.

There's a vast amount of information on strategies and products to achieve financial security in retirement. Much of it is complex and confusing, and some material is produced by people and institutions who are specifically focused on selling their products and services. It was a very important goal of mine for this book to distill this mountain of information into effective, straightforward strategies that ordinary workers could understand and implement. I've been helped tremendously by many talented people who simply want to provide useful and unbiased information to help older Americans grapple with these serious retirement planning issues.

I've been very fortunate to work closely with Wade Pfau, PhD, and Joe Tomlinson, FSA, on our research on retirement income projects for the Stanford Center on Longevity, in collaboration with the Society of Actuaries. Many of the strategies in this book result from research projects that they co-wrote with me. Wade and Joe reviewed several chapters in the financial security section of the book and provided invaluable comments.

Anna Rappaport, FSA, and Pete Neuwirth, FSA, both reviewed many chapters in the financial section and also provided helpful comments and suggestions. Anna was the first person I interviewed for this book at the *Living to 100 Conference* sponsored by the Society of Actuaries, and her enthusiasm encouraged me to proceed. In addition, I'm deeply indebted to Steve Siegel, Andy Peterson, and Barbara Scott at the Society of Actuaries for sponsoring much of the research on retirement income strategies that's featured in this book.

Andy Landis, author of *Social Security: The Inside Story*, provided invaluable feedback on Chapter 5, covering Social Security. I've also gained valuable insights on Social Security from the research conducted by John Shoven, PhD, former director of the Stanford Institute for Economic Policy Research. I've had several occasions to use his famous quote on retirement math, featured in Chapter 12 on working longer.

To fine-tune my understanding of investing strategies, I benefited significantly from my interviews with Allan Roth, a financial writer for AARP and the author of *How a Second Grader Beats Wall Street: Golden Rules Any Investor Can Learn*, and David Blanchett, director of retirement research at Morningstar Investment Management LLC. A delightful lunch with Bill Sharpe gave me a chance to compare notes with his comprehensive work on investing and drawdown strategies.

Diane Omdahl, founder of Sixty-Five Incorporated, helped sort out the complex world of Medicare, Medigap, and Medicare Advantage plans, covered in Chapter 10. Anna Rapport also provided helpful review of this chapter.

Chapter 11 on health strategies posed a challenge similar to financial security: There's a mountain of potentially confusing and conflicting information on steps you can take to maintain and improve your health. Several experts helped me sort out the latest research on health strategies. My interview with Jack Rowe, MD, was extremely insightful, and he was very generous to allow me to quote from his book, *Successful Aging*. I also benefited tremendously from my interview with Ann Marie Chiasson, MD, co-director of the Fellowship at the Arizona Center for Integrative Medicine at the University of Arizona. Ann Marie reviewed Chapter 11 and provided many helpful comments. She also introduced me to Andrew Weil's groundbreaking book, *Mind Over Meds*.

Christopher Gardner, PhD, nutrition researcher at the Stanford University Medical School, fit me into his busy teaching and research schedule for a helpful interview. He was very generous to lend some of his informative material on nutrition, and I benefited from his review of Chapter 11. I also benefited significantly by reading Dr. Michael Greger's book on healthy nutrition, *How Not to Die,* and he graciously allowed me to quote from his book.

Anne Friedlander, PhD, a professor at Stanford University who researches physiology, exercise, fitness, and health, also squeezed time into her busy schedule for an interview with me, and she provided keen insights on exercise. I've had many impromptu and wide-ranging conversations on a variety of health-related topics with Ken Smith, director of the Mobility Division at the Stanford Center on Longevity. Ken introduced me to Christopher Gardner and Anne Friedlander. He also reviewed Chapter 11 and provided helpful comments, particularly on interpreting the health statistics in the *Sightlines* project produced by the Stanford Center on Longevity.

I thought I was finished writing Chapter 11 on health strategies until I heard a talk about hearing loss from Amy Yotopoulos, director of the Mind Division at the Stanford Center on Longevity. Amy was very helpful in pointing out the critical importance for your health of maintaining your hearing abilities in your later years.

Chapter 12 on working longer posed yet another challenge, as there are many ways to think about working in your retirement years. I started by interviewing old friends who were very helpful: Mark Miller, creator of the RetirementRevised website, and Helen Dennis, author of *Project Renewment: The First Retirement Model for Career Women.* Mark then introduced me to Kerry Hannon, author of *Great Jobs for Everyone 50 +: Finding Work That Keeps You Happy and Healthy...and Pays the Bills,* and Chris Farrell, author of *Unretirement: How Baby Boomers Are Changing the Way We Think About Work, Community, and the Good Life.* Both Kerry and Chris shared their keen insights and suggestions in my interviews with them.

I was lucky to fit into the busy schedule of Marc Freedman, founder of Encore. org, and Marc introduced me to Marci Alboher, author of *The Encore Career Handbook: How to Make a Living and a Difference in the Second Half of Life.* Both Marc and Marci provided valuable insights into the encore career movement, which also helped guide my own encore career.

A few members of AARP's staff have been particularly helpful regarding this book. Staci Alexander and Ramsey Alwin helped me navigate their extensive resources for helping older workers. I've also benefited from my correspondence over the years with Debra Whitman, who provided an insightful quote.

I've also gained valuable insights from research on the circumstances of older workers and retirees by the Transamerica Center for Retirement Studies. Catherine Collinson, the Center's president, has always been a font of helpful information about the challenges that older workers face.

Sally Hass is a fierce advocate of the value of older workers, as well as the issues with working longer for both employers and employees. I've benefited from many conversations I've had with her over the years on this topic. She also reviewed the chapter on working longer and provided helpful comments.

I met Phyllis Mitzen at the Society of Actuaries *Living to 100 Conference*, where she was enthusiastically talking about retirement housing alternatives. Anna Rappaport formally introduced me to Phyllis, and both Anna and Phyllis lent their time generously with interviews and review of Chapter 13 on choosing the best place to live in retirement. I've also gained helpful insights over the years from reading the many "Best Places to Live in Retirement" lists, started by Richard Eisenberg when he was at *Money* magazine. He graciously approved a quote on the insights gained from these lists.

Like all the other topics in the book, there's a wealth of information on the topics I cover in Chapters 14 and 15 on well-being, ranging from well-intentioned self-help books to rigorous academic research. Many people helped me sort through the respected research and distill it into usable strategies for our readers. Laura Carstensen and Amy Yotopoulos were my first "go-to" people for help in this area. Amy generously reviewed Chapter 14 and provided helpful edits, and her delightful story about her 99-year-old grandma was a great way to start that chapter.

Tamara Sims, PhD, director of the *Sightlines* project at the Stanford Center on Longevity, has also been very helpful with her extensive knowledge of the state of the health and social engagement among Americans of all ages.

Carol Dweck, PhD, author of *Mindset: The New Psychology of Success*, provided keen insights during our interview into the importance of keeping an open mind regarding the many challenges that older workers face when planning for retirement. Morten Hansen, PhD, and author of *Great at Work: How Top Performers Do Less, Work Better, and Achieve More*, generously provided his insights on discovering your passion and purpose.

My wife, Melinda, and I have enjoyed our many interactions with our chi gung instructor Susan Ezra, who also had a long career as a hospice nurse. She is masterful at integrating Western and Eastern philosophies on life and health. We also benefited from our delightful dinner interview with Gay Luce, PhD, and David Patten, who founded the Nine Gates Mystery School. In the 1970s and 1980s, Gay founded SAGE, a groundbreaking program on successful aging that became a prototype for many programs to follow. Gay and David both provided unique perspectives on aging, and they're powerful role models for aging with vigor and purpose.

I also benefited from the research on how your state of mind can influence your health, conducted by Stanford researcher Alia Crum, PhD. My good friend, Tom Soma, helped me by sharing his writing about his four-point compass for healthy integration of life's events as we age.

Marti DeLiema, PhD, and Martha Deevy, both at the Stanford Center on Longevity, are two of the nation's top experts on financial fraud and abuse of older Americans. Marti generously reviewed the section in Chapter 15 on financial fraud and provided helpful comments.

Research conducted by Merrill Lynch, in collaboration with Age Wave, has been particularly useful on a variety of topics in this book. Surya Kolluri of Merrill Lynch has graciously shared these reports and invited me to briefings as the reports were released. I've also gained numerous insights and information from interactions with many retirement industry professionals, including Stephen Chen, Matt Fellowes, Doug Fisher, Sasha Franger, Neil Lloyd, Nag Odekar, Stig Nybo, Andy Reed, Ken Steiner, and Jeanne Thompson.

Many friends have taken an interest in the book and provided helpful suggestions. For example, Deborah Jones introduced me to Ann Marie Chiasson, MD, who was so helpful with the chapter on health strategies. Dan Milder, a good friend who is a tax accountant, gave us helpful insights over coffee on the misconceptions that many retirees have about income taxes. Ben Wada is my yoga friend, with whom I've had many valuable conversations while sitting on our mats before yoga class begins.

Many other friends and family also contributed their thoughts and provided encouragement, and I'm grateful for their help. Our kids and their spouses or partners — Jeff, Mary Kathryn, Emily, Taras, Bonnie, and Spencer — all provided input and helped keep us motivated.

Retirement Game-Changers wouldn't have been published without all of this help, so I'm very grateful to be part of such a wonderful community.

REFERENCES

Introduction to Our Challenges and Opportunities

1. Dublin, L.I., and Lotka, A.J. *Length of Life.* New York: The Ronald Press, 1936.
2. National Center for Health Statistics. "Health, United States, 2015." *U.S. Department of Health and Human Services, Centers for Disease Control and Prevention, National Center for Health Statistics.* June 2017. https://www.cdc.gov/nchs/data/hus/hus15.pdf
3. Copeland, Craig, Greenwald, Lisa, and VanDerhei, Jack. "The 2017 Retirement Confidence Survey." *The Employee Benefit Research Institute.* March 2017. https://www.ebri.org/pdf/surveys/rcs/2017/IB.431.Mar17. RCS17..21Mar17.pdf
4. Transamerica Center for Retirement Studies. "17th Annual Retirement Survey." *Transamerica Center for Retirement Studies.* December 2016. https://www.transamericacenter.org/retirement-research/17th-annual-retirement-survey

Chapter 1: Plan for a Long Retirement

1. Martin, Courtney E. *The New Better Off: Reinventing the American Dream.* Berkeley: Seal Press, 2016.
2. Adam, Stephane, Bonsang, Eric, and Perelman, Sergio. "Does Retirement Affect Cognitive Functioning?" *Journal of Health Economics,* Volume 31 (March 2012).
3. Rohwedder, Susann, and Willis, Robert. "Mental Retirement." *Journal of Economic Perspectives,* Volume 24 (Winter 2010).
4. Manheimer, Ronald J. *The Second Middle Age: Looking Differently at Life Beyond 50.* Canton Township: Visible Ink Press, 1995.
5. O'Hara-Devereaux, Mary. "Healthy Longevity — Get Ready for Your Second Middle Age." *GlobalForesight.* 2014. http://global-foresight.net/extreme-longevity-get-ready-for-your-second-middle-age/
6. AgeWave and Merrill Lynch. "Leisure in Retirement: Beyond the Bucket List." *AgeWave and Merrill Lynch.* 2016. https://agewave.com/wp-content/uploads/2016/05/2016-Leisure-in-Retirement_Beyond-the-Bucket-List.pdf
7. Abraham, Sarah, Chetty, Raj, and Stepner, Michael. "The Association

Between Income and Life Expectancy in the United States, 2001-2014." *Journal of the American Medical Association*, Volume 16 (April 2016).

8. Greenwald and Associates. "2015 Risks and Process of Retirement Survey." *The Society of Actuaries*. January 2016. https://www.soa.org/Files/Research/Projects/research-2015-full-risk-report-final.pdf

9. Jaworski, Dominika, Reed, Andrew, and Vernon, Steve. "The Decision to Retire: Research-Based Recommendations for Individuals and Employers." *Stanford Center on Longevity*. September 2016. http://longevity.stanford.edu/blog/2017/03/03/the-decision-to-retire-research-based-recommendations-for-individuals-and-employers/

Chapter 2: Motivate and Inspire Yourself

1. Baumeister, Roy and Tierney, John. *Willpower: Rediscovering the Greatest Human Strength*. New York: Penguin Books, 2011.

2. Stanford Center on Longevity. "The Sightlines Project: Seeing Our Way to Living Long and Living Well in 21st Century America." *Stanford Center on Longevity*. February 2016. http://longevity.stanford.edu/the-sightlines-project/

3. TD Bank. "Visualizing Goals Influences Financial Health and Happiness." *TD Bank News Releases*. January 20, 2016. https://www.prnewswire.com/news-releases/visualizing-goals-influences-financial-health-and-happiness-study-finds-300207028.html

4. Hershfield, Hal E., et al. "Increasing Savings Behavior Through Age-Progressed Renderings of the Future Self." *Journal of Marketing Research*, Volume 48 (November 2011).

5. Aaker, Jennifer. "Harnessing the Power of Stories." *Lean In*, 2013. https://leanin.org/education/harnessing-the-power-of-stories/

6. Cohen, Geoffrey L. and Sherman, David K. "The Psychology of Change: Self-Affirmation and Social Psychological Intervention." *Annual Review of Psychology*, Volume 65 (January 2014).

Chapter 3: Take Your Financial Inventory

No references for this chapter.

Chapter 4: Manage the Magic Formula for Retirement Income Security

No references for this chapter.

Chapter 5: Optimize Your Best Retirement Paycheck – Social Security

1. Pfau, Wade, Tomlinson, Joe, and Vernon, Steve. "Optimizing Retirement Income by Integrating Retirement Plans, IRAs, and Home Equity: A Framework for Evaluating Retirement Income Decisions." *Stanford Center on Longevity*. November 2017. http://longevity.stanford.edu/scl-publications/

2. Board of Trustees of the Federal Old-Age and Survivors Insurance and Federal Disability Trust Funds. "2017 Annual Report of the Board of Trustees of the Federal Old-Age and Survivors Insurance and Federal Disability Trust Funds." *Social Security Administration*. July 2017. https://www.ssa.gov/oact/tr/2017/tr2017.pdf

Chapter 6: Complete Your Portfolio of Retirement Paychecks

1. TIAA. "2016 Voices of Experience Survey Results." *TIAA*. 2016. https://www.tiaa.org/public/about-tiaa/news-press/press-releases/pressrelease642.html

2. WillisTowersWatson. "Annuities and Retirement Happiness." *WillisTowersWatson Insider*. September 2012. https://www.towerswatson.com/en/insights/newsletters/americas/insider/2012/annuities-and-retirement-happiness

3. Vernon, Steve. "Should You Accept a Lump-Sum Pension Cashout?" *CBS MoneyWatch*. November 2014. https://www.cbsnews.com/news/should-you-accept-a-lump-sum-pension-cashout/

Chapter 7: Deploy Retirement Bonuses

1. Vernon, Steve. "The Next Evolution in Defined Contribution Retirement Plan Design: A Guide for DC Plan Sponsors to Implementing Retirement Income Programs." *Stanford Center on Longevity*. September 2013. http://longevity.stanford.edu/blog/2013/10/10/soa_scl/

2. Pfau, Wade, Tomlinson, Joe, and Vernon, Steve. "Optimizing Retirement Income Portfolios in Defined Contribution Retirement Plans: A Framework for Building Retirement Income Portfolios." *Stanford Center on Longevity*. May 2016. http://longevity.stanford.edu/blog/2015/07/14/optimal-retirement-income-solutions-in-defined-contribution-retirement-plans/

3. Pfau, Wade, Tomlinson, Joe, and Vernon, Steve. "Optimizing Retirement Income by Integrating Retirement Plans, IRAs, and Home Equity: A Framework for Evaluating Retirement Income Decisions." *Stanford*

Center on Longevity. November 2017. http://longevity.stanford.edu/ scl-publications/

4. Kinnel, Russel. "Fund Fees Predict Future Success or Failure." *Morningstar.* May 5, 2016. http://news.morningstar.com/articlenet/article. aspx?id=752485

5. Harbron, Garrett L., Roberts, Daren R., and Rowley, James J. "The Case for Low-Cost Index-Fund Investing." *Vanguard.* April 2017. https:// personal.vanguard.com/pdf/ISGIDX.pdf

Chapter 8: Build Your Retirement Income Portfolio

1. Pfau, Wade, Tomlinson, Joe, and Vernon, Steve. "Optimizing Retirement Income by Integrating Retirement Plans, IRAs, and Home Equity: A Framework for Evaluating Retirement Income Decisions." *Stanford Center on Longevity.* November 2017. http://longevity.stanford.edu/scl-publications

2. Vernon, Steve. "How to 'Pensionize' any IRA or 401(k) Plan." *Stanford Center on Longevity.* November 2017. http://longevity.stanford.edu/ scl-publications

Chapter 9: Buy Just Enough

1. Greenwald and Associates. "2015 Risks and Process of Retirement Survey." *The Society of Actuaries.* January 2016. https://www.soa.org/Files/Research/ Projects/research-2015-full-risk-report-final.pdf

2. Transamerica Center for Retirement Studies. "The Current State of Retirement: A Compendium of Findings About American Retirees." *The Transamerica Center for Retirement Studies.* April 2016. https://www.trans-americacenter.org/docs/default-source/retirees-survey/tcrs2016_sr_retiree_ compendium.pdf

3. Bureau of Labor Statistics. "A Closer Look at Spending Patterns of Older Americans." *Bureau of Labor Statistics, U.S. Department of Labor.* March 2016. https://www.bls.gov/opub/btn/volume-5/spending-patterns-of-old-er-americans.htm

4. Fellowes, Matt. "Living Too Frugally? Economic Sentiment and Spending Among Older Americans." *United Income.* May 2017. https://unitedincome. com/documents/papers/LivingTooFrugal.pdf

5. JPMorganChase Institute. "Seniors Lead the Slowdown in Local Consumer Finance." *JPMorganChase Institute.* July 2017. https://www.jpmorganchase. com/corporate/institute/insight-deceleration-in-lcc.htm

6. T. Rowe Price. "New Retirees and Those Approaching Retirement Age Are

Faring Well." *T. Rowe Price Press.* July 2014. https://www3.troweprice.com/usis/corporate/en/press/t--rowe-price--new-retirees-and-those-approaching-retirement-age.html

Chapter 10: Make Smart Choices for Health Insurance

1. Bureau of Labor Statistics. "Employee Benefits in the United States, News Release." *Bureau of Labor Statistics, U.S. Department of Labor.* July 2017. https://www.bls.gov/news.release/pdf/ebs2.pdf
2. My Medicare Matters. "How Much Does Medicare Part D Cost?" *National Council on Aging.* 2017. https://www.mymedicarematters.org/costs/part-d/
3. American Association for Medicare Supplement Insurance. "2017 National Medicare Supplement Price Index." *American Association for Medicare Supplement Insurance.* 2017. https://medicaresupp.org/medicare-supplement-insurance-costs/
4. American Association for Medicare Supplement Insurance. "Medicare Supplement Insurance Statistics and Data." *American Association for Medicare Supplement Insurance.* 2017. https://medicaresupp.org/medicare-supplement-statistics/

Chapter 11: Invest in Your Health

1. Fidelity Investments. "Fidelity Couples Study." *Fidelity Investments.* June 2015. https://www.fidelity.com/about-fidelity/individual-investing/fidelity-couples-study
2. Nationwide. "Annual Nationwide Survey Finds Pre-Retirees Fear Health Care Costs, But Are Not Taking Action." *Nationwide Press Release.* December 2015. https://www.nationwide.com/about-us/120915-nf-health-care-survey.jsp
3. Age Wave and Merrill Lynch. "Health and Retirement: Planning for the Great Unknown." *Age Wave and Merrill Lynch.* Summer 2014. http://agewave.com/wp-content/uploads/2016/07/2014-ML-AW-Health-and-Retirement_Planning-for-the-Great-Unknown.pdf
4. MassMutual Financial Group. "Health, Wealth, and Happiness in Retirement: The Impact of Health on Retiree Lifestyles and Satisfaction with Life." *MassMutual Financial Group.* March 2015. https://www.mass-mutual.com/~/media/files/health-wealth-happiness-report-2015.pdf
5. Matt Blake. "The Healthiest Old Person on the Planet Explains How to Stay in Shape." *Vice.* April 2016. https://www.vice.com/en_us/article/nn9xzg/charles-eugster-fittest-oap-on-planet

6. Acharya, Mosiqi. "104 year-old Fauja Singh Runs the Mumbai Marathon." *SBS*. Jan 2016. http://www.sbs.com.au/yourlanguage/hindi/en/article/2016/01/17/104-year-old-fauja-singh-runs-mumbai-marathon

7. Sturman, Robert. "The World's Oldest Yoga Instructor Turns 97 Today." *Mindbodygreen*. August 2015. https://www.mindbodygreen.com/0-20942/the-worlds-oldest-yoga-teacher-turns-97-today-happy-birthday-tao.html

8. Vernon, Steve. "How Good Health Will Pay Off During Retirement." *CBS MoneyWatch*. April 2014. https://www.cbsnews.com/news/how-good-health-will-pay-off-during-retirement/

9. Stanford Center on Longevity. "The Sightlines Project: Seeing Our Way to Living Long and Living Well in 21st Century America." *Stanford Center on Longevity*. February 2016. http://longevity.stanford.edu/the-sightlines-project/

10. Michael Greger, MD. *How Not to Die: Discover the Food Scientifically Proven to Prevent and Reverse Disease*. New York: Flatiron Books, 2015.

11. Campbell, T. Colin, and Campbell, Thomas M. *The China Study: Revised and Expanded Edition: The Most Comprehensive Study of Nutrition Ever Conducted and the Startling Implications for Diet, Weight Loss, and Long-Term Health*. Dallas: BenBella Books, 2016.

12. NutrionFacts. "Standard American Diet." *NutritionFacts.org*. https://nutritionfacts.org/topics/standard-american-diet/

13. Dean Ornish, MD. *Dr. Dean Ornish's Program for Reversing Heart Disease: The Only System Scientifically Proven to Reverse Heart Disease Without Drugs or Surgery*. New York: Ivy Books, 2010.

14. Behan, Donald, and Cox, Samuel. "Obesity and Its Relation to Mortality and Morbidity Costs." *Society of Actuaries Committee on Life Insurance Research*. December 2010. https://www.soa.org/research-reports/2011/research-obesity-relation-mortality/

15. Huffington, Arianna. *The Sleep Revolution: Transforming Your Life, One Night at a Time*. New York: Harmony Books, April 2016.

16. MacMillan, Amanda. "7 Ways to Keep Your Brain Sharp as You Age." *Time Magazine*. September 7, 2017. http://time.com/4931877/keep-brain-sharp-prevent-alzheimers/

Chapter 12: Find Work That's Right for You

1. Pfau, Wade, Tomlinson, Joe, and Vernon, Steve. "Optimizing Retirement Income Portfolios in Defined Contribution Retirement Plans: A Framework for Building Retirement Income Portfolios." *Stanford Center*

on Longevity. May 2016. http://longevity.stanford.edu/blog/2015/07/14/optimal-retirement-income-solutions-in-defined-contribution-retirement-plans/

2. Adam, Stephane, Bonsang, Eric, and Perelman, Sergio. "Does Retirement Affect Cognitive Functioning?" *Journal of Health Economics,* Volume 31 (March 2012).

3. Rohwedder, Susann, and Willis, Robert. "Mental Retirement." *Journal of Economic Perspectives*, Volume 24 (Winter 2010).

4. Farrell, Diana. "Is the Online Platform Economy the Future of Work?" *JPMorgan Chase Institute.* November 2016. https://www.jpmorganchase.com/corporate/institute/insight-is-online-platform-economy-future-of-work.htm

5. Merrill Lynch and Age Wave. "Work in Retirement: Myths and Motivations." *Age Wave.* March 2014. https://agewave.com/what-we-do/landmark-research-and-consulting/research-studies/work-and-retirement-myths-and-motivations/

6. Collinson, Catherine. "The Current State of Retirement: Pre-Retiree Expectations and Retiree Realties." *Transamerica Center for Retirement Studies.* December 2015. https://www.transamericacenter.org/docs/default-source/retirees-survey/retirees_survey_2015_report.pdf

7. Munnell, Alicia H., Sanzenbacher, Geoffrey T., and Rutledge, Matthew S. "What Causes Workers to Retire Before They Plan?" *Boston College Center for Retirement Research.* September 2015. http://crr.bc.edu/working-papers/what-causes-workers-to-retire-before-they-plan/

8. Employee Benefit Research Institute and Greenwald & Associates. "2017 Retirement Confidence Survey." *Employee Benefit Research Institute.* March 2017. https://www.ebri.org/surveys/rcs/2017/

Chapter 13: Choose the Best Place to Live

1. Hoagland, William G., Bell, Steve, Akabas, Shai, Collins, Brian, Megan, Kenneth, and Ritz, Ben. "Securing Our Financial Future: Report of the Commission on Retirement Security and Personal Savings." *The BiPartisan Policy Center.* June 2016. http://bipartisanpolicy.org/wp-content/uploads/2016/06/BPC-Retirement-Security-Report.pdf

2. Sass, Steven. "Is Home Equity an Underutilized Retirement Asset?" *Boston College Center for Retirement Research.* March 2017. http://crr.bc.edu/briefs/is-home-equity-an-underutilized-retirement-asset/

Chapter 14: Nurture Your Well-Being

1. Age Wave and Merrill Lynch. "Leisure in Retirement: Beyond the Bucket

List." *Age Wave and Merrill Lynch.* 2016. https://agewave.com/wp-content/uploads/2016/05/2016-Leisure-in-Retirement_Beyond-the-Bucket-List.pdf

2. Transamerica Center for Retirement Studies. "The Current State of Retirement: A Compendium of Findings About American Retirees." *Transamerica Center for Retirement Studies.* April 2016. https://www.trans-americacenter.org/docs/default-source/retirees-survey/tcrs2016_sr_retiree_compendium.pdf

3. Nationwide Retirement Institute "The Nationwide Retirement Institute Consumer Social Security PR Survey." *Nationwide Press Release.* September 2017.

4. Gorry, Aspen, Gorry, Devon, and Slavov, Sita. "Does Retirement Improve Health and Life Satisfaction?" *NBER Working Paper.* July 2015. http://www.nber.org/papers/w21326

5. Stanford Center on Longevity. "The Sightlines Project: Seeing Our Way to Living Long and Living Well in 21st Century America." *Stanford Center on Longevity.* February 2016. http://longevity.stanford.edu/the-sightlines-project/

6. Zahart, Octavia H., and Crum, Alia J. "Perceived Physical Activity and Mortality: Evidence From Three Nationally Representative U.S. Samples." *American Psychological Association.* July 2017. http://www.apa.org/news/press/releases/2017/07/slackers-health.aspx

7. Carol D. Ryff, PhD. "Psychological Well-Being Revisited: Advances in Science and Practice of Eudaimonia." *Karger Psychotherapy and Psychosomatics.* Volume 83, 2014. https://www.karger.com/Article/FullText/353263

8. Perls, Thomas. "The New England Centenarian Study." *Boston University School of Medicine.* 1995-ongoing. http://www.bumc.bu.edu/centenarian/

9. Hill, Patrick L., Turiano, Nicholas A., and Mroczek, Daniel K. "The Value of a Purposeful Life: Sense of Purpose Predicts Greater Income and Net Worth." *Journal of Research in Personality.* Volume 65, December 2016. http://www.sciencedirect.com/science/article/pii/S0092656616300836

10. English, Tammy and Carstensen, Laura L. "Selective Narrowing of Social Networks Across Adulthood is Associated with Improved Emotional Experience in Daily Life." *International Journal of Behavioral Development.* January 2014. https://www.ncbi.nlm.nih.gov/pmc/articles/PMC4045107/

11. Carol S. Dweck, PhD. *Mindset: The New Psychology of Success.* New York: Random House, 2016.

Chapter 15: Prepare for Your Frail and Final Years

1. Associated Press-NORC Center for Public Affairs Research. "Long-Term Care in America: Views on Who Should Bear the Responsibilities and Costs of Care." *Associated Press-NORC Center for Public Affairs Research.* 2017. http://www.longtermcarepoll.org/Pages/Reports/who-should-bear-the-responsibilities-and-costs-of-care.aspx

2. Ira Byock, MD. *The Best Care Possible: A Physician's Quest to Transform Care Through the End of Life.* New York: Avery Publishing, 2013.

Chapter 16: Leave Your Legacy

1. Age Wave and Merrill Lynch. "Leisure in Retirement: Beyond the Bucket List." *Age Wave and Merrill Lynch.* 2016. https://agewave.com/what-we-do/landmark-research-and-consulting/research-studies/leisure-in-retirement-beyond-the-bucket-list/

2. Stanford Center on Longevity. "The Sightlines Project: Seeing Our Way to Living Long and Living Well in 21st Century America." *Stanford Center on Longevity.* February 2016. http://longevity.stanford.edu/the-sightlines-project/

3. Stanford Center on Longevity. "Hidden in Plain Sight: How Intergenerational Relationships Can Transform our Future." *Stanford Center on Longevity.* June 2016. http://longevity.stanford.edu/scl-publications/

4. Hill, Patrick L., Turiano, Nicholas A., Mroczek, Daniel K., and Burrow, Anthony L. "The Value of a Purposeful Life: Sense of Purpose Predicts Greater Income and Net Worth." *Journal of Research in Psychology.* September 2016. https://www.sciencedirect.com/science/article/pii/S0092656616300836

5. Carr, Dawn, Fried, Linda P., and Rowe, John W. "Productivity & Engagement in an Aging America: The Role of Volunteerism." *Daedalus.* 2015. https://www.mitpressjournals.org/doi/abs/10.1162/DAED_a_00330?journalCode=daed

6. Butrica, Barbara A., Johnson, Richard W., and Zedlewski, Sheila R. "Retaining Older Volunteers is Key to Meeting Future Volunteer Needs." *The Urban Institute.* December 2007. https://www.urban.org/research/publication/retaining-older-volunteers-key-meeting-future-volunteer-needs

Chapter 17: Track Your Progress with the Retirement Reality Check

No references for this chapter.

INDEX

ABOUT THE AUTHOR

For more than 40 years, Steve Vernon, FSA, has analyzed, researched, and communicated about the most difficult retirement topics, including finances, health and lifestyle. He had a 30-year career as a consulting actuary with Watson Wyatt and Mercer, helping Fortune 1000 employers manage and communicate their retirement programs. During that time, he worked on the front lines of the extraordinary shift that's taken place in retirement plans, as employers switched from traditional, defined benefit pension plans to 401(k) and other defined contribution plans.

Steve has served for more than five years in his encore career as a Research Scholar at the Stanford Center on Longevity. He's also president of *Rest-of-Life* Communications, a company he founded that delivers retirement planning workshops and conducts retirement education campaigns. He has never sold insurance, annuities, or investments; this enables him to be unbiased in his writing and recommendations.

Currently, Steve writes a regular blog column for CBS *MoneyWatch* where he addresses the critical topics facing people in retirement. His previously published works include:

- *Money for Life: Turn Your IRA and 401(k) Into a Lifetime Retirement Paycheck. Rest-of-Life* Communications, 2012.

- *Recession-Proof Your Retirement Years: Simple Retirement Planning Strategies That Work Through Thick or Thin. Rest-of-Life* Communications, 2009-2014.

- *The Quest: For Long Life, Health and Prosperity* (a DVD/workbook set). *Rest-of-Life* Communications, 2007.

- *Live Long & Prosper! Invest in Your Happiness, Health and Wealth for Retirement and Beyond.* Wiley, 2005.

- *Don't Work Forever! Simple Steps Baby Boomers Must Take to Ever Retire.* Wiley, 1995.

A Fellow in the Society of Actuaries, Steve graduated summa cum laude from the University of California, Irvine, with a double major in mathematics and social science.

Steve lives in Oxnard, California, with his wife, Melinda, where they're following the advice in this book for their own retirement and rest-of-life. For more information, visit www.restoflife.com.

89325693R00175

Made in the USA
San Bernardino, CA
23 September 2018